Women of India

Their Status Since the Vedic Times

Arun R. Kumbhare

B.E.(Civil), M.E.(Public Health Engg.),M.Sc.Civil Engg.,
MCSCE (Life), Former Member APENS.

iUniverse, Inc.
New York   Bloomington

Women of India
Their Status Since the Vedic Times

iUniverse books may be ordered through booksellers or by contacting:

iUniverse
1663 Liberty Drive
Bloomington, IN 47403
www.iuniverse.com
1-800-Authors (1-800-288-4677)

Because of the dynamic nature of the Internet, any Web addresses or links contained in this book may have changed since publication and may no longer be valid.

ISBN: 978-1-4401-5600-7 (sc)
ISBN: 978-1-4401-5602-1 (dj)
ISBN: 978-1-4401-5601-4 (ebk)

Printed in the United States of America

iUniverse rev. date: 7/13/2009

DEDICATED
TO
THE WOMEN OF INDIA

Contents

India; they were, in fact, indiginous Indians. (Ref.32) In any case it was 500 BC when Alexzander the Great attacked the northwest frontier. Later in the history many invaders followed; the Arabs, the Turks, the Mongols, the Afghans and so on. Each has left its imprint on the cultural and social canvas of India and each time women were the ones who were affected the most. It was around 1200 AD that the Mughals established their rule, which lasted till the nineenth century after which the British ruled India until 1947 when India became a free country. Prior to this many invaders such as Ghaznavids, the Ghurids, etc had been venturing incursions into northern India and had been successful in causing largescale destruction of Hindu temples, plundering the Indian countryside, carrying out rapes and murders creating a reign of terror. Later Mughals came to rule and to establish their empire in India. Their main objective was to loot but while carrying out the collection of precious things they also destroyed important temples and arteffects; primarily destroying the cultural symbols and they also took women with them as slaves or for sexual gratification to become a part of their "haram". In their culture women were considered a "possession" just like any other material goods. The Hindu population was considered slaves and "Kafirs", (meaning infidels), who were, according to Islam, ought to be either converted to Islam or killed. To get rid of such a large Hindu population was practically impossible so the Mughal rulers levied a heavy tax on the non-Muslim population called, Jazia, which was the price a Hindu must pay to be a Hindu. They also severely restricted their religious practices and their women were raped or taken as slaves without any impunity. Conditions got somewhat relaxed during the rule of Akaber the Great but again worsned soon after his death and reached their lowest ebb during the rule of Auranjeb, the last of the emperors ruling a large territory and the most ruthless. The impact on Indian society, however, was mostly confined to north where the Moghul influence was most predominant and where the Mughal Empire was mostly confined. South India was left unaffected by the Muslim influence. But the Christain missionaries had reached Kerala where they had gained a beachead and were successful in spreading their religion.

Beginning from the earliest Vedic times, followed by the "puranic" period, the medieval period, the long Mughal rule, the British Raj and lastly the post-independence period are the major divisions of Indian history and also represent the major cultural periods and the status of Indian women should be studied with these periods as the main distinctive influencing periods. This study will also be useful in appreciating the background for the contemporary condition of the Indian society, particularly the women.

The evidence of what the status of women was in the earliest history is found in the sacred Hindu texts, the Vedas. There are four Vedas: *Rig Veda, Yajur Veda, Atharva Veda and Saam Veda.* Each one of these texts is quite voluminous, the *Rig Veda* being the largest and the oldest. It is important to note that the hymns contained in these texts were composed by various eminent sages and during different time periods. We shall see that some of the hymns in the *Rig Veda* had been composed by eminent women sages, a proof of the fact that women during those times were quite learned, great thinkers and of course, emancipated. The Vedas provide good and credible information about the social conditions during the Aryan civilization and the place, which women occupied in that ancient period. The precise period during, which the Vedas were produced is difficult to establish but one thing is certain: they belong to a very antiquated period. They are, no doubt, the oldest texts in the history of the world:

> "Vedas are the heritage of mankind. Even though the credit
> for preservation of these without adding a syllable here or
> a dot there is that of the Indians, the verses in these have
> come down to us from remotest antiquity when forefathers
> of all the peoples of this wide world were living together"
> S.D.Kulkarni claims. (Ref.32, p.372).

Many scholars have estimated their antiquity. Vedas are the most important religious texts of the Hindus or more precisely, the followers of *Sanatana Dharma,* the correct name for Hinduism, which literally means a religion, which has been in existence since the beginning of time. The reason why the name Hindus came into being is that the foreigners who first came through the northwest passage came across the mighty river *Sindhu* and they pronounced it as Hindu and named the people living along the river and beyond as Hindus. Mughals introduced Islam to India in a very cruel and ruthless manner. This had a devastating effect on the Hindu religion, Buddhism and all its symbols, temples and written material. The great ancient universities of Nalanda and Taxsila were, for example, plundered, burned and completely destroyed by Mughal invaders. Finally, Christanity, which had gained its foothold in the south, arrived in full force with the British conquet of India, and conversion of Hindu women to Christanity began. Islam and Christanity both engaged in massive conversions. It is the result of their vigoros conversions that we now find such large number of Muslims and Christians in India today. Population of Hindus converted to Islam far exceed those converted to Christainity because the Muslims used force in conversions wereas the Christians used pursuation, gifts and other forms of bribes. Mughals also ruled for much longer period than the British. Christians also made the best of the caste system within Hinduism and its associated discriminatory treatment of the lower castes, provided dignity to lower castes as incentive to join Chriastinity. The introduction of different religions and the socio-political changes associated with each new invasion had enormous adverse impact on the female population of India. The example of the life of Pundita Ramabai is a prime example of a Hindu woman getting converted to Christianity out of frustration. Her life story is included in the chapter containing prominent women.

The British Raj brought a foreign culture, an imposition of a foreign language, under a general pretext that the native Hindus were uncivilized and backward. None of which helped in the improvement of the condition of women. Initial period of the East India Company is full of the Company employees keeping harams containing a number of Indian women. This practice ended when Britain formally made India a colony of their Empire and women from England were allowed to come to India either to join their men or in search of eligible partners. Also the British introduced a strict policy of discrimination wich prohibited the British from mixing with local population.

In the nineententh and twentith centuries, certain social reformers took great initiatives and dedicated themselves to the improvement of the status of women. The Indians who came in contact with the British, and who went to England and closely observed their society, greatly felt the need for improvements in Indian society. One big positive influence of the British rule was the introduction of an organized system of education based on modern concepts. The age- old Brahminic system, which had practically shut the women from getting educated, became passé and the new system came into vogue, which encouraged education among women. The change had its labor pains but the end result was beneficial for the Indian society in general. The British also studied the Indian texts to improve their knowledge of India and its civilization and culture, an unbiased effort of certain British scholars, adopted, rightly or wrongly, the Manu Smiriti as their guide to introduce legislation.

The departure of the British in 1947 brought freedom to India and the independent India adopted a very forward-looking constitution, a social document, which made important provisions for the protection and emancipation of women and to free them from the age-old yoke of confinement and religious impositions, which were completely unnecessary and unsuitable for this day and age. The constitution has enshrined clauses, which give equal rifgts to women, makes discrimination against women illegal and punishable, and violence against them also punishable as well. It also makes generous provisions for encouraging women's education. The effects of these constitutional provisions are making a difference but on the ground improvements in the status of women across the country as a whole are very slow, especially in the rural areas. The large-scale corruption in India and limited resources dedicated to education in the rural areas are some factors among others, responsible for lack of progress in the improvement of the conditions of women.

Being from India, and having spent my first thirty years in that country, I was strongly of the opinion that women in India were treated with great respect and enjoyed good freedom but this was not quite true. After leaving the country and taking a closer look at the situation from the outside reveals some alarming information. The status of Indian woman is far from satisfactory when one takes into account the country as a whole. Her status varies depending on to which caste or class she belongs, the level of her parent's education and their financial status; to which part of the country she belongs and so on. Conditions are quite different in the cities. Rural areas are still caught up in the age- old traditions and practices, which suppress women. This work is taking a closer look at the condition of women in India; not only does it traces her status through the centuries long history but also discusses the influence of foreign religions and cultures, which came in to India in the form of invaders and adversely affected the Indian society and women particularly. Pundit Jawaharlal Nehru, the first Prime Minister of India, and who was himself strongly influenced by the Muslim and British cultures, has stated: "You can tell the condition of a nation by looking at the condition of the status of its women." Dr. Radhakrishnan who has been the President of the India, and a product of traditional Indian upbringing as opposed to Jawahar Lal Nehru, has also expressed similar sentiments. None of these great persons would be happy to learn about the condition of women in India today and would demand quick improvements. Many other Indian philosophers and thinkers have expressed similar opinions. It is hoped that the reader will enjoy reading about the status of Indian women through the past many centuries and about their present condition. I have dedicated the book to "The Women of India" because they have suffered a lot, always made great sacrifices and yet preserved our values, our culture and have been a backbone of our morality and our civilization. In chapter 7 lives of some great women of India have been presented. I hope that this book will serve as an inspiration to everybody in appreciating the conditions under which women of India marriage", a problem, which came into existence in later centuries and still persists in many parts India today. The Vedic texts created in those ancient times, and later compiled systematically, must have taken considerable time to formulate and compose, since the texts contain compositions by several sages who happened to have lived during different time periods. And it must have taken several centuries to reach the kind of sophistication exhibited in these texts. The texts have been preserved meticulously, in their original form through centuries by committing them to memory, a practice, which is still in vogue. Committing these texts to memory happened to preserve and save them during the Moghul invasions and rule at which time the invaders were bent on destroying all Hindu scriptures and texts along with their places of worship.

During that time Hinduism was the prominent religion in India. The real name of the religion was and still is *"Sanatana Dharma"*. How the religion started being called Hinduism has already been explained in the introduction.

It is, therefore, most appropriate to refer to these most ancient scriptures to begin enquiry into the status of women during that earliest period of history of India and for that matter, the history of the world. Out of the four Vedas, the *Rig Veda* is the earliest and the largest. A short sample of some of the hymns from the *Rig Veda,* which pertain to women, and would provide an idea of the type of life during that time, is presented in Appendix I. Some hymns from the *Atharva Veda* are also included. It is not the intent to provide a complete list of such stanzas since that would be fairly extensive and would require a separate work. However, the important hymns are included.

Women's education during Vedic times:

There was a great emphasis on education during the Vedic times. The culture of the Vedic times required both women and men to get educated and opportunities for acquisition of knowledge and education existed in plenty and for both sexes. The Vedic hymns repeat many times that the women ought to be educated to the same degree as men, which indicates the importance of this matter. During the Vedic period anybody who wanted to get educated used to go to an ashram and if accepted by the guru, used to stay in the ashram, receive education and while pursuing studies used to help and contribute in the day-to-day functioning of the ashram. This helping in the running of the ashram was an important part of education since it is in this process the student learnt practical aspects of day-to-day living. There was no discrimination based on gender with respect to opportunities for receiving education and the sages who were teaching made no difference in imparting education to women. The girls who were educated were regarded with great respect, since to be educated and learned was considered worthy of respect. This idea has continued to dominate the Indian society ever since. Vedic literature praises a scholarly daughter and says: "A girl also should be brought up and educated with great effort and care" (*Mahanirvana Tantra*). The importance of a girl's education is stressed in *Atherva Veda, which* states, "The success of a woman in her married life depends upon her training during the *Brahmacharya* , that is, the student life. To explain the meaning of *Brahmacharya,* the following explanation is given:

During the Vedic times the life of a person was ideally divided into four parts or *Ashrams,* based on assuming the length of an average person's life being one hundred years. The first period or a person's twenty five years was designated as *"Bramhacharya Ashram",* during which one was to practice celibacy, acquire knowledge and skills necessary for life and for his/ her chosen profession and to prepare him/her for entering the next stage, which was designated the *"Grehastha Ashram"* in which one spent a life with his/her spouse and raised a family. This stage was for the next twenty five years after which comes the *"Vanaprastha Ashram"* from age 50 to 75 during which the conventional family life was supposed to end and one was supposed to live with or without his/her spouse, spending time in meditation and contemplation and away from the crowds. This is why it was called *Vanaprastha,* meaning "on way to the forest", withdrawn from the main stream of life. The next and last period of a person's life was called *"Sansaya Ashram",* during which he/she become a complete hermit and gives up all his/ her material belongings and lived by begging for alms. He/she spends all time in meditation and contemplation till death comes. In this last period one has to ideally accomplish complete control of desires and spends all the time in meditation. In this stage one is supposed to completely surrender to the almighty by entirely giving up one's ego.

The girls were entitled to *Upanayana* (to receive the sacred thread), which is a ceremony formally signifying one's entry into the *Brahmacharyaya Ashram,* and to the privilege of studying Vedas, just as the boys. Women performed religious rites after completing their education under guidance of a guru. They were also entitled to offer sacrifices to gods. Women were allowed to perform the last rites of their fathers if a son was not available for this purpose. The practice of only the son performing this last rite came into being later and everybody prayed to have a son so that he will perform the ritual of the last rite for the father. According to *Shrastas and Grihya Sutras,* women chanted mantras along with their husbands while performing rituals.

While at the guru's ashram, like all other students, the girls helped in the daily running of the facility. The help they provided included chores such as going to the forest to fetch firewood, cooking, serving food, tending the cows of the ashram, which included cleaning their stables, bathing them, milking and feeding them, and the processing of milk to produce buttermilk and butter etc. Chanting relevant mantras to offer the prepared food to the gods prior to eating it was a routine practice. In addition to receiving education in general subjects of arts and sciences, women also received education in martial arts. There are certain outstanding examples, which are well known where certain women have displayed their knowledge and skill in martial arts. Such examples include Kaikai, the young and devoted queen of king Dasharatha, the famous father of Ramchandra, who accompanied him into the battlefield to provide crucial and timely help. Another famous example is that of princess Subdhra, who drove the great warrior Arjuna away in a chariot. Satybhama killed the demon Narkasur. Rig Veda refers to women engaged in warfare. One queen Bispala is mentioned. Even as late as fifth century BC, *Megasthenes,* the Greek ambassador, left by Alexzander the Great, mentions heavily armed women guards protecting *Chandragupta's* palace. Girls belonging to the *Khatria,* or warrior class, in particular, received this type of training and education.

Girls also received training and education in finer arts such as painting, dancing and decoration. Chitralekha, for example, was a famous painter. That is why her name is also Chitralekha. A Sanskrit word made of two words: Chitra, meaning a painting and Lekha, meaning the one producing or making it. Brahmin girls received education to suit their life style, the type of life they were going to lead after their education ended. This education would place greater emphasis on learning the Vedas, the religious philosophy and ritual practices, ethics and morality, among other things. There is a quotation by a woman in the *Udyogaparva of Mahabharatha, (Mahabharatha* being a great Indian epic), which states, " I am seventy years old. I have been through many ashrams and got educated." She had been unmarried all that time and wished to marry at that late age! This is cited as an example to show that women during those times had the liberty to keep on getting educated to their heart's content and also had the freedom to get married as they wished.

One is able to learn a great deal about the conditions of women in the ashrams during those times by reading the works of famous writers, poets and composers such as *Kalidasa and Bhavabhuti.* Their descriptions of the ashram of *Kanva* rishi, where the famous character in the whole Indian history *Shakuntala* was brought up and educated. Boys and girls both received education together in this ashram. The description of the ashram in its natural beauty, and the clean and pure life, which they lead is, even today, makes one desire such an education for their child. In *Utterramchiritamanas,* there is a mention of one girl student who had to go to a separate class because she was not able to keep pace with *Laav and Kush,* the twin sons of the famous incarnation of god, king *Ramchandra.* They were getting educated in the ashram of the great rishi *Valmiki,* where *Sita,* their mother, was living in exile. This is yet another proof that the girls were receiving the same education as the boys. A question may be asked whether these eminent poets have described the conditions pertain to their own time or to the epic periods in question. Whatever the answer to this question may be it is certain that co-education was practiced during those ancient Vedic times.

There has also been a great emphasis placed on the practice of celibacy during the perid when the boys and girls were in the process of getting educated, the *Bramhacharya* period. It was believed that engaging in sexual activity during this period posed a great distraction and a great hinderance in acquiring education, which required a complete dedication to learning and concentration. This is also the period during which one is supposed to become physically fit and strong in preparation for the rest of their lives, especially the *Grahastha Ashram,* which is quite physically and mentally demanding. The Vedas clearly state that one should not be paying attention to opposite sex during the *Brahmacharya ashram.* This idea is deeply ingrained in the Indian psyche. Even today it is not considered good to look at girls while one is a student. This type of behavior is looked- down upon by better and edcated families in India. With the world becoming smaller, western cultural influence in India is on the increase and Indian youth are fast discarding the older practices and trying to imitate western style practices.

While on the topic of celibacy a word with respect to the importance, which celibacy occupies in Buddhism would be in order. The emphasis, which Buddhism places on the practice of celibacy can not be overstated. Buddhism also recognizes the four divisions of human life but when it comes to one wishing to get ordained as a Buddhist monk one is required to practice celibacy very strictly. This commitment by a person is far more serious than the commitment, which a Roman Catholic priest makes. The loosely practiced celibacy in Roman Catholism is quite apparent and is well known world over since these priests are paid and they accept to remain celibate as a condition

well as that of the "wooer" (vara), in the formal wooeing was a formality, though it was an essential preliminary to the marriage ceremony.

The uncomplimentary references to some sons-in-law (VIII. 2. 20; I. 109. 2), suggest that in some cases a "brideprice" was paid by a not very desirable son-inlaw. Similarly, when girls had some physical defect, dawries, it seems, had to be given (VI. 28. 5; X. 27. 12).

The *Swayamvaras,* (a form of marriage in which the bride chooses her would be husband, was a very popular form of marriage ceremony. Some of the famous Swayamvaras such as that of *Sita*, the princess of Janakpuri, where a number of prominent kings and princes were invited in a bid to win her favour is well known.) But this form of marriage was not restricted to royalty only. Common folk were also getting married in the same way, which reaffirms the freedom, which the women of the day enjoyed with regard to their marriage. This is in stark contrast to the practice of later ages when the parents decided who their daughter would marry.

Many marriages, as is the case in the later day Hindu society today, involved the intercession of the families on both sides, but a maiden was consulted and her wishes taken into account when the matrimonial alliance was discussed. The marriage hymns 139 in the *Rig Veda* and the *Atherva Veda* indicate that the parties to marriage were generally grown up persons competent to woo and to be wooed, qualified to give consent and make choice.

Young girls had the choice and freedom to go out to attend fairs, festivals and assemblies: the seclusion of women was not practiced. There is a reference to certain occasional festivals or gatherings called *Samanas* organized to help young boys and girls to get together. The *Rig Veda* described *Samanas* as where:

"Wives and maidens attire themselves in gay robes and set fourth to the joyous feast; youths and maidens hasten to the meadow when the forest and field are clothed in fresh foliage to take part in dance. Cymbals sound and seizing each other lads and damsels gaily moving around." A girl often chose one of the suitors whom she met in these *Samanas* who she would choose as her would-be husband.

To get dressed up and wear ornaments to make themselves attractive was something, which the young maidens used to do during the Vedic times. This is not quite different from the modern-day girls who also spend a lot of time in making themselves presentable. The descriptions of ornaments etc., which are described in the Vedas do not compare with the modern day multi-billion dollar industry but the idea appears to be the same. Several ornaments are mentioned in the *Rig Veda*. The *Karnasobhana* was an "ornament for the ear", apparently for the use of men (VIII. 78. 3), and that it may have been a gold ornament is suggested by I.122.14, which refers to the deity as gold-eared (*hiranya-karna*) The *kurika* was some kind of a head-ornament worn by females, specially brides. The same may be said of *nyochani* (X. 85. 6), a bride's ornament. *Khadi* was a kind of a ring, worn as an armlet or an anklet (I. 166. 9; Vii. 56. 13). *Nishka* was a gold ornament worn on the neck. *Mani* was some kind of jewel worn around the neck (I. 122. 14). *Rukma* was an ornament worn on the breast (II. 34. 2, 8). Men used to wear garlands (IV. 38. 6; V. 53. 4). There are also descriptions of the hairstyles (X. 114. 3). It seems from the descriptions of Rudra and Pushan that men wore their hair plaited or braided, and the Vasishtas were noted for wearing their hair in a plait or coil on the right (VII. 33. 1). The beard and moustache are mentioned, but shaving is also referred to (X. 142. 4).

With respect to marriage ceremony, the *Rig Veda* mentions the seven steps and vows taken based on mutual respect:

> "*A friend thou shall be having paced these seven steps with me. Nay, having paced the seven steps we have become friends. May I retain thy friendship, and never part from thy friendship? Let us unite together: let us propose together: Loving each other and ever radiant in each other's company, meaning well toward each other, sharing together all enjoyments and pleasures, let us join our thoughts.* (Source: Taittiriya Ekagnikanda, I iii, 14. Sastri, 1918)

The bridegroom and party used to proceed to the bride's house (X. 17. 1), where the well-adorned bride remaind ready (IV. 58. 9) to join the marriage feast. The guests were entertained with the flesh of cows killed for the occasion (X. 85. 13). The ceremony proper then used to begin. The bridegroom used to grasp the hand of the bride and used to lead her around the fire (X. 85. 36, 38). These two acts used to constitute the essential part of the marriage and after which the bridegroom became the husband who takes her by the hand (*hasta-grabha,* X. 18. 8, 10, 24-27, 42). Then the marriage consummation used to follow, which was signified by the purification of the bride's garment (X. 85. 28-30, 35). (Ref.39).

9

Prayers for perfect harmony and happiness in conjugal life were offered to bless the couple and wished for sons and grand sons (VIII. 31. 5-9; X. 34. 11; 85. 18, 19, 42). The fulfillment of the desire for offspring, and male offspring in particular, was the primary aim of marriage. Abundance of sons is constantly prayed for along with cattle and land, but no desire for daughters was expressed. The desire for a son is understandable in a patriarchal form of society. The son alone could perform the funeral rites for the father and continue the line. Sonlessness was deplored as much as poverty (III. 16. 5). A son could be adopted but not favoured (VII. 4. 7,8).

Polygamy was permitted during the Vedic times but monogamy may have been the general practice (I. 62. 2; 71. 1; 104. 3; 105. 8; 112. 19; 186. 7; Vi. 53. 4; VII. 18. 2, 26. 3; X. 43. !; 101. II, etc.). Also, (I. 124. 7; IV. 3. 2; X. 71. 4). Polygamy was mostly practiced by the *Rajyanya* class (the ruling class).

There are a few references to lovers and love- making (I. 134. 3; VIII. 17. 7). A *raha-suh* "bearing in secret" is mentioned in II. 29. 1. A protégé of Indra is referred to as the "castaway" (*paravriji* or *paravrikta*), presumably as the offspring of illigimate love. Incest was strictly prohibited. The so-called incestuous intercourse between father and daughter in the story of Prajapati (X. 61. 5-7), and between brother and sister in the dialogue between Yama and Yami (X.10) can be satisfactorily explained on a mythological or astronomical basis. *Rig Veda* X.40. 2 and X 18.7, 8 point to the practice of requiring a childless widow to cohabit with her brother-in-law until the birth of a son. This *niyoga* is a kind of short-term levirate. These passages and I.24.7 are clear evidence that the remarriage of widows was permitted in certain circumstances, though there is no definite reference to it in *Rig Veda*. (Ref. 39)

Dowry as such was not practiced. It appears that the bride's parents gave gold, cattle, horses, and valuable articles, which she carried to her new home. She had the right to deal with it as she pleased. No doubt the dowry the girl brought with her made her more desirable, as mentioned before in (10. 27. 12).

Marriage was an established institution in the Vedic age. It was regarded as a social and religious duty, not a contract. (Marriage even today is not a contract within Hindu society, which is entirely different from either Islam or Christianity). The husband and wife stood on equal footing and prayed for long and lasting love and friendship. In the wedding, the bride also used to address the assembly in which sages were present. (*Rig Veda 10.85.26-27*).

Marriage was not compulsory for a woman and an unmarried woman who stayed back in the house of her parents was called *Amajur,* a girl who grew old at her father's house. An unmarried person, however, was not eligible to participate in Vedic sacrifices, which is an indication of her lower status. A woman, if she chose, could marry even after the child-bearing age. For example, Gosha, a well-known female sage, married at a late stage in her life (her husband being another well-known scholar of that time, Kakasivan). Widows were allowed to remarry if they so desired: and faced no condemnation and isolation.

A girl, when after her marriage, moved into another household where she became part of it. Her "*Gotra*" used to change to that of her husbands. (It is still the case among Hindus. The term is used to indicate the family lineage, traced over the past about seven generations). (In Hindu marriages, the practice even today is not to marry within the same *Gotra.*) She participates in the performances of *yagnas* (religious sacrificial offerings) for *devas* (gods), and *pitras* (forefathers) of her husband's family. This indicates that she now completely belongs to her husband's family. The bride takes charge of her new family that includes her husband, his parents, brothers and sisters along with any others who lived in the household for some reason. She takes charge of taking care of her husband's parents who are old and retired. Others are younger and junior in family hierarchy.

The *Rig Veda* hymn (10.85.27), the wedding prayer, indicates the rights of a woman as wife. It is addressed to the bride sitting next to bridegroom. It touches upon some other issues as well: (Ref. Appendix I)

> *"Happy be you (as wife) in future and prosper with your children here in the house: be vigilant to rule your household in this home (i.e. exercise your authority as the main figure in your home). Closely unite (be an active participant) in marriage with this man, your husband. So shall you, full of years (for a very long life), address your company (that is, others in the house listen to you, and obey and care about what you have to say)". (Rig Veda 10.85.27).*

The famous marriage hymn (10.85) calls upon members of the husband's family to treat the daughter-in-law (invited into the family" as a river enters

new husband, with prosperity and happiness. The *Rig Veda* praises *Ashwin*, gods for protecting widows: (10.40.8)

> **10.40.8:** *Krsa and Sayu ye protect, ye Asvins*
> *Twain: ye Two assist the widow and*
> *The worshipper;*
>
> *And ye throw open, Asvins, unto those*
> *Who win the cattle-stall that thunders*
> *With its sevenfold mouth.*

The 14 stanzas in the 18th sukta of the 10th book deal with treatment of widows.

The hymn 10.18.8 is quite specific regarding the treatment of widows. The dead man's brothers and others recite this hymn for requesting the widow to release her husband's body for cremation. The hymn also commands the widow to return to the world of living beings, return to her home and to her children and grand children:

> *"Rise: woman, (and go) to the world of living beings;*
> *Come, this man near whom you sleep is lifeless;*
> *You have enjoyed the state of being*
> *The wife of your husband,*
> *The suitor who took you by the hand."(10.18.8)*

The same hymn also confers upon her the full right over the house and properties of her deceased husband. (It was only in 1995 that the Supreme Court of India interpreted Section 14(1) of the Hindu Succession Act to allow Hindu widows full ownership rights over properties she inherits from her deceased husband.) . *Rig Veda* also sanctions the marriage of the widow with the brother of her deceased husband and to live with her family with full dignity and honor. Scholars also say that the widow did not necessarily had to marry the brother of her deceased husband. She could marry any other person of her choice, but a male relative of her husband was generally preferred.

Rig Veda (10.18.9) blesses a woman at her second marriage with progeny and prosperity in this lifetime:

> *"Go up O woman to the world of living;*
> *You stand by this one who is deceased;*

Come! to him who grasps your hand,
Your second spouse (didhisu),
You have now entered into the relationship
Of wife and husband."

(18.3.4) Blesses the widow to have a happy life with present husband:

"O ye inviolable! (The widow), tread the path of wise
In front of these and choose this man (another suitor),
As thy husband.

Joyfully receive him and may the two of you,
Mount the world of happiness."

Guidance for marriage, gender equality and different marriage styles with examples:

The *Vedas* state that eligible men and women ought to both look for their life partners as mentioned earlier. And the marriage should take place by their mutual consent only. The *Vedas* have given a lot of guidance on what to look for in choosing a life partner to make the married life a success. It has been emphasized that both the bride and the groom should, among other things, have the same level of education, for the sake of compatibility and better enjoyment of a happy married life. It is also stated that compatibility of both parties in terms of their nature and overall outlook on life is also essential. The responsibility of choosing the life partners was entirely that of the parties (the prospective bride and groom) concerned. It is recommended in the *Vedas* that relationship be between two who live farther apart, distance wise. This, they say, is good for a healthier progeny and marriage. In all cases, it is important to know the correct information about each other. In the olden days, information about the girl and the boy was obtained through relatives or by sending special agents in disguise. For prince or princesses, quite a bit used to be known by their general fame. In most cases, vital information used to be declared by the parents. This was a fundamental requitement before any decisions were made. Even today the parents of the girl and the boy make information about them formally known to each other including photographs etc. In addition, answers to any questions, which either party may have, are readily provided. Verification of information provided is done discreetly. Relevent Vedic hymns have been cited in Appendix I for reference.

Swayamvara, literally meaning marriage by personal choice, is one form of accepted Hindu marriage. The marriage of Sita with Ram is a prime example of this style of marriage. Princess Sita's father, king Janak, had invited a number of eligible kings and princes to his court and had posed a test for them to pass to qualify for her hand. That test was to lift the mighty bow of lord Shiva and string it. All the invited guests tried but failed. Only prince Ram of Auyodhya was successful and hence got married to Sita. This is one of the classic *Swayamvaras* described in detail in the great epic *Ramayana,* first by the world's first poet, Valmiki Rishi, and later by Sant Tulsidas in his composition called "*Ramchirata Manas.* Tulsidas's composition is in Hindi, a language more popular and easily understood by common folk and therefore is extremely popular. Valmiki's composition is in Sanskrit and difficult for average person to understand. It is a text fit for scholars of Sanskrit to study.

Another famous example of the *Swayamvara* is the marriage of princess Draupadi. Here also, many promising princes and kings were invited and the test posed was to pierce the eye of a fish, which was moving in a circle at the ceiling and one had to take aim at the fish by looking down at the reflection of the fish in a pool of water on the floor. Only prince Arjuna, one of the Pandava princes, could pass the test and married Draupadi.

These two examples are from a period, called *Tretayuga,* the second out of four ages of Hindu mythology, in Indian History popularly known as the epic period. This epic period consists of two great epics, the *Ramayana* and the *Mahabharata.* This period occurred just after the Vedic period, but the strong influence of the Vedic period had persisted. Vedas were the primary reference for deciding right from wrong. Ramayana, the life story and the glorious work, which Lord Ramchandra, an incarnation of Vishnu, did during his lifetime, occurred prior to Mahabharata. Mahabharata depicts the conflict between the Kauravas and the Pandavas, and the life, work and teachings of Lord Krishna, a later incarnation of Vishnu.

The princesses were not the only ones who had the privilege of marrying in the Swayamvara style. Ordinary women also enjoyed these rights. It would also be important to know that the fiercest battle fought in the entire Indian history, the battle of Mahabharata, was primarily fought for the honor of Draupadi, who had been insulted by the Kauravas in their court. The great battle, which lord Ramchandra fought with the mighty demon king Rawana, was also for the sake of saving the honor of Sita, whom Rawana had abducted.

Shakuntala's marriage with king Dushyanta is a very well known and important love story, which ought to be mentioned. Shakuntala, who was abandoned by her mother just after her birth, was found by a group of hermits and was raised by them in their ashram. She grew up to be a very beautiful girl, accomplished in all the arts etc. She used to play and spend time in the ashram with the other girls of the ashram. The environs of the ashram were very rich in natural beauty. There were beautiful flowering shrubs emenating sweet smells, a variety of green tropical trees loaded with healthy foliage, small bushes bearing flowers of a diverse variety, bumble bees buzzing around sucking nector from flowers and the whole ashram resembled a large professionally landscaped garden. Anybody entering this ashram would just marvel its beauty and feel pleased and relaxed. There also were wild animals of a friendly variety such as deer rabbits etc., who had become quite friendly with the residents of the ashram.

Shakuntala used to spend her time loving the environment and playing with the animals. She used to get so much absorbed in the nature that she used to talk with the flowers, especially the beautiful red water lilies. She had become one with the environment and used to know and communicate with the plants and animals. Life was very good and enjoyable till one fine day the ruler of that kingdom, king Dushantya happened to appear on the scene. He was in the area on a hunting trip and had lost his way back to his camp. He accidently arrived in the ashram and at once became enchanted with its beauty. While he was looking around with awe, he happened to spot beautiful Shakuntala. It was love at first sight. He saw Shakuntala fighting off a big black bumblebee, which was bothering her. King Dushyanta conveniently came to her resque. Their eyes met and a very famous and historical romance began. The famous Indian poet, *Kalidas,* (370-450 AD), has composed his very famous Sanskrit drama, *Shakuntalam,* based on this immortal love story. The composition has impressed art world of the West. The play was first translated into German and English in the 18th century, and greatly impressed the great poet and playwright Jonathan Wolfgang von Gothe, who was so much influenced by it that he created an "introduction in the theater" to his *Foust* and helped to spread knowledge of *Kalidasa* in the West. As an interesting note, the name *Kalidasa* is made up of the two Kali, the name of one manifestation of the mother goddess, and dasa, meaning slave. The literal meaning then is slave of Kali.

Having spent some time with Shakuntala, they decided to get married. They wanted to get married in private without the usual pomp and ceremony associated with the regular marriage, called the *Brahmay Vivah*. This type of marriage is permitted in the Hindu religion and is designated as "*Gandharva Vivaha*".

King Dushyanta returned to his capital, giving his royal ring to her as a token of his love and asked her to present the ring when she comes to his capital to join him at his court. After the departure of king Dushyanta, Shakuntala used to be immersed in his memory, always lost in thought, gazing in the emptiness. She was always remembering the good time they had together and the anxiety of meeting him again. One day when she was deep in her thought, a hermit came by that way and asked her for directions. But Shakuntala did not hear him since she was deep in her trance. The hermit shouted loudly to get her attention but by the time she came to her senses, the impatient hermit had already jumped to the conclusion that she had insulted him by ignoring him. He immediately cursed her stating,"The one in whose romance you have got lost, will forget you when you will meet him." This was a big blow to Shakuntala. Curses spelled by hermits in those days used to come true. For poor Shakuntala this was a great punishment. She begged the hermit for his mercy. The hermit then revised his curse and told her that her lover will remember her but after some time. While Shakuntala was on her way to meet his beloved, her ring slipped in the water while she was crossing the river in a boat. When she asked king Dushyanta to accept her, he had completely forgotten her and she did not have the ring, which he had given her as a token of his love. Devasted, Shakuntals had to return to her ashram. But the sages at the ashram also denied her permission to stay because she was pregnant and legally unmarried. The ashram could not take her word for what had happened. Shakuntala had to go out in the forest and survive on her own. She gave birth to a handsome boy whom she named *Bharat*. In the meantime, a fisherman caught the fish, which had swalloed the ring, which had slipped out from Shakuntala's finger. Being a ring bearing the royal insignia, the fisherman ran to the court in the hope of getting a reward. As soon as king Dushyanta saw the ring, his memory came back. He again went to the same area where he had his first encounter with Shakuntala. He observed a little boy who had captured a lion cub and was defending himself against an angry lioness protecting her cubs. He was very much impressed by the boy's courage and bravery. He then saw Shakuntala who came looking for her son, Bharat. They all meet. King Dushyanta apologizes profusely. He was delighted to meet his son, Bharat. Dushyant and Shakuntala return to the capital and ruled as king and queen for many years thereafter. Their son, Bharat, grew up to be a brave handsome man, expanded his kingdom, which covered the whole of the Indian sub-continent for the first time in the history of India. It is after his name that the country India is officially called "Bharatvarsha" or simply "Bharat". One would notice that an Indian postal stamp states "Bharat" on it.

The story of Shakuntala has been cited here since it is a remarkable illustration of marriage by choice and love. It is also represents the social conditions in which this type of marriage was accepted. Marlin French in her book, titled, "The History of Woman", a three-volume work, an excellent work, mentions the story of Shakuntala but she portrays her as being a victim of persecution. I disagree with her. In my opinion, Shakuntala was a victim of circumstances. Marlin is coloring everything from a "feminist" perspective and therefore her interpretations are biased in that manner. While on the subject of Marlin's writing, she has also harshly criticized the *Ashwamedha Yagna*. According to her, the queen is made to copulate with the horse, which is sacrificed in this important yagna. The purpose of this, according to her, is to exhibit male superiority. This again is a gross distortion and misrepresentation of this very sacred ceremony. Lord Ramchandra has performed this ceremony and he is a Hindu god and an incarnation of lord Vishnu, most revered in all of India. Hindus would be furious if they knew that such a degrading comment has been made by Marlin. If such a comment had been made about a Muslim religious character, the reaction could be furious, similar to Salman Rushdie's *The Satanic Verses*. Hindus won't react like Muslims. It is also interesting to note that in the chapter on India, all her references were from female sources.

There are a number of ways of getting married as prescribed by *Rig Veda*. The most common marriage ceremony is called Bramhya Vivah: This is the procedure, which is generally preferred by respectable people. It is a fairly elaborate and is fairly detailed marriage ceremony. The main objective is the father giving away the daughter called "*Kanyadaan*" in Sanskrit. Kanya means daughter and Daan means donation. It is relevant to cite some of the vows, contained in this ritual:

> ---*Oh bride! For the sake of future happy married life, which you desire, I accept you. Not just for my sake. All this wealth belongs to you. Just as nature is the cause for the production of all kinds of grain, similarly, you are also going to fulfill all the desires. Therefore, I, representing the Earth, accept you in the form of a goddess*

> .----*Stanza used for Kanya Daan: "This beautiful daughter, all decked in ornaments, is being given to you, you representing lord Vishnu, for fulfilling your desire of obtaining "Bramha Loka."*

Kanya daan is an essential part of all marriages in Hinduism. It has been acceptable to Hindus for the past many millennia. It has never been objected to by any feminists or women's equality advocates on the basis that to treat one's girl as something, which can be "donated" as if it were property or any material belonging. It could, however, be picked up by western feminists as one more point of male dominition in the Hindu society.

All other forms of marriage are described in the following pages. In Hinduism, marriage is conceived of as something, which happens by the grace of god; something of a matter of destiny, pre-arranged in the heavens. This belief is in the same vein as the other important concept of a Hindu marriage, considering the relationship between husband and wife as being permant, lasting not only over this life but also over the next seven lives. The purpose of marriage, according to the religious texts, is not just to spend a happy married life, but with the ultimate goal of obtaining "Brahma Loka". Loka means place and Brahma Loka means the place of residence of "Brahma", i.e. obtain release from the cycle of birth and death.. When one reaches this stage, one attains freedom from all the worldly things called *Samsara*. This, according to Hindu religion, should be the aim of a human life. Husband and wife, together, going through the *Grahestha Ashram,* are supposed to gain valuable experience, learn from this experience and realize that worldly pleasures are not everlasting. The only permanent source of happiness is the knowledge of "reality", that is Brahman. The hymns remind the couple of this ultimate goal, which they should bear in mind and try to accomplish jointly. So the purpose of marriage, according to Hindu religion, is not limited to a happy married life but has a higher purpose. One cannot reach such a high goal unless one spends a life of high moral character, cultivate purity of heart and adhere to certain ideals. Easier said than done. In any case, the marriage has a very lofty purpose in Hinduism. Marriage also is not limited only for the welfare of the married couple themselves or their immediate family but for the good of the society in general. *Rig Veda* contains the following wedding prayer:

> *This wedding prayer indicates the rights of a woman as wife. It is addressed to the bride sitting next to bridegroom. It touches upon a few other issues as well.*
> *"Happy be you (as wife) in future and prosper with your children here (in the house): be vigilant to rule your household in this*

home (i.e. exercise your authority as the main figure in your home). Closely unite (be an active participant) in marriage with this man, your husband. So shall you, full of years (for a very long life), address your company (i.e. others in the house listen to you, and care about what you have to say)." (Rig Veda 10.85.27).

The famous marriage hymn (10.85), calls upon members of the husband's family to treat the daughter-in-law (invited into the family "as a river enters the sea") as the queen *samrajni*. She is welcomed in many ways:

"Come O desired of the gods, beautiful one with tender heart, with the charming look, good towards your husband, kind towards animals, destined to bring forth heroes.
May you bring happiness for both our quadrupeds and bipeds."
(Rig Veda 10.85.44)

"Over thy husband's father and thy husband's mother bear full sway.
Over the sister of thy lord, over his brothers rule supreme." (Rig Veda 10.85.46)

"Happy be thou and prosper with thy children here:
Be vigilant to rule over your household, in this home." (Rig Veda 10.85.27)

Later in the marriage ceremony, the mother of the bride presents an auspicious necklace, called *Mangal- Sutra* to the bride. This necklace is of special significance in that it has to be worn by a married woman all her life to signify her good fortune and to signify that she is married. This is just like a diamond ring with a band a wedded woman wears in the west. A widow is not allowed to wear this ornament (the Mangal Sutra). The bride's mother while she is putting this ornament around the bride's neck says:

" O the one who is devoted to her husband!
I am putting this auspicious Mangal- Sutra,
Around your neck.
Oh beautiful! May you live for one hundred years!"

- The husband does not have to wear anything to signify that
he is married

Equality of sexes emphasized:

Throughout the *Vedas*, equality among sexes has been emphasized. Women were not to be confined to do the domestic work, as is the popular belief. They were carrying out all types of responsibilities, just like men. None of the jobs were the forte of men only. Vedas state that women can and should do almost all the jobs, which men do. Even going to the battlefield and taking part in the combats has been mentioned. The *Vedas* demand that the women ought to be physically strong. There are particular professions recommended for women, such as teachers, judges, writers, administrators, community leaders, and of course, housewives. The job description of a housewife was quite different during the Vedic period. The wife had complete control of the household, the finances and supervision of all the servants and staff. There was no interference from the husbands. Whatever the husbands earned, they used to give it all to the wife and did not question her about how she spent it.

In ancient India women played an important part in art and religion. Dr. *S. Radhakrishnan,* a world renouned philosopher and one time president of the republic of India, recalls some examples of the active part played in intellectual and social life by women in ancient India: " Brahmin girls were taught Vedic wisdom, girls of the *Khatrya* community were taught the use of the bow and arrow. The *Barhut* sculptures represent skillful horsewomen in the army. *Patanjali* mentions the famous spear-bearers (*sakitikis*). *Megasthenes* speaks of *Chandragupta's* bodyguard of *Amazonian women*. *Kautalya* mentions women archers in the houses as well as in the forest universities of India, where boys and girls were educated together. *Atrai* studied under *Valmiki* along with *Lava* and *Kusha,* the twin sons of *Lord Ramchandra*. In *Malatimadhava,* the great poet, *Bhavabhuti,* makes *Kamandaki* study with boys." Prominent women like *Gayatri, Maitreyi, Anusuya* were renowned seers of their time. This shows that women had the right to religious teachings. Appendix II lists important women sages who had composed hymns, which are included in the *Rig Veda*. Looking after the household, bringing up children, teaching them during their very early years, providing full support to husband and fully participating in all the affairs of the household affairs was supposed to be an important part of a good woman's life. As mentioned before, it was customary that a man would give all his earnings to his wife and she would be the one who would spend it as she pleased without reporting to her husband. As mentioned in the *Vedas,* a good woman is expected to do every thing to enhance the glory of her husband's family and that of her own family.

Klaus K. Klostermair has written an excellent book entitled "A Survey Of Hinduism" and in it, in chapter 23, he has described the position of women in Hinduism. The following portion from that chapter describes the status of women during the *Vedic* times as follows:

> " *Minoti Bhatacharya*, herself a Hindu woman, argues that in Vedic times women and men were equal as far as education and religion were concerned. Women participated in the public sacrifices alongside men. One text mentions a female rshi *Visvara*. Some Vedic hymns are attributed to women such as *Apala*, the daughter of *Atri, Ghosa*, the daughter of *Kaksivant*, or *Indrani*, the wife of *Indra*. Apparently in the early Vedic times women also received the sacred thread and could study the Veda. The *Haritasmiriti* mentions a class of women called *bramhacharyani* who remained unmarried and spent their lives in study and ritual. Panini's distinction between *achrya* (a teacher) and *acharyani* (a lady teacher), and upadhyaya (a woman preceptor) and an upadhyayini (a preceptor's wife) indicates that women at that time would not only be students but teachers of sacred lore. He mentions the names of several noteworthy women scholars of the past such as *Kathi, Kalapi, and Bhvici*. The *Upanishads* refer to several women philosophers, who disputed with their male colleagues such as *Vychaka*, who challenged *Yajnavalka*."

In order to illustrate the importance of women during the Vedic period, the following examples are cited. The Vedic pantheon includes a substantial number of female goddesses. There are beautiful hymns to *Usas*, the dawn, imagined as an alluring young woman:

> *"Dawn on us with prosperity, O Usas, daughter of the sky,*
> *Dawn with great glory, goddess, lady of the light, dawn thou*
> *With riches, bounteous one...*
>
> *O Usas, graciously answer our songs of praise with bounty and*
> *with brilliant light.... Grant us a dwelling wide and free from*
> *foes...."*
> (*Rig Veda, Sukta on Ushas*)

One of the most important of all Vedic hymns, the so-called Devi-sukta, is addressed to Vak (speech, revelation), the goddess who is described as the companion of all the other gods, as the instrument that makes ritual efficacious

> ."*I am the queen, the gatherer –up of treasures....*
> *Through me alone all eat the food that feeds them....*
>
> *I make the man I love exceedingly mighty,*
> *make him a sage, rsi and a Brahmin....*"
>
> *It is not unimportant, that, that Earth (Prithvi)*
> *is considered female,*
>
> *The goddess who bears the mountains*
> *and who brings fourth vegetation....*"

There are more examples of worship of goddesses. The idea of equality of sexes is expressed in the *Rig Veda* thus:

> "*The home has , verily, its foundation in the wife*",
> "*The wife and husband, being equal*
> *Halves of one substance,*
> *are equal in every respect;*
>
> *Therefore both should join and*
> *take equal parts in all work,*
> *Rreligious and secular.*" *(Rig Veda 5.61.8).*

This clearly illustrates the importance given to feminity and presents argument that males alone did not dominate the society. It is important to point out that Mahatma Gandhi advocated the same thing in the twentieth century but the idea was not new. In the Vedas, they do not just limit themselves to equal sharing of household work, which Mahatma Gandhi refered to, but the wives were also supposed to be knowledgeable about the husband's business so that she could take over in case the husband becomes disabled or dies or is absent for a long time. It was certainly a very advanced concept, even from today's standards. They could not do this unless the women were well educated. Not only that, in all-important matters, a woman had to be present and made decisions jointly with her husband. Her presence at all religious ceremonies and sacrificial rituals was absolutely essential; her absence would make the ceremony or ritual invalid. A good example of this is the *Ashwamedha Yagna* performed by lord *Ramchandra*, mentioned in the great epic, *Ramayana.* Since queen *Sita* was not with him for the performance of this very important yagna, Lord *Ramchandra* installed a gold statue of her to satisfy this important requirement.

> A wife was called *Patni*,(the one who leads the husband
> through life),   "   *Dharmapatni,* (the one who guides
> the husband in dharma), and
> *Sahadharmacharini,* (one who moves with the husband on
> the path ofdharma).

The edicts *patni* and *dharmapatni* are in common usage even today.

Vedas have given a great importance to *Usas,* meaning dawn, a feminine gender; the phenomenon of dawn, described as a feminine goddess, the topic had been mentioned earlier. The quality of poetry in dealing with this topic is particularly noteworthy. The poetry and imagination is indicative of the deep conviction of the composer, who, in dealing with this subject, which, of course is not to be found in any other religious literature. Nor is it found in ordinary literature. The beautiful natural phenomenon of "Usas", i.e. dawn, has been given the simile of a beautiful and virtuous lady who is the deliverer of prosperity, brightness, freshness, purity and so on. It must also be appreciated that the composers of these stanzas were keen observers and appreciators of the beauty of nature. They, in describing this natural phenomenon, chose to compare it with another beauty, that of a woman. Built in these compositions also is respect and admiration for women. There is also a strong suggestion that a woman should possess the virtues of *Ushas.* Some examples of stanzas in praise of *Ushas* are:

> *Hymn 7.75:*
> > *Born in the heavens the Dawn hath flushed*
> > *And showering her majesty is come as*
> > *Law ordaineth.*
>
> > *She has uncovered fiends and hateful*
> > *Darkness; best of Angirases, hath waked*
> > *The pathways.*
>
> > *Rouse us this day to high and happy fortune;*
> > *To great felicity, O Dawn,*
> > *Promise us.*

> *Vouchsafe us manifold and splendid riches,*
> *Famed among mortals, man-befriending,*
> *Goddess.*

This is a portion of this hymn. There are a number of hymns devoted to *Ushas*: Hymns 7.76, to 7.81, 1.48, 1.92, 1.123 and 124, 5.79, 6.64 and 65, 8.47, and 10. 172. This shows the importance of *Ushas* in *Rig Veda*.

In addition to conceiving Usha as a goddess, very beautiful and virtuous, she has also been conceived of as incarnation of "power" in one of her other form. She is, in this form, the destroyer of evil and protector of good. She is the destroyer of darkness and an illuminator of the world; giver of happiness and energy to all.

The wise and learned sages who have composed these stanzas have used the natural phenomena such as dawn, rain, earth and its qualities of growing vegetation, lightning, rivers, etc. as similes to describe the virtues of a woman.

CHAPTER 2.
STATUS OF WOMEN IN THE POST-VEDIC AND EPIC PERIODS:

The status of women described in the Vedic period did not continue in the periods, which followed. The Vedic period is enshrined in remote antiquity and from the information available, mainly through the Vedas, it is safe to conclude that women during that period enjoyed remarkable freedom and independence, gender equality prevailed, education for women was freely available and encouraged. Certain evil traditions, such as child marriages, restrictions on widows and Sati were unheard of. Women were well educated, well respected in the society and had contributed in arts, literature, philosophy and in other areas of human endavour. As the time passed, it was felt that women needed to be protected and their freedom got gradually curtailed.

The great epics of Ramayana and Mahabharatha:

The period, which followed the Vedic times, is a long and colorful one containing the wonderful mythological stories of glorious characters, their lives, and what extra-ordinary things they were able to achieve during their lifetimes. There are a large number of *"Puranas"*, (Mythical literature), containing these stories. The main theme, which runs through all of them is that the characters in each one of these great sagas follow the dictums of the religious texts, i.e., the Vedas, and live a righteous life; face and overcome enormous difficulties in an effort to practice the path of the *Dharma*. They never wavered from their *Dharma,* and surmounted the obstacles with faith, courage and dignity without caring for the price they had to pay; in many cases it was a matter of sacrificing their life. There were, on one hand, these other characters, who had given up the path of the *Dharma* and had chosen to live the life of the immoral and devilish beings. Their main objective was to harass the followers of the righteous path of *Dharma* and take over the reins of power in their hands. The long sagas of the two most important epics, the *Ramayana and the Mahabharatha,* which are well known all over the world, have this theme running through them right from the beginning till the very end. In both these epics, a fierce battle goes on between the forces of good and the forces of evil and in each and every case the good ultimately triumphs over the evil. The forces of evil are generally stronger and a point comes when it becomes certain that the forces of evil will win when devine intervention occurs and saves the good and righteous. At the center of each epic there is a woman. In the case of *Ramayana, Sita,* the wife of prince Rama, of *Ayodhya,* had been abducted by the demon king *Rawana.* The whole saga is, in nutshell, the story of how prince Rama gathers an army, fights with the demon king and brings about the release of his wife, *Sita.*

At the center of the great saga, the *Mahabharata,* is again a woman, *Draupadi,* the very beautiful, highly accomplished wife of the *Pandavas,* the rightful heirs to the throne of their ansisteral kingdom, which had been illigeally taken over by their own cousins and they also tried to disrobe *Draupadi* in the court. Again, devine intervention, in this case that by lord *Krishna,* prevents this from happening. This, in short, is the story but there is considerably more in this epic, including the great war fought between the *Pnadavas and* the *Kauravas,* which ends with the victory of the forces of good, that is, that of the *Pandavas.* The forces of the evil, the *Kauravas* were larger and more powerful and victory of *Pandavas* seemed unlikely, but again the devine intervention, in this case, help of lord *Krishna,* tipped the odds in favour of the good. *Draupadi* was thus able to avenge the insult that was meted to her in the court.

There are countless other *Puranas,* such as *Vishnupuran, Shivpuran, Naradpuran, Garudpuran* and so on, to name a few. In each one of them runs the same theme of the fight between the good and the evil, with a woman being in the center of each episode, in most cases. These stories teach certain important things: firstly, that a woman's honor is to be protected, secondly, the forces of good always win in the end and that is why following the path of rightousness and *Dharma* is the correct path to follow, thirdly, one should not be afraid in this struggle, have faith and god will always protect those following the path of the *Dharma.* All the teachings of the Vedas were followed by people whom the devine forces helped.

In most of the *Puranas* a woman has been portraid as being physically weak and is overpowered by evil men who harass her in many ways. She begs for god's help and she gets it in one form or other and is relieved from her distress. But a woman is not always depicted as a weakling all the time. The motherly love, which a woman has for her child is a powerful thing and a mother does everything in her power to protect her child, nurish it and provides it the best possible environment for growth and development. That is why a mother is always worshipped. Worship of the mother is a fundamental tenant of Hinduism and the child is taught this as a first lesson. The idea is extended in the religion where a *Devi* or universal mother is worshipped. She is the mother of all. She protects everybody just like a mother protects her child. A mother's care for her child never ends; it begins as soon as a child is born and continues even after the child has grown up and is completely independent and capable of taking care of himself as well as his mother. That is a virtue, which a mother intrinsically possesses. The worship of mother goddess in Hinduism is a unique phenomenon and is not found in any other religion anywhere in the world. In Christianity it is the father in the heaven who is worshipped. The trinity consists of the father, the son and the holyghost. There is no place for a female in this ensamble. Christians do worship a female deity in the form of Maddona in certain parts of the world but this is on a much smaller scale compared to the worship of the *Devi* in India. She is worshipped in every household on a daily basis.

The worship of the universal mother occupies a very important place in Hinduism. Each year there are several festivals specially dedicated for her worship and the woman of the house has a central role to play in these festivities and *pujas* (worships). The most important of these festivals is, of course, Deepawali, known all over the world as the festival of lights. On this day the goddess *Laxumi* is worshipped. She is one of the nine manifestations of the universal mother and is the one who is the giver of wealth and prosperity. The lady of the house is supposed to receive gifts on this auspicious ocassion, which should generally consist of a gold ornament and a new dress (a saree), which she wears in preparation for this special puja. Also, the other members of the family also get new garments. The whole house is thoroughly cleaned, freshly painted and tastefully decorated in preparation for this event. In the evening lights are placed all around the house and is illuminated in the dark night. All houses and buildings are similiarly lit up. *Laxumi pujan* is performed in the evening with all members present. A special feast is then served. This is actually the culmination of a nine-day long festival called the *Navaratri*, literally meaning nine nights. On each one of these nine days nine different manifestations or forms of the mother goddess are worshipped. These nine days are considered to be the most auspicious in the entire year. It is believed that a person receives rewards many folds if he/she does a good deed such as performing a puja or giving donations in charity during this period. There are many more festivals devoted to the worship of the mother goddess spread throughout the year but they are not as important as Diwali. And in all these festivals the housewife is the central figure and occupies the most important position. Without her these celebrations cannot take place.

A housewife is called *Grahalaxumi*, that isto say that she is the creator of wealth and prosperity in the household. It is, therefore, believed that wealth and prosperity comes to a house where the housewife is loved and respected. Where a housewife is unhappy, disrespected and suppressed, poverty and destruction results. All religious texts state this and as will be cited later, the *Manu Smiriti* states this quite clearly and explicitly.

Worship of goddesses in Hinduism, a glorification of motherhood and feminity:

Worshipping of goddesses is not a recent phenomenon. It is an age-old tradition, which can be traced back to the Vedic times. There are certain hymns in *Rig Veda*, which are dedicated to the praise and worship of certain goddesses. These goddesses are, of course, not the same as described above but represent natural phenomena. Some of these hymns are cites here to illustrate this point:

There are three Great Goddesses invoked in the ten apri-suktas. One of them is Bharati, as the very name suggests, was the tutelary deity of the Bharatas. Mention of the goddesses, Bharati, Ila and Saraswati has been made in Suktas, 2.3 8., 3.4.8, 7.2.6 & 8, 9.5.8 and 10.70.6 & 8. The following is a sample from Rig Veda:

> *"Sarasvati who prefers our devotion, Ila*
> *Divine, Bharati all surpassing—*
> *Three Goddesses, with power inherent,*
> *Seated, project this holy Grass, our*
> *Flawless refuge"! (2.3.6)*

> *"You I address Saraswati and Bharati, and Ila, all:*
> *Urge ye us on to glorious fame" (Rig Veda 1.188.8)*
> *"Saraswati, who prefers our devotion, Ila devine, Bharati all*
> *surpassing;*
> *Three goddesses, with power inherent, seated, protect this holy*
> *Grass, our flawless refuse!" (Rig Veda 2.3.8)*

*"With eulogy I call on Raka swift to hear: may she auspicious
hear us, and herself observe.*

*With never-breaking needle may she sew her work, and
Give a hero son most wealthy, meet for praise" (Rig Veda
2.32.4)*

The following hymn is devoted to Night and Dawn, as goddesses:

*"Here in this shrine may Dawn and Night,
The daughters of Heaven, the skilful
Goddesses, be seated."*

*"In your wide lap, auspicious, willing Ladies
May the Gods seat them with a willing
Spirit". (10.70.6).*

As is wellknown, *Saraswati* and *Mahi* are also names of rivers; they are
being worshipped in the same spirit as the river *Ganges* is worshipped today.
The *"Mother Ganges"*, very much revered by Hindus. To conceive these rivers
in the form of goddesses is quite natural since they were of immence benefit
to the Aryans. The flow of river *Saraswati* has since gone underground; till it
surfaces at *Trivani,* meaning the confluence of the three, at *Prayag,* renamed
by Moghul Emperors, Allahabad.. The trivani is believed to be a very sacred
place for Hindus and they believe that bathing in the waters, which are a
mixture of the rivers *Ganga, Yamuna* and *Saraswati*, washes one's sins away.
The whole object of citing these hymns is to illustrate that Aryans, during
the ancient Vedic times also used to worship female deities. So worshipping
female deities is not something recent in Indian history. It is a long established
tradition.

It is also important to note that the worship of a female goddess, a goddess
riding a tiger, had been in practice in Harrapa, a civilization very ancient and
anticident to that of Aryan. Archiological findings clearly substantiate this.
So this supports the view that worship of a female deity had been practiced
for a long time; practically as far as the history takes us and no bias against
females is indicated.

In the *Rig Veda,* there are a number of hymns devoted to the praise and
worship of *Usha* (Dawn). The beautiful and spellbounding phenomenon of
the play of light and color just prior to the sunrise, *Usha* had captivated the

vivid imagination of the Rishis of that time. Not only are there a lot of hymns on the subject of *Usas*, the poetry in these compositions is also exquisite. In the words of B.K.Ghosh (Ref. 37, chap. XVI): "The hymns addressed to Heaven's daughter, *Ushas*, are perhaps the oldest and certainly the most beautiful. They have something of a lyric and beauty and love of nature of Shelley and Wordsworth, and one cannot help feeling that they were inspired by the sight of the sunrise over the snow clad peaks of the Himalayas." A few stanzas of the first hymn to *Usas* (1.48) will suffice to reveal the spirit of simple adoration, which invokes the goddess:

> 1. *Light us with happiness, O Ushas, daughter of heaven,*
>   *With great lusture, O radient one, with wealth,*
>   *O beautiful goddess.*

> 5. *Like a fair maiden comes Ushas, gladdening (all),*
>   *she comes awakening four-footed beasts, and*
>   *makes the birds rise into the air.*

> 9. *O Ushas, shine with shimmering radience, O daughter of*
>   *heaven, bringing us simple happiness, as you shew*
>   *your light upon the daily sacrifices.*

> 10. *The breath and life of the whole world is in you,*
>   *O noble one, as you shine forth;*
>   *As such, O resplendent one with towering chariot,*
>   *Give ear to our cry, O bestower of various gifts.*

> 11. *O Ushas, win then (for us) the prize*
>   *that is admired among human folk.*
>   *With that hasten to the sacrifices of your worshippers,*
>   *The sacrificers who are chanting your praises.*

> 14. *Whoever were the Rishis of old that invoked you*
>   *for protection and support, O noble one,*
>   *Yet accept our hymns and bestow on us a gift in token*
>   *Of your satisfaction, O Ushas, with brilliant lustte.*

Here is simplicity and not greed that is begging of the goddess, gifts and more gifts. Later, in the great epic, *Ramanaya*, there is, for example, a mention of the worship of *Devi*. It is mentioned in the *Ramcharit Manas* of

Tulsidas that *Sita,* prior to her *Swayamvar* visits the temple of her *Devi*, to seek her blessings, especially to reward her with a suitable husband.

Here is yet another example from the *Rig Veda:*

"I am the victorious one: may my husband
recognize my strength. O Gods!

It is I who made the sacrifice from which
The great and glorious Indra deriveth
All his strength."

Again it is Aditi who embodies the whole relm
Of nature and is the
"common mother of Gods and men."

Under whatever aspect the ancient *Aryans* worshipped the mysterious forces of nature, the feminine principle always received more than its generous share of adoration. The idea of all-encompassing motherhood as the highest principle was firmly accepted in Vedic times, transmitted to all later periods, and has throughout all ages formed the basis of the exceptional degree of reverence paid in India to the *mother.*

The difference between the ancient Vedic times and now is that then women were really respected and gender equality was really practiced. Now that sort of respect for women does not exist. The idea just exists in the mythology and iin the temples.

Examples of gender equality as practiced in Hindu mythology and worship:

The mutuality of man and woman in the Indian tradition strikes one as an early intution of the finding of modern science that masculinity and feminity are matters of degree rather than bipolar: that human beings are bisexual, possessing both male and female hormones and characteristics, though distributed in varying degrees. It is being increasingly recognized by modern scientists of human personality that it is a combination of what are generally regarded as masculine characteristics such as strength and self-confidence and the feminine virtues like patience, forgiveness and self-effacing service that makes the finest human beings. The glorification of the female principle as illustrated earlier, it should not be surprising that the greatest of the India's life-giving rivers be worshipped as mother *Ganges* (in contrast to Egypt's father Nile), and the country itself is regarded as *Bharat Mata.* We have seen how goddesses are worshipped in the above-mentioned examples. It is important to point out that in Hinduism all the female deities are associated with their male-god counterparts. They form the famous male/female pairs in an unseparable manner. Each deity by itself is conceived of as incomplete without the other. Some very primordial deities, such as Lord *Shiva,* for example, is not complete without *Shakti or Parvati,* the goddess of power and the pair *Shiva and Shakti* is always worshipped together. A very common prayer in praise of Shiva is:

> *Karpur gauram karunavatram*
> *Sansara saram bhujagendra haram*
>
> *Sada vasantam hridayarvinde*
> *Bhavam bhavani sahitam namami*

Meaning: You are white like camphor, and are mercy incarnate;
You are the essence of the world, and wear a garland of snake.

Your lotus heart is always pleasant like spring;
I pray you along with goddess Bhavani.

The last line is important to note where the prayer states that I pray you along with *Bhavani,* (another name for *Shakti).* Mother goddess assumes many forms and is known by many names such as *Parvati, Annapurna, Durga, Saraswati, Chamunda, Kali, Laxumi,* etc., according to the various manifestations, such as, the giver of knowledge and learning, (*Saraswati),* giver of wealth and prosperity (*Laxumi),* destroyer of evil *Durga or Chamunda),* giver of peace and motherly love, giver of bravery and so on. *Shiva* and *Shakti* are complementary to each other. This is why he is also known by the name, *Ardhanari Nateshwara. Ardhanari* literally means half woman and half man and *Nateshwara* means the God of Cosmic Dance.

The following *Stotra* is recited in the worship of the mother of the whole universe, *Annapurna* :

> *Annapurne sada purne, shankar prana wallabhe*
> *Gnayana, Vairagya siddhyartham, Bhikshyam   dehi   che*
> *Parvati*

34

Meaning: O Annapurne (meaning the one who is the giver of food, and who is never short of it), thou art very dear to Lord *Shankara*, (another name of Shiva), I beg you to give me Knowledge (*Gnyana*) and detachment (*Vairagya*). It is a very powerful stotra in which a devotee prays the goddess and begs for her blessings and wants to get the power to become knowledgeable and also to become detached from the worldly pleasures and attachments. These are the two most important pre-requisites for spiritual advancement, as per the Hindu philosophy and eventually obtaining *Moksha,* (the release from the cycle of birth and death). Mother goddess is the one who has the power to bestow the devotee with this power if he prays to her with pure conscience.

Similarly, Laxumi, the goddess of wealth, complements Lord *Vishnu* and they are worshipped together as *Laxumi Narayana*. *Sita* is inseparably associated with Lord *Rama*, the incarnation of the Supreme- being, Lord *Vishnu*. In doing their *Puja*, Sita's name is taken first and they say, *Sita Ram*. Yet another example is that of Lord *Krishna*, yet another incarnation of the Supremebeing, who is always worshipped in association with *Radha*. And again, her name is taken first, *Radhye Krishna*. These examples illustrate the point under discussion, that is, gender equality. It would be wonderful if this lofty spirit be put into practice!

In the words of S.Das, (Ref. 15):

> " *Significant is the place given to female deities in this ancient worship, an honor equal to, if not exceeding, that of the gods. From the very dawn of Indian philosophy—embodied in the hymn known as the Rig-Veda – the conception of the duality, male—female, of divinity held sway. Each god was closely linked with his shakti, or female principle; the god was energy, the goddess the form through which alone it could pour itself out and find expression":, the female principle went forth hought the universe as the abiding force of the creator of the world"*

> *"Aum" is the mistic logos, and voice*
> *or speech is a goddess,*
> *The wife of the creator.*

> *It is She who sounds throughout the universe,*
> *whose vibrations has created all things;*

-*"in unison with whom and by whom
the creator accomplishes His creation".*

Under whatever aspect the ancient Aryans worshipped the mysterious forces of nature, the feminine principle always received more than its generous share of adoration. The idea of all-encompassing motherhood as the highest principle was firmly accepted in Vedic times, transmitted to all later periods, and has throught all ages formed the basis of the exceptional degree of reverence paid in India to the *mother*. An extremely important hymn called *Shree Suktam, or Laxumi Suktam,* from the Vedas, is always recited while worshipping the mother goddess in any of her manifested forms. The complete hymn consists of sixteen stanzas. It is difficult to appreciate the beauty of this very auspicious hymn without the knowledge of Sanskrit and therefore instead of citing this hymn in its entirety, the fourth stanza is chosen as an example:

*Kaam sosmitam hiranaya prakaram
Ardram jwalantam triptam tarpayantim;*

*Padme sthitam padma varanam
Taamhopvahe shriam. (4)*

Meaning: O who has a smiling countenance, living in the midst of gold, born under the influence of the "Ardra" planet, glorious, the one who always fulfils the desires of her devotees, dwels in the lotus flower, her color is that of a rose colored lotus, O mother Laxumi! I invoke you.

An example of a very common prayer in honor of *Devi* is as follows:

*Namo Devi maha Devi Shivayyi sattanmaha
Namah prakartayi bhadrayi niata pranata smrita.*

Meaning: Prayer to you Devi, O great Devi, you ever
           belong to Lord Shiva; prayer to you who
           control the nature, I remember you and pray
           you always.

The following prayer is popularly taught to children in almost all Hindu families:

Matru devo bhavo, Pitre devo bhavo, Acharya devo bhva

Meaning: Mother is god, father is god and teacher is also god. The order in which the statement states the god-like praise of these persons is very important; the noteworthy point is that the mother comes first and foremost. In learning to respect his elders, a child must make a beginning from his mother; father and teacher come after mother, in that order. This gives the mother the highest ranking and respectability the first one to be respected in the hierarchy. Yet another prayer for the *Devi* is as follows:

Sarva mangal manglayye Shive sarvaarth sadhike
Sharanaye triambeke Devi Narayani namostute

Meaning: O the one who is auspicious and creats everything
             auspicious for all, accomplishes every thing for
             Shiva, I take refuge in you, O Narayani, I worship
             you with folded hands.

Adi Shankaracharya, a very prominent Hindu religious philosopher of the seventh century, and proponent of the non-duality principle of the *Advaita Vedantic* philosophy, has composed two beautiful *Stotras*, or compositions in Sanskrit in praise of the mother- goddes. They are: the "*Dayaparadhkhamapana Strotra*" and the "*Bhavanaykashtakam Stotra*. " Again, one with the knowledge of Sanskrit can really understand and appreciate these compositions. But the importance of worshipping the mother goddess is the point to be stressed.

There may be a great number of additional hymns and *Strotras*, which may be quoted in support of the deep and sincere belief in the power of the universal mother. Her worshippers firmly believe in her power and that she will answer their prayers and fulfill their desires. The religious literature is, therefore, replete with exquisite compositions for her praise and prayers. Having said that, It ought to be pointed out that in Hinduism, there is a lot of freedom allowed for a devotee to make an individual choice about which god or goddess one wishes to dedicate himself and select his/her own personal deity for worship. Some choose the worship of *Devi* because they find satisfaction and happiness in the experience of the motherly love, others choose Vishnu or Shiva etc, and worhip them with full devotion. Most pray many deities and sing their prayers without particular focus on any one. In some localities there are old temples of certain deities and people of that locality worship that particular deity. There is generally some history or mysticism associated with these places. For example, in certain cities in Rajasthan, the Rajput king or chieftan had established a temple of *Devi* many centuries ago and the Rajputs, whenever they went to the battlefield, worshipped the *Durga* or *Chamunda* prior to their departure and begged for victory. This temple and the deity, therefore, has a very special place in that city or community and the deity is worshipped regularly

Most of these citations belong to the post -*Vedic* period. The worship of feminine deities in the Vedic period has already been dealt with. In spite of all the evidence in support of the respect with which women had been treated in the Vedic and post-Vedic periods, the place of a woman, in many ways, had never been exactly equivalent to that of a man. The situation worsened with time. For example, in *Mahabharatha*, King *Dharamraja*, while gambling, placed his queen, *Draupadi*, on the bet and ended up losing her. This illustrates that a husband could treat his wife, an individual in her own right, like a possession. The question, which may then be asked is:"Doesn't the woman not have her own independent existence? A probable answer is: "A wife did not have a life independent and separate from her husband. She always had a subservient role."

Mother, the first teacher:

In the Vedic period a great emphasis was placed on the care, development and education of a child. It was recognized that the very early impressionable age of a child is very critical for his/her healthy development. And any thing learnt or experienced during that critical age has a lasting impression on the child. Whatever the child sees and experiences during this critical period creates a very deep and long lasting impression on the child's mind, which he/she carries throughout his/her life. It was, therefore, thought that the mother, who is the child's first care- giver, the first teacher, be well educated and knowledgeable, so that she would provide the proper environment for the child for his/her healthy development both mentally and physically. An educated and knowledgeable mother, it was thought, will do a much better job of providing the right atmosphere and care necessary for a child's healthy growth. The Vedas clearly state that the mother is the first teacher of the child and they emphatically state that all women should be well educated. (Please refer to hymns 1.49.2, 1.113.8, 1.113. 2, 1.113.20 and others in the Appendix). This is why the *Vedas* insist on educating women. The mother was, therefore, the most important person in the life of any person. This is why during those times in introducing oneself it used to be customary to state the name of one's mother. A very wellknown example is from the great epic, *Mahabharata*. In it the great warrior Arjuna always introduced himself as son of *Kunti*, his mother. This type of introduction shows his pride in being raised by a lady of *Kunti's* stature and whatever ability and status he has attained, is the result of the upbringing and teaching of his revered mother. It also states that he will not do anything to belittle his mother's reputation and glory. On the contrary, he will do his best to enhance the glory and good name of his mother. In this great epic, one of *Arjuna's* names is *Kaunteya,* which in Sanskrit means "son of Kunti". If one reads the Hindu religious text, the "*Bhagwad Geeta*", consisting of a long conversation between Lord *Krishna* and *Arjuna,* one will notice sometimes the Lord calling *Arjuna* by the name *Kaunteya.*

Contained in this important text is he Lord's teaching to *Arjuna,* the great *khtria* warrior and through him to the whole world, the essntial philosophy for a human being for successfully attaining *Moksha.*

There has also been a great reverence for the mother, not just in the Vedic times but also throughout the Indian culture and tradition, the likes of it not found in any other culture in the world. This continues even now without any diminution. This is why one will notice that in India, especially the Hindus, things, which are revered are given the names of mother. Most common examples are: *Bharat Mata,* India, my motherland, *Ganga Mata,* Mother Ganges, *Dharti Mata,* Mother earth, *Davi Mata,* mother goddess, *Saraswati Mata,* goddess of learning, *Gau Mata,* mother cow, and so on.

The *Manu Smriti* states:

> *The teacher is ten times more venerable*
> *Than a sub-teacher,*
>
> *The father a hundred times more than a teacher,*
> *But a mother a thousand times more than the father*

Mothers used to take pride in their children and openly displayed their confidence in their children by making statements such as: "My son (or daughter) will never do any thing like this…"They could do this because they were very confident about what their children had learned from them. The mothers were very confident and sure as to what to expect from their children. This was, therefore an excellent way to teach the children the morality, the discrimination between right and wrong and "Dharma", that is, their duty. This understanding of Dharma used to be developed further by their father and then by their teachers. But the basic foundation used to be laid by the mother.

Sita, an example of an ideal woman:

If one reads the great Indian Epic, the *Ramayana*, one will learn about the most ideal woman, *Sita*. *Ramayana* is the story of Lord *Ramchandra's* life, a true historical fact. He was the eighth incarnation of Vishnu and *Sita* was his wife. Both *Ram* and *Sita* are considered to be ideals, an ideal man and an ideal woman. That is why lord Ramchandra is called *Mariaada Purushottam*. This Sanskrit title means the best amongst the men and a completely ideal person who possesses a flawless character. Reading this great epic will enlighten the reader about the character of *Sita*. It is really impossible to do any justice to elaborate on the absolutely flawless character of this divine lady who is considered an incarnation of the divine mother herself. She was an ideal wife, an ideal daughter, an ideal mother, an ideal daughter-in-law, an ideal sister-in-law, and totally ideal in every way. She is worshipped in each Hindu home along with Lord *Ramchandra*. She is cited as an example to follow for every woman in an Indian Hindu family. It is recommended that the readers read the *Ramcharita Manas* by the great Hindi poet, *Sant Tulsidaas* or *Ramayana* by the great Sanskrit poet, *Valmiki*, who wrote the Ramayana for the first time. His writing is a poetic composition in Sanskrit. Translations of both works are available in English.

In her book, *From Eve To Dawn*, *Marlyn French* has described *Sita* as a persecuted woman. She is wrong in categorizing her in this way. It is, therefore, necessary to clarify this. It is true that lord *Ramchandra* had sent *Sita* away in exile. But one has to understand the background for his action. When lord *Ramchandra* fought with the demon king *Rawana* in order to free *Sita* whom *Rawana* had abducted, *Rawana* was defeated and was killed. *Sita* then returned to lord *Ramchandra*. But lord *Ramchandra* did not accept her as such. Since she had lived under the custody of the demon king for some time, she went through the "*Agni pariksha*", or the fire test to prove her purity before being accepted back by lord *Ramchandra*, even though lord *Ramchandra* had no doubts about her purity personally, this test was considered necessary to satisfy the doubts of public in general. *Agni pariksha* is a test in which the woman sits on a funeral pyre and the pyre is lighted. If the woman is pure, then the fire does not burn her. Lord *Ramchandra* had thus accepted her having successfully passed the "*Agni Pariksha*" (the fire test, which involves a woman being tested for her purity, has to sit in a fire. If the woman survives unscathed, it proves her purity.). After this lord *Ramchandra* returns to the capital, *Ayudhya* with *Sita* and others and starts ruling the kingdom. During this time the wife of a washerman goes out of town and does not return till the next day since the river in her path was flooded and crossing was impossible. When she returned home the next day, the washerman refused to let her in the house and said, "I am not like the king who accepted his wife even though she had lived with the demon king *Rawana.*" The news of this incident reached king *Ramchandra*. He sent secret agents across his capital and the kingdom to gage the feelings of his subjects regarding this matter. The agents reported back to the king. The news was not favourable. People were dissatisfied with the king. Lord *Ramchandra*, therefore, sends *Sita*, his very dear wife, into exile against his personal wishes but to satisfy the general demand of his subjects. He took this action in the capacity of the king and his responsibility as a king not as a husband. As a husband he was deeply disappointed by having to send his wife in the jungle. He did not wish his wife to go and live in the austere ashram, leaving the luxury of the palace. He himself also made a change in his personal living. He did continue to live in the palace but he did not sleep on the comfortable bed. He prepared a bed of grass on the ground and slept on it just as Sita would be doing in the ashram. He also spent all his life style to exactly the conditions of ashram conditions and vowed to continue that way till Sita would return back from the forest. So strong was his love for *Sita*. One must understand the clear difference between his duty as a king and his personal duty as a husband. For him, his duty to his subjects was far more important than his personal duty as a husband. He considered the happiness and welfare of his subjects his foremost duty and priority. He ran his administration very democratically. His governance is regarded as an ideal and even now the Hindus of India long for it. There is also a political party in India based on the principles of the governance of lord *Ramchandra*. It is called, *Raam Raj Parishad..*

It ought to be appreciated and understood that both lord *Rama* and queen *Sita* suffered personally but both were very sensitive to the need of their subjects. It was their first responsibility to make sure that their subjects were happy and had complete confidence in their leadership no matter whatever personal suffering they might have to endure. That is exactly what they did. For setting up such high moral ideals, they are worshipped by all the Hindus and regard them as ideals to be followed. Even after so many millenniums, the devotion of Hindus for them continues and is probably on the rise.

Status of woman in the great epic, Mahabharata:

The Mahabharatha teaches:

The wife is half the man, (Sanskrit: Ardhangini)
The best of friends,
The root of the tree of life;
and of all that will help him in the other world.
With a wife a man does mighty deeds;
With a wife man finds courage...
A wife is the safest refuge
...
A man aflame with sorrow in his soul,
or sick with disease,
finds comfort in his wife,
as a man parched with heat
finds relief in water.
Even a man in the grip of rage
Will not be harsh to a woman,
Remembering that on her depend
The joys of love, happiness, and virtue.
For woman is the everlasting field,
In which the Self is born

.

This passage leaves no doubt about the respect and esteem in which women used to be held during this important period in the history of India. The teaching of Mahabharata is of particular importance since this great epic is highly regarded by the majority of the population in India, particularly the Hindus. The epic is as popular today as it might have been many centuries ago. A recent revival of this epic was done when it was made into a video and DVD formats. Both Hindus and non-Hindus have watched this epic on these new formats and has resulted in its revival. The recent reproduction of this great epic on a set of DVDs revived once more the deep respect Hindus have had for the legendary epic of *Ramanaya* containing lofty ideals and important teachings. This is such an important and popular epic that all Indians are very well versed with every little detail contained in it. In every home and in the society, every body's character is judged against on the basis of characters in this epic, especially women. There is no doubt that a new presentation of this epic in electronic format has rekindeled interest in the ideals this epic depicts. It certainly has had a very positive effect on the general population.

Shakuntala, a prominent example of marriage by mutual consent, "Gandharva Vivah":

The famous story of Shakuntala, her love with Dushyanta and their marriage in the *Gandharva Vivaha style* has already been described in detail.

In the words of S. Das: " The relationship between husband and wife likewise is still one of confidence, trust and joy. "Consumed by the troubles of the soul, afflicted by reverses, men find pure delight in their wives, as creatures suffering from heat find it in the freshness of water."

"In the immortal story of *Shakuntala*, the heroine further defines this high ideal, according to her a wife is:

> *"An object of honor in the house; it is she who rears the children.*
> *The bride is the breath of life to her husband, and she is all devotion*
> *to her master. She is the half of man, the best of his friends, the*
> *source of well-being, wealth and happiness, the root of the family*
> *and of its prosperity... sweet-spoken wives are ever partakers in joy,*
> *ministering helpers in hours of sorrow and sickness... men who*
> *have wives perform the sacred ceremonies well and fulfill the*
> *duties of happiness; salvation is assured to them. Wives are*
> *friends in the wilderness, giving consolation by their gentle discourse:*
> *they are like fathers in the serious duties of life, they become like*
> *mothers in times of distress; Whoever has a wife is sure of support;*
> *that is why wives offer the best of refuge in life."*

Shakuntala, the forest-reared maiden, that "lotus in water, sparkling flame of life" , had married for love by a mere exchange of vows." Beautiful words of sanction were spoken over her union: "a soul unites itself by to another; a soul finds refuse in another; a soul gives itself to another; such is the rule traced out for thee by divine law". What a difference between the spirit of this union and present day marriage in India!" "

Swayamvara of Damayanti: (Nal/Damayanti story)

Another very beautiful example of a marriage in which the would-be bride chooses her life mate, the *Swayamwara,* is that of *Damayanti.* The *Nal/ Damayanti swayamvara* story is a very famous and popular one in the Indian mythology. It is said that *Damayanti* was so beautiful that even gods from heaven came to seek her hand and presented themselves for the occasion. *Damayanti's* love for king *Nala* was well known and there was no doubt in anybody's mind that she was going to place the garland around his neck. The gods decided to transform themselves as perfect copies of *Nala* and sat around him also holding a beautiful lotus flower in their hand just like him. It would, therefore, be impossible for anybody to find out the real *Nala. Damayanti* looked at the assembled wannaby bridegrooms and was able to successfully recognize the real *Nala* by the condition of the lotus flower in his hand, which was drooping a little bit and not as fresh fresh looking as all the others. The flower in *Nala's* hand was affected by the heat of his body. The flowers in the hands of the gods looked extremely fresh due to godly powers. This was a clever way of recognizing *Nala.*

As soon as Dayamanti recognized *Nala* and placed the garland on him signifying her choice, the gods from the heavens showered her with rosepetals in appreciation of her intelligence and unwavering love for *Nala.*

Many more examples of *swayamvara* style marriages are available in Indian literature and mythology. These examples are spread over many centuries, starting from the ancient times right up to the present day.

There is, of course, no other comparable story of love like *Nala and Damayanti* or the example of an ideal woman like *Sita.* But there are a large number of examples of women who have been very loving and devoted wives. They have also attained greatness and fame. People sing their praises.

.The status of women of Vedic era began to decline with time. Gender inequality started creeping into the society. Slowly women's status degraded to such an extent that they were not given the freedom, which was available to even Sudraas, (the lowest cast of ancient Hindu society). They were not given the basic rights. They were debarred from religious practices. They lost their political freedom as well. As the Vedic age progressed, the status of women became worst. And till the time of *Smiritis*, (religious scriptures of Hindus), the condition became so bad that women were not allowed free access to education. They were just given enough education to make them good for running the households. This process of deterioration in the status of women began just after the end of the Mahabharata period. This denotes the end of the epic period. The kind of insult to which queen Draupadi was subjected to in the court of king Dhritrashtra, is a good indication of the moral degradation of the society at that time. She was dragged into the court, filled with all categories of people including her the king her brothers-in-laws, ministers, respected teachers, her maternal grand father, other high class courtiers and orders were given to forcibly make her naked by taking her clothes off! This would be considered a height of moral degradation in any society at any time. This degradation kept on continuing. The ideals of goddess worship and the respect, which women should receive, as per the instructions of the Vedas, all remained in the books only. And this, unfortunately, also remains that way even now. The hypocrisy in the Hindu culture is very apparent. A small example in the life of Mahatma Gandhi would be interesting to note. While the Mahatma was in South Africa, busy in reforming the caste system and setting up an example, he asked his wife, Kasturba, to clean the latrines. These were not the flush toilets of today. They were the very crude things where one would just have a cast iron tray underneath. Kasturba, having come from a respectable "Vaisha", (business class), family up-bringing, had never in her wildest dream had thought that she would be asked to do such a task! She crossed the line of an Indian wife always obeying the orders of her husband and refused to obey. The Mahatma was very upset and asked her to leave his house for not obeying him. Later he realized that he was wrong and they made up but the important thing to note is that even the great Mahatma, who is now considered a person who is supposed to have contributed greatly in the cause of women, expected his wife to obey him without questioning. In his hearts of hearts he expected his wife to obey in accordance with the Indian/Hindu tradition and culture. With regard to this incident, one may ask: "Why did the Mahatma himself set an example by cleaning the latrines himself?" This question had never been asked. If you believe in something you must set an example by doing it first before asking somebody else to do it.

Status of Women in Jainism and Buddhism:

Buddhism, which began as a religion about 500 BC, was very popular in India during the time of the Mauryan Empire (324 to 183 BC). (Ashoka the great, (270 to 237 BC), was the best example of this period. Buddhism treated men and women on an equal basis in the sense that in terms of attaining the highest state, that is "Nirvana", both were considered equally eligible. This was considerably different from the Brahminic tradition of treating women at a lower and in a way not quite eligible to reach the highest state of "Mukti". That is why women were not permitted to perform the religious rituals. Buddhism made a departure from this tradition. The arrival of Buddhism was a welcome change for both the women as well as the lower caste Hindus and many women and lower caste Hindus got converted to Buddhism to escape from the degraded status they were given in the powerful and corrupt Brahmin dominated Hindu society. Joining Buddhism immediately raised the status of the women as well as the Shudras. It may also be mentioned in this context that the lower status given to the Shudras in particular, has also been an important factor in conversion of Hindus to Christianity. That is why the orthodox Hindus treat the Christians and Buddhists as if they were Shudras.

Buddhism does not consider women as being inferior to men. Buddhism recognizes the biological differences between men and women but consider both sexes to be equally useful to the human society. The division of society into four castes, as practiced in Hinduism is not a part of Buddhism. In Buddhism there is emphasis on the important role, which a woman plays as a wife, a mother, a sister, and a daughter, etc. But there is also emphasis on sharing responsibilities of the household between a husband and wife. A husband, according to the teachings of Buddha, should consider his wife as his friend, a companion and an equal partner in all aspects of family and in decision –making, which is not at all different from the message of the Vedas. (Refer to *Rig Veda* 5.61.8 in Appendix I). If the husband, on account of certain reasons, is unable to make decisions or becomes incapable, the wife should immediately take his place. This implies that she should be quite familiar with and be knowledgeable about the husband's business and affairs. Buddhism does not restrict women from getting educated or having religious freedom. This was also the message of the Vedas and a part of Vedic life style, which got degraded and women were later prevented from getting educated. Buddha permitted women into the Religious Order. In Buddhism women occupied responsible positions in the Bhikkuni Sangha. This is not very much different from the functions and responsibilities of a wife as given in the ancient Vedic society, which got changed due to the corruption in the Hindu society with the Brahmins becoming very powerful and corrupt. Buddhism rejected the sati tradition, which was prevalent during that time. The Jains also did not approve of this evil practice. In fact, Jains declared that to commit suicide by self-immolation was a sin.

The Buddhist texts have records of eminent saintly Bhikkunis, who were very learned and who were experts in preaching the Dhamma. During the time of Ashoka, certain Bhikkunis were sent to Ceylon to spread Buddhism.

The Buddha did not consider that there was much virtue in producing sons. His view was that any and all people could produce sons, even animals. The Indo-Aryan belief that it was important to have a son since, a son's performance of the last rites of his father will save him from going to hell, be rejected by the Buddha. Also, the other aspect of Hinduism, which believed in the Brahminical rituals to wash away the sins committed, was also not acceptable to Buddha. For Buddha it was not necessary for men or women to get married and raise a family. To him it was important that for anybody to rise to a higher level of spirituality, one must learn to exercise self-control, (control over one's senses and desires), and practice celibacy. It is important to point out in this context that in Hinduism the same is being preached, that is, practice of self-control, but the difference is that in Hinduism, self-control and celibacy are not in contradiction with getting married and raising a family. It used to be in the earlier times that a person would have to renounce the "world", that is, the *Samsara,* and go in the forest to meditate, but later on that concept underwent revision since it became clear that to achieve renunciation and sense control, which is basically a mental exercise, one does not necessarily have to leave the samsara. The concept of self-control as advocated in Buddhism is, therefore, not a new concept in the spiritual philosophy of India. The Vedas are full of stanzas, which highly recommend exercising *Brahmacharya.* (Celibacy). The *Bhagwad Gita,* a very important text of Hindu religion also preaches control of senses for achieving perfection and to experience "reality".

In Buddhism marriage was not considered an inviolable sacrament. According to Buddhism, one could get out of the marriage bond at any time without any adverse consequences to take to the religious life. This is different from the Hindu concept. In Hinduism a married life is not considered a non-religious life. In fact, to marry and to have a family and to raise children is considered a natural process. In Hinduism, the sole aim and purpose of the human life is to attain "Mukti", that is, to get out of the cycle of birth and death and get one with the absolute reality and therefore the advice is that the complete life of a person right from the birth till death and any act, which a person commits ought to be regarded and done as a form of a prayer to the almighty. The *Bhagwad Gita* teaches this very well.

Buddhism was in favor of widow marriage, which was a refreshing change from the rigidity in Hinduism, which came about in the post-Vedic period, preceding the birth of Buddhism. In a Buddhist text called *Anguttara Nikaya*, the following passages have been found:

> *"To whatever husband your parents will give you in*
> *marriage-anxious for your good, seeking for your happiness*
> *—for them, you will rise up early, be the last to retire, be*
> *willing workers, order all things sweetly and speak*
> *affectionately. Train yourselves thus, girls.*
>
> *And in this way also, girls: You will honor, revere, esteem*
> *and respect all whom your husband reveres, whether mother,*
> *father, recluse or Brahmin and on their arrival, will offer*
> *seat and water. Train yourselves thus, girls.*
>
> *"And in this way also girls: You will be deft and nimble at*
> *your husband's home crafts, whether they be wool or*
> *cotton, making it your business to understand the work,*
> *so as to do it and get it done. Train yourselves thus, girls.*
>
> *"And in this way also, girls: whatever your husband's*
> *household consists of—servants, messengers or workmen*
> *—you will study the work of each one of them, and know of*
> *each, what has been done and what not done; you will study*
> *the strength and weakness of the sick; you will portion off*
> *the solid food and soft food, to each according to his need.*
> *Train yourselves thus, girls.*
>
> *"And in this way also, girls: The treasure, silver and the corn,*
> *that your husband brings home, you will keep safe watch*
> *and not act as a robber, thief, carouser or wastrel in*
> *respect of these. Train yourselves thus, girls.*
>
> *"Indeed, girls, possessed with these five qualities women, on*
> *the breaking up of the body, after dying, will arise among*
> *nymphs of lovely form."*

The same text also states:

> *"Monks! Those families where mother and father are honored*

*are like unto heaven of Brahma; worthy of honor are such
families; Brahma, monks, is a term for mother and father.
Why? Because mother and father do so much for the children,
bring them fourth, nourish them, and introduce them to the
world."(These ideas are, again, not different from teachings of
Hinduism)*

Buddha has stated that there are seven types of wives:

One resembles a murderer, the second a soberer; the third a mistress; a fourth a mother; the fifth a sister; the sixth a friend; and the seventh a servant. According to Buddha the seventh, the servant type is the most preferable. The most that was expected of a wife was obedience and fidelity like a servant; the Buddha, considered the position of the wife as subordinate to that of her husband, but he did not believe in the unity and inseparability of husband and wife.

Position of women in Jainism:

Jainism is another important religion, which came about almost at the same time as Buddhism, and was started by Mahaveer Swami, a couple of centuries earlier than Buddhism, also gave women similar status as in Buddhism. Jainism, just like Buddhism, was another escape for the frustrated and oppressed women and lower class Hindus. And they joined this religion for the same reasons as they joined Buddhism. In Buddhism and in Jainism, women were admitted and ordained as priests. They were allowed to preach and were able to enjoy a status equivalent to that of men, albeit, in Jainism, the belief was that a woman, despite all her austerity and strict adherence of the religion, wouldn't achieve "Nirvana" on account of being a woman. She would have to be reborn as a man to attain that stage.

These two religions dominated the Indian sub-continent and even spread in countries adjoining India, more so Buddhism than Jainism. Buddhism spread in countries such as Afghanistan, China, Burma, and Sri Lanka, to mention the important ones. Ashoka the Great, who after his mighty bloody battles got converted to Buddhism and became a devout Buddhist, sent emissaries far and wide to spread Buddha's teachings. He also erected monuments and obelisks on which he etched inscription, which give us valuable information. Jain religion, on the other hand, was not as well organized as Buddhism and whatever Jain literature is now available, is not well classified and organized as the Buddhist. Ahoka also erected monuments at various places with Buddha's important teachings inscribed on them. There is not a great deal of information pertaining to the condition of women during the Mauryan Empire, which covered most of India in 250 BC, (see map), except the popularity of these two religions.

In the three-way fight between Buddhism, Hinduism and Jainism, around the eighth century AD, Buddhism almost disappeared from India except some remnants in the east, while Jainism survived on account of the many concessions, which it made with the Brahmanism. This is also the prime reason why one finds a greater commonality between Jainism and Hinduism. It recognized the supremacy of the Brahmin ritualism. It is, therefore, the practice of Jains to have Brahmins come and officiate over their domestic rituals and religious ceremonies.

In the early period of Jainism, marriage did not involve any indissoluble ties. And men were free like the Buddhists, to leave their wives and take to the monastic life if they so chose. In the earlier stages of Jainism, wives too had the choice of leaving their husbands and joining convents, but later, as inter-marriage with the Hindus became common among the Jains, the practice came under censure. All Jains, whether *Digambers or Swatambers,* maintain that in the monastic life the position of the nun is inferior to that of a monk, a view uniformly held by all great religions. The nuns are prohibited from reading certain texts such as *Mahaparijana* and *Arunopapata* and *Drishtiwada.* Adultery in Jainism was punished very severely but there was a more tolerant attitude towards nuns who committed adultery. Nuns, unlike the Buddhists or the Christians, did not have regular convents. They used to be generally wandering from place to place and were quite vulnerable to harassment and attacks from wicked men. There are accounts available of nuns being raped and became pregnant. In such cases, the religion required that they be taken good care of and not subjected to humiliation or ex-communication. The children born in such cases were also not condemned.

Jainism emphasizes self-denial for the sake of individual salvation and hence considers marriage a sort of hindrance in the path of spiritual progress. There are stories recorded of certain monks leaving the religious life and going back and getting married and living as a householder. This "back-sliding" was not considered good. It was, therefore, recognized that any one joining the order should be evaluated for his/her stage of spiritual attainment and strength of determination. Jainism recognizes that individuals are at different stages of spiritual development and, therefore, not every person was considered eligible for joining the order. As a comparison, the eligibility of persons joining the

Catholic Brotherhood is relatively lax. In Catholic system, the brothers live a relatively comfortable life. The condition that they will practice celibacy is a requirement but a large number of the ordained priests are unable to live up to this oath and the results have been disastrous: there are a large number of sexual abuses committed by the Roman Catholic Priests involving native Indian children and others resulting in the Church paying large sums of money in compensation in addition to apologies and loss of reputation. One big reason for the violation of their oath is that people who choose to join the order, are motivated by the comfortable living the priesthood offers rather than the hunger for spiritual upliftment. This is not the case in Jainism and Jainism also allows the freedom to get back to the *grehastha* stage without recrimination.

In Jainism, four types of marriages are recognized. They are: marriages arranged by parents, Swayamwara, Gandharva, and Asura. Out of these, Swayamvara is not mentioned in the *Gryha Sutra.* The rest are the same as in the *Gryha Sutra,* the Hindu text of Dharma Shastra. Even though not mentioned, the swayamvara was quite a common form of marriage at that time. A number of important examples of this type of marriage have been cited.

Though there are references in Jain literature about the desirability of a woman, in general, women, by nature, women were considered bad and an undesirable distraction, having a corrupting effect on men engaged in making spiritual progress. In the *Tandulaveyaliya* are given etomologies of various types of "women". For example, she is called Nari (Na-ari) because there was no worse enemy for man than her; she is called Mahila, because she charms by her wiles and graces; she is called Padma, because she accelerates man's passion; she is Rama, because she delights in coquetry; she is called Angana, because she loves the anga or body of men; she is Josiya, because by her tricks she keeps men under her subjection; she is Vanita, because she caters to the taste of men with her various blandishments. It is further stated that:

> *" Intelligent may know the sands of the earth, the waters of*
> *the oceans, the size of the Himalayas; but a woman's heart*
> *they may not know. They weep and make you weep; they*
> *tell lies and make you believe them. A woman is like sugar*
> *when she has fallen in love, but the very same woman*
> *surpasses*
> *the bitter Neem (a tree quite common in north India. Its*
> *leaves are very bitter but have medicinal value), as soon*

> *as her love has ended. Delighting in various love*
> *sports, unstable in their affections are like the color of*
> *turmeric.*
> *Crual in their hearts, and charming in their body, speech*
> *and glance, girls resemble a knlfe inlaid with gold."*

In spite of these monkish tales, the Jains generally consider women desirable since they marry and without them procreation is not possible. Some of them even thought of them very highly. Jain kings considered women as one of the fourteen crown jewels of royalty, and generally loved to display their splendor by the number and quality of women they possessed. Ladies of the royal clans used to observe a sort of Purdah to prevent them from being seen by wicked eyes. Trishla, mother of *Mahaveera*, the founder of the Jain religion, said to have listened to the interpretation of her dreams, which foretold the birth of her illustrious son, by sitting behind a curtain. Women of the middle and lower classes were free and could go about without a veil. *Vivagnasuya,* a Jain text, gives accounts of how many wives were possessed by kings and states that some powerful kings at that time had hundreds of wives in their harems. The usual methods of recruiting women to the harem were by marriage, purchase, or capture and Jain texts mention many instances of high-handedness of royalty in this matter.

The life of a Jain nun is very hard and challenging: no good place to stay, always wandering bare foot, begging for food, which she is required to do only once a day in the noon, and eat only once a day, wear coarse white clothes of which she is only allowed one set, wash her own clothes, sleep on bare ground without a bedding, keep the head always shaved. No creature comforts are allowed; no fine arts or sensual enjoyment, even the food begged is collected in one pot, all mixed up so she can't taste individual items. Compared to her life the living conditions of a Christian nun would appear to be luxurious. The primary idea is, again to control and conquer the senses including the mind, which is essential in making spiritual progress. The same philosophy is followed in both Hinduism and Buddhism, the eastern religions. The Roman Catholics follow it to a certain extent only in that the monks are supposed to practice celibacy. But they live a comfortable life. The Pope lives in luxurious quarters whereas the Dalai Llamma or the Sankaracharya live a very austere life with minimal requirements for themselves and they follow a very rigrous religious practice involving hours of meditation and worship along with fasting etc.

The influence of these two religions started waning somewhere around 300 AD, at which time Hindus started waking up and started reacting to the decline in their popularity. After the breakdown of the Maurya and Shunga empires, there was a period of uncertainty that led to renewed interest in traditional social norms. This was the time (between 200 BC and 200 CE), when certain texts, known as Dharma-shastras were written. These texts were in response to the threats to the Brahminical tradition. In Thaper's view, "The severiety of the Dharma- shastras was doubtless a commentary arising from the insecurity of the orthodox system in an age of flux."

What Manu Smiriti and Other Dharma Shastras state about women:

A discussion of the status of women of India would be incomplete without the mention of some important texts called the *Dharma Shastras,* which were produced during the time when Buddhist influence was on the decline. This time period is approximately 600 AD. Some of these texts, such as the Manu Smiriti, were produced much earlier. This period is of interest in the history of Hinduism since it marks the rise of Hinduism having gone down on account of the popularity of Buddhism and the corruption of Brahmins. An important factor in the awakening and rise of Hinduism was the tremendous contribution of the great Hindu philosopher, the *Jagat Guru Adi Shankaracharya,* who engaged the Buddhist elite in high level philosophical discussions, which resulted in the Buddhists accepting "defeat". This famous debate boosted the validity of the fundamental principles of Hinduism and restored its popularity and prestige. In any case, these texts have given to the Hindus the laws or codes, which a householder must follow. These codes cover a wide range of subjects including regulations, which govern women's lives and a householder's for ritchous living. There are a number of *Dharma Shastras* among them about twenty are considered more important. But out of all the law books the Manu Smiriti is considered the most authoritative and most exhaustive. Manu Smiriti and Yajnavalkya Smiriti are the ancient law books dating a couple of centuries before the start of the Christian era. The other law books belong to a later period, between seventh and twelfth centuries when Buddhism had almost subsided in India and Brahminism had come back in power. This was also the time when Mughals had started attacking India and conquring parts of its territory and Islam was taking a foothold. Manu Smiriti consists of a large number of stanzas and lays down laws for everybody, especially women. There are passages in which the sage shows respect for women whereas in other cases he has curtailed their basic human rights. Some of the laws pertaining to a woman make her completely dependent on her husband. The *Dharma Shastra* texts were not based on the authority of the Vedas. Hence this was a departure from the earlier traditions and this is an important point, which must be understood since the guiding principles of Hindu society experience a change at this point in the history of Hindu religion. The principles laid down in the Vedas were no longer applicable, especially so far as the women were concerned; their freedoms, which they were enjoying during the Vedic times had been drastically curtailed. The argument advanced in support of this curtailment was that the social conditions, which existed during the Vedic period cease to exist. The authors did not reject or disagree with the principles laid down in the Vedas but argue that the change in the social conditions required a change in the codes.

The Manu Smiriti was also one of the first Sanskrit texts studied by the British in an effort to understand the religion and culture of India, the country, which they intended to govern. Sir William Jones, the founder of Indology, was the first one to translate the text into English. His version was published in 1794. A portion of the text is as follows:

According to the sage *Manu*, a woman:

> *Should do nothing independently*
> *Even in her own house.*
> *In childhood subject to her father,*
> *In youth to her husband,*
> *And when her husband is dead to her sons,*
> *She should never enjoy independence….*
> *She should always be cheerful,*
> *And skilled in her domestic duties,*
> *With her household vessels well cleansed,*
> *And her hand tight on the purse strings….*
> *In season and out of season*
> *Her lord, who wed her with sacred rites,*
> *Ever gives happiness to his wife,*
> *Both here and in the other world.*
> *Though he be uncouth and prone to pleasure,*
> *Though he have no good points at all,*
> *The virtuous wife should ever*
> *Worship her lord as a god.*

Almost all the codes, whether earlier or later, establish the abject dependence of woman on man. *Manu* says,

> *"In childhood, a woman is to be dependent on her father,*
> *in youth on her husband and in old age on her son;*
> *a woman is never fit for independence"*

Manu was in agreement with the epic and post-Vedic writers with regard to the base nature of woman:

> *"Women do not care for beauty, nor is their attention*
> *fixed on age; thinking it is enough he is a man,*
> *they give themselves to the handsome and the ugly.*

> *"Though their passion for men, through their mutable*
> *temper, through their natural heartlessness, they*
> *become disloyal towards their husbands, however*
> *carefully they may be guarded in this world."*

> *Knowing their disposition, which the Lord of Creatures*
> *laid in them to be such, every man should most strenuously*
> *exert himself to guard them*

> *When creating them, the Lord of Creatures allotted to women*
>   *a love of their bed, of their seat and of ornaments,*
> *impure*
>   *desires, wrath, dishonesty, malice and bad conduct.*

> *For women no sacramental rite is performed with sacred*
>   *texts, thus the law is settled; women (who are) destitute*
> *of*
>   *strength and destitute of the knowledge of Vedic texts,*
> *are*
>   *as impure as falsehood itself, that is the fixed rule."*

> *Further, "three persons, a wife, a son and a slave, are*
> *declared by law to have no wealth exclusively their own;*
> *the wealth they may earn is regularly acquired for the man*
> *to whom they belong." In marriage while a man's eligibility*
> *was judged by his intellectual and spiritual accomplishments*
> *, the girl's desirability was solely dependent upon her*

> *physical attractions. She was to be "free from bodily*
> *defects, should have an agreeable name, should be of*
> *graceful gait like a swan or an elephant, should have*
> *moderate quantity of hair on the body and on the head,*
> *small teeth and soft limbs." A man was not to marry*
> *"a maiden with reddish hair, nor one who has a redundant*
> *member, nor one who is sickly, nor one either with no*
> *hair (on the body) or too much, nor one who is garrulous*
> *or has red eyes". An Aryan was not to eat with his wife;*
> *"nor look at her while eating, sneezing, yawning or sitting*
> *at her ease."*

The dictates of Manu are in stark contradiction with the teachings of the Vedas as one can see by reading the stanzas from the Rig Veda. The Smiriti does not derive its authority from the Vedas as stated earlier. So the development of these codes has been done independently. The *Bhagwad Gita,* an authoratitave text contradicts many statements contained in the Manu Smiriti. In northern and southern India, *Shivaism* and *Vaishnavism* were the common religious traditions and the teachings of the Manu Smriti was not as widely followed or wellknown. (Shaivaism is that aspect of Hinduism in which the belivers worship lord Shiva; just as in Vaishnavism they worship lord Vishnu only). The text (*Manu Smriti*) was never followed universally or acclaimed by the vast majority of Hindus. It came to the world's attention through a late eighteenth-century translation by *Sir William Jones*. He mistakenly exaggerated both its antiquity and its importance. They are, however, anathema to modern thinkers and particularly the feminists. The excerpt from the *Manu Smriti* cited here would give the reader a clear idea of how things were stacked against women of that time. But this is a very small sample out of the total of about 2,685 verses, as counted by *Surendra Kumar.* (Ref.35). He also found that only 1,214 are authentic, the other 1,471 being interpolations on the text. The position taken by the *Manu Smiriti* about women has also been debated. While certain verses glorify the status of women, others seem to limit their freedom. For example, a statement such as "where a woman is respected, gods dwell", clearly contrast the stanzas quoted above. On balance it can be concluded that this document does impose certain restrictions on the freedom of women, making their position in the society subordinate to that of men.

As has been mentioned earlier, the condition of women in the Indian society had started declining toward the end of the Vedic period. The important changes, which had taken place included marriages of girls prior to acquiring maturity, restricted their education; just limiting it to domestic work, no access to the study of Vedas and withdrawal of rights to perform religious rituals. Women were also excluded from any major decision making at practically all levels. The Brahmins had made a drastic departure from the ideals laid down in the Vedas and had concentrated much on the acquisition and concentration of power in their own hands. This was also the time when Buddhism and Jainism became more attractive alternatives for women. This decline in the Hindu religion continued for a few centuries till the *Adi Shankaracharya* appears in the picture around 700 AD. The contribution made by his holiness the *Adi Shankaracharya* is a historical monument in the Hindu religious philosophical history of India. It was he who revived the Hindu religion and substantially reduced the influence of Buddhism and Jainism in India. This is the reason why these two religions, especially Buddhism, practically disappeared from India and continued in countries such as China, Japan, Burma, Indonesia, and other far-eastern countries.

Gupta dynasty ruled in North India after the great Mauryan Empire. This period is called the "golden period" in Indian history. During this period arts and crafts, poetry, literature flourished and other great things of social welfare and occurred. The greatly acclaimed poet and drama writer, *Kalidas,* belonged to this period. From what is known of this period, the empire was very progressive in its outlook and not in any way oppressive to women. Hindus were practicing their traditional ways and the State did not interfere in their practice. It is, therefore, safe to assume that the condition of women remained unchanged from what it used to be after the introduction of the Manu-smriti and the Dharma-shastras. During the period of Ashoka, the State policy was to give complete religious freedom to everybody and that tradition continued in the Gupta period as well. Please refer to maps of India showing the extent of the Gupta and Mauryan Empires.

There are other important sutras or religious texts, which are important from the point of view of the position of women in the Indian society. The *Grihya Sutra* is one, which ought to be considered. This sutra throws light on the domestic and social life of the Indian society in the post-Vedic period. It deals with the rules of conduct and ceremonies to be performed by a Hindu householder. The *Grihya Sutras* pertain to that period in Brahminism when the Vedic religion was well established in the south as well as in the north of the Vindhyas; (the mountain range dividing north and south), the sutra writers, several in number, had written to meet the needs of the Inian communities following different customs and usages, but efforts were made to create some basic unity in the fundamentals.

Historically, it is estimated that the main Sutra period may have started by about the sixth century B.C. and continued till the rise and spread of Buddhism under Ashka in the third century B.C. The early sutras were contemporaneous with the *Brahmanas* and *Upanishadas;* especially the *Grahya Sutras* owe much to the *Brahmanas* as both emphasize the importance of ritual as distinct from the intellectualism of the *Upanishads.* The *Gryha Sutras* would prescribe the daily life of a Hindu householder under the religion, giving daily religious rituals to be performed daily as well as all other rituals required to be performed on special occasions such as birth, death, marriage, *Yagno pavitam or Upanayanam* (initiation into the *Brahmacharya Ashram,* popularly known as thread ceremony, an important event in the life of a Brahmin. This is why he is called a *Dwija* or twice born), child naming ceremonies, and so on. It also included ceremonies for the dead and departed, which are more elabrate in Hinduism than any other religion. The principal writers of the *Gryha Sutras* were: *Asvalayana, Apasthamba, Sankhayana,* and *Bharadwaja.* They were not contemporaries; lived in different times and in different parts of the country; wrote for different regions taking into consideration local traditions. But there is no disagreement in existing texts attributed to them regarding the fundamentals.

Types of Hindu Marriages:

In the *Grhya Sutras, Asvalayana* has classfied the various types of marriages. They are:

> 1) Brahma, 2) Daiva, 3) Prajapatya, 4) Arsha, 5) Gandharva, 6) Asura, 7) Paisacha, 8) Raksha. The first one is the most desirable and the last one the least, the rest inbetween are in descending order for respectable couples.

The Brahma form involves the main item the ceremony in which the father of the bride gives away his daughter to the bridegroom. The bride is decked with ornaments and many gifts are given to the groom. This was the most common form of marriage among the Brahmins and it still is the common form of marriage ceremony among Brahmins, Ksatrayas and the Vaishyas in the Indo-Aryan society.

In the Daiva form, a girl was given in marriage to a learned priest offering at an important sacrifice in recognition of his vast learning and efficient performance of the sacrifice. In this case, the girl is not necessarily the daughter of the householder. But in most cases she is. It was in the capacity of the host of the sacrifice that he gives away the girl. Such giving away of girls to a vastly learned priest eventually results in the priest acquiring many wives.

The prajaptya form of marriage is similar to the Brahma, except that the guardian of the bride gives her away in this case instead of her father.

In the Arsha form of marriage, the marriage is performed in accordance with the religious rites except that the bride's father receives a pair of cattle, a cow and a bull. This form of marriage did not continue beyond the Mauryan period as mentioned by Megasthenese, in his accounts of India. He was the Greek envoy in the court of Chandragupta Maurya.

The Gandharva form of marriage is a love marriage. The girl and the boy, or the woman and man fall in love and decide to get married. There are some prominent examples of this type of marriage in the hiatory of India. Shakuntala's marriage to king Dushyanta is one such example, described in detail later and is also the subject of the famous Sanskrit composition of the famous poet Kalidas, called "Shakuntalam".

In Asura style of marriage, the bride is purchased. The price is not a token like a cow etc, but a real price negotiated between the bride's father and the groom and was required to be paid prior to the marriage. Imagine the status of woman/girl in this situation. Pishcha form of marriage is very brutal since in this case the bride is drugged and raped. The *Grhya Sutra* does not explain how rape could be legalized, but in Vatsyayana's *Kama Sutra,* valid excuses for this type of marriage are given.

Raksha is a marriage by capture. This type of marriage was prevailent in the ancient world and in the heroic age of Hindus it was almost a point of honor for the martial classes to capture their brides after defeating the parents and forces of the bride's side. An example of this type of marriage is that of Prithviraj Chauvan with Sainyogita.

Of these eight forms of marriages, Asvalayana considered the first four alone as becoming of the righteous. The Brahma form ennobled ancestors of twelve generations, Daiva fourteen, Prajaptya eight, and Arsha seven.

An account of the status of women during the period of Mauryan Empire has been available, as mentioned earlier, from the notes of the Greek ambassador, Megasthenese in the court of Chandragupta Maurya. But not all his writings are available; but from what is available, he has described the condition of women during that time. According to him:

> *"The Brahmins do not admit their wives to their philosophy;*
> *if they are good, they might leave their husbands, since no*
> *one who has learnt to look with contempt upon pleasure and*
> *pain, upon life and death, will care to be under another's*
> *control."*

It would appear that the denial of Vedic wisdom to women was partly inspired by fear of sacrilege and partly by the selfishness of men. Meganesthese also noticed that"the son succeedes the father". The wealthy were polygamous in Mauryan India. He also mentioned that child marriages were common in south India where girls were married at the young age of six or seven. In the Mauryan Empire the minimum age for marriage would appear to have been twelve as fixed by *Kautlya*. (Kautlya is the author of the famous tretise called *"Artha Shastra"*) Theis text gives advice on matters pertaining to politics, finance and other matters pertaining to State administration among other things.

Later law- givers were harsher than Manu. The law -giver, Daksha, states that a good wife is not born she is made. "A wife was always to be taught her place; if out of misplaced affection, she was allowed to have her own way, she becomes uncontrollable like a disease neglected; all wives are like leeches; even if daily gratified with ornaments, dresses and good food, they never cease to extort a man."

Another law-giver, Atri, was of the opinion that "a man shall not take food in the house of a barren woman even if she is his own daughter; he who takes food out of love, goes to hell". Further, "a woman, who, during the lifetime of her husband fasts while performing a religious rite, robs the longevity of her husband. Such a woman goes to hell". According to Atri, there was no need for a woman to hazard a long journey for the sake of taking a holy bath in sacred waters. She can obtain the benefit of such a bath by washing the feet of her husband and drink the water!"

Most lawgivers, both earlier and later, believed that a woman should worship her husband like a god even if he were a drunkard, gambler or debauchee. This was the general attitude of most of the lawgivers towards the women of higher castes. As a rule, they were not allowed to own property, not to be given freedom or the benefits of litracy and were to be constantly kept under male survelliance.

There are certain other codes found, which consider women respectable. In the formulation of these codes there is a hand of what are known as the "Tantrics. The tantrics had always held a high opinion of women but they did not express this openly. According to some passages contributed by the Tantrics, a woman was always pure. "The moon has conferred purity on women, the Gandgarvas (these are demi gods) sweet speech, fire the most exhalted state of holiness; therefore women are most holy. If a woman commits adultery, she gets purified by her menses." According to Angiras:

> ---*A woman is purified by her menses, just as a river by its current.*
> ---*There is no Sastra superior to the Veda; and no elderly person*
> *superior to the mother.*
>
> ---*A woman is not sullied by being known by another person; nor is a Brahmin sullied by harmful Vedic rites; nor is the water (of a river) by urine or excreta; nor fire by burning impure things.*
>
> ---*Women were first enjoyed by celesticals; then by the moon , the Gandharvas and by fire. Afterwards men came to enjoy them.*
> *They are never affected by any sin.*
>
> ---*When woman conceives by being known by an Asavarna (asudra) she remains impure as long as she does not give birth to her child. After the delivery, the menstrual blood is seen, the woman becomes purified like pure gold.*
>
> ---*If despite her unwillingness, a woman is known deceitfully, forceably, or stealthily, that woman, unaffected by any sin, should not be renounced*

With regard to the last stanza, it has always been a question of debate whether a woman abducted, raped or gets pregnant in the process, as was what happened to many women at the hands of Muslims, should she be accepted again. It was considered desirable to accept them by all Hindus, including the orthodox. The main authority for this decision was the sanction of the lawgivers like Atri.

It has been mentioned that a woman gets purified by her menses but it is a common practice (not observed any more in most households who consider themselves modern) to let her remove from the household activities and she is made to become "untouchable" for a period of three days. During these three days no body touches her nor does she touches any body; she does not freely move in the house, does not do any work and is strictly prohibited to enter the kitchen or the place of worship (puja room). The lawgiver, Angiras describes her three days as: "on the first day of the mensus, the woman (of whatever high caste she may otherwise be) becomes a chandala, on the second day a murderess of a Brahmin, and on the third, a washerwoman; on the fourth day, she is putified."

Marriage Systems of South India:

Invadors who came to India all came from the northwest and conquered the fertile Indo-Gangetic plain. They generally did not venture into the south since they were not left with enough energy after their actions in the north. Even the earliest invaders, the Aryans, settled in the north, and just tried to consolidate their hold and properly establish themselves in their new homeland. The original inhabitants, having been defeated got pushed into the south. The present "Dravidians" and Tamils are the remanants of the early dwellers of the Indus valley civilization. The customs of the Aryans did not influence the Dravidians since the latter resisted the Aryan influence and Brahminism. The customs and traditions of the Tamils are, therefore, different from the people in the north.

The approved form of marriage among the ancient Tamils was *Kalau* or secret. This was love marriage, pure and simple. Marriage used to be a private affair between a young man and a girl, and no marriage ceremonies or nuptual rites were performed. No details are available as to the successful working of this type of marriage but there are elaborate details of courtship are available in works such as *Sitapadikaram*. It is believed that this style of marriage is instrumental in giving rise to a Matricharcal form of family in the south. In this the female is the head of the family. *Karpu*, is an open form of marriage. In the ancient Tamil literature, in which the wedding ceremonies have been described as performed in public, with witnesses, was an introduction by the *Ayara*. (Tamil corruption of Aryans; in south India, the Brahmins are even now distinguished by the honorific *Ayar*). The *karpu* in ancient days, was considered an undesirable innovation, an exotic fashion from the north, not suitable for the warm climate of the south. The approved forms of marriage according to the Sanskrit Samhitas were the unapproved forms to the Tamils and were, known as Poruntak-kaman.

Kerala, the southern most part of India is, by its geographical location, quite isolated and protected from any foreign influences, not even the powerful Aryan. This society has been based on the matriarchal pattern for a very long time. Hindus in Kerala are the Sudras who are not subject to the Indo-Aryan *Dharma Sastras* but follow their own traditional customs. The matriarchal tradition is so deeply rooted in Kerala that kings of Kerala who were Kshtriyas, and as such Indo-Aryans, were compelled to follow it. In the royal houses of Cochin and Travencore, the heir to the throne was not the Maharaja's son but his sister's son. Even the *Nambudari* Brahmins to whom Parsurama had given Kerala as a gift to be enjoyed in perpetuity, had to come to terms with the matricharcal social system sacrificing some of their cherished ideals and transforming the laws of Manu and other Indo-Aryan legislators.

The matricharcal system in India has now practically gone and mostly the system is patriarchal except in the villages of Kerala it is still alive. The *Nayars* are the dominant matriarchs of Kerala. For the Nayars, marriage was a simple affair. When a girl came of age, she was married according to the rite known as *Sambandham* (the word "sambandh" literally means relationship). The sambandham was not sacramental; a few relatives were called on the occasion and the bridegroom presented to the bride a set of clothes called *Pudava*, and the guests were treated to light refreshments; there was no elaborate procedures with the chanting of Vedic hymns, the holy fire and rituals and feasts with music, which is typical in an Indo-Aryan marriage ceremony in the north.

After the marriage, the girl does not leave her house to go and live in her husband's house and continues to live in her with her own people, which is quite contrary to the northern Indo-Aryan marriage in which the girl is required to go to the house of the husband and there is an elaborate ceremony dedicated for that event. The husband, likewise, lived in his own house, but visited his wife at night for conjugal rites and returned home in the morning. The marrying parties mostly belonged to the same village and their homes were not too far from each other so that the husband could easily walk to his wife's house. Divorces among *Nayers* were very simple. If the husband wanted to divorce his wife, all he had to do was to stop visiting her at hights. This would amount to a divorce. On the other hand, if the wife wants a divorce, she would indicate that the husband is politely told that he is not welcome in her house any more. The children born are brought up and supported by the wife's family. The husband is not at all responsible for bringing up the children or to provide any financial support for them.

The system of the *Nambooderi* Brahmins of Kerala is again quite different. In their case, the eldest son in the family is the only one eligible for marriage. When he marries a girl from a particular family, all the sisters of this girl also marry him. This meant unlimited polygyny. The marriage of the eldest male in the family also was financially very beneficial since he brings in a substantial dowry. The younger brothers marry girls from *Khastria* or Brahmin families but they are not allowed to bring them home. The children born in this type of *sambandham* belonged to the caste of the wife and were also brought up by the wife's family; the husbands had no responsibilities in this regard. The Indo-Aryan traditionl belief that a son is the one who after the death of his father saves him from going to hell by performing the last rites, is not a religious injunction in the south Indian traditions. This, therefore, reduces the importance of having a son considerably.

Condition of Widows:

In Indian society, for a woman to become a widow had been a very unfortunate thing in the woman's life, not because she had lost her husband, even though to lose her husband is in itself a very terrible thing, but mainly because the ill treatment she would receive as a widow, from the members of her family and the society. In the very early period in the history of India, that is, in the Vedic times, the widows were not treated badly. Certain references found in the religious texts indicate that widows were neither treated as unwanted nor was their life made miserable. The following references are cited:

1. Atharvaveda, 9.5.27 and Rig Veda, 10.40.2 indicate that widows were allowed to remarry.
2. *Baudhayana Dharmashastra* 4.1.18 and *Vashta Dharmashastra* 17.19.20 also support the widow marriage.
3. *Parashara Smiriti* 4.30, *Garuda purana* 107.28 and *Agni purana* 154.5, classical texts of Hinduism also permit marriage of widows.
4. *Manusmriti* 9.76: in certain cases permits a married woman to marry another person if her husband was to go abroad for a very long period of time.

The condition of widows did, however, deteriorated after this period and kept on deteriorating till the seventeenth century when this issue caught the attention of some social reformers. But the life of a widow did not change much until later in the twentith century when the reforms started making their effects. But these changes, which improved the life of widows, had their effect in only the educated and reform minded families. The hard-core believers, uneducated and mostly rural people continued to treat the widows badly and are still continueing to do so.

The status of a woman changes immediately after becoming a widow. Widows were unwanted, shunned from all family and community functions since her presence at all religious and auspicious ceremonies was considered inauspicious. She loses her place of respect and finds herself isolated. She is required to wear only white, no ornaments are allowed neither is she allowed to indulge in any make-up. Her presence at any auspicious occasion was prohibited and she was not allowed to indulge in any enjoyments such as music or fancy food. Widows were also required to shave their heads to make them look less attractive. This treatment of widows has been prevalent since the medieval time. A recent movie, called "Water", is a good presentation of the condition of widows. The conditions depicted in this movie dates back to the 1930s, but such conditions existed for a long time prior to this date. In the words of *Pundita Ramabai*, written towards the close of the 19th century, continued to be a largely true description of the plight of the widow in Hindu society, specially among the so called higher castes, till the 1930s:

> *"Throughout India widowhood is regarded as the punishment*
> *for horrible crimes committed by a woman in her former existence.*
> *But it is the child widow upon whom in an especial manner falls*
> *the abuse and hatred of the communit. Among the Brahmins*
> *of the Deccan the heads of all widows must be shaved regularly*
> *every fortnight. The widow must wear a single coarse garment*
> *. She must eat only one meal during the twenty-four hours of the*
> *day. She must never take part in family feasts. A man or woman*
> *thinks it unlucky to behold a widow's face before seeing any*

> other object in the morning. In addition to all this, the young widow
>   is always looked upon with suspicion, for fear she may some
>   time bring disgrace upon the family by committing some improper
>   act. Her life, then destitute as it is, of the least literary knowledge,
>   void of all hope, empty of every pleasure and social advantage,
>   becomes intolerable, a curse to herself and to society at large."

The usual benediction when a married woman bows respectfully before her elders is: " Long may you remain unwidowed." There is a widely observed tradition of the wife fasting and praying on certain days of the year for the long life of her husband. Becoming a widower was no great hardship. He could, and usually did, marry again. The young widow is also quite vulnerable to sexual advances by other young males within her family or in certain circumstances by males outside the family. This places the widow in a very dangerous situation especially if she is good looking.

The widows in the Muslim communities, lower caste Hindus and women belonging to other religions did not share the same fate as the widows of the higher caste Hindus. In the lower castes remarriage was permitted. The widows were not looked down upon as social out castes and curses upon the families and the society.

Widows were expected to spend their time in worship, reading of the epics and other religious literature, go to temples and attend discourses on religious issues. This type of activity probably suited to older ladies but for a young widow, who is yet a child or in the prime of her life, it was not at all interesting. In case the girl was married at a tender age of 8 or 10, it was no less than a life sentence. There was no possibility for her or any other widow to further her education or skill or to be of any use to the society or for engaging herself in a meaningful activity. This is even worse than the condition of a person incarcerated for life, since he can work within the jail premises, read, study, and socialize with fellow inmates. In many prisons the inmates are taught skills such as carpet weaving and they produce excellent carpets and get paid certain minimum wages. The widow does not have even this opportunity!

The Custom of Sati:

The ritual of dying at the funeral pyre of the husband is known as "Sati" or *Sahagaman*. The word Sahagaman is made of a combination of two words, *Saha*, meaning together, and *Gaman* meaning to go. So the joint word literally means going together. In this case it means the going of the wife with her husband. According to *Agni Puran*, a Hindu mythological text, a woman who dies at the funeral pyre of her husband goes straight to heaven and this act by a woman has been regarded as praiseworthy. (Ref.11). Initially it was not obligatory for a woman to "go sati". *Ibn Batuta* observed that Sati was considered praiseworthy by the Hindus; without being obligatory. Those who committed Sati, did it because they were very devoted to their husband and their love for their husband was so strong that they did not wish to live even for a minute without their husband. Scholars of the Puranas trace the origins of the suicide of *Satidevi* in the *Yagnakunda* (sacrificial fireplace) of Lord *Brahma*, while a few attribute it to the pre-caste Vedic system of Indian society. A very ancient example of sati is the case of the wife of Indrajit, the eldest son of the famous demon king *Rawana*. When Indrajit got killed in battle with lord *Ramchandra*, his wife who was extremely devoted to him and loved him very much, died by sitting on her husband's funeral pyre. This incident dates back to the period of the famous epic *Ramanaya*, several centuries before Christ. Yet another example of sati is found in the great epic of *Mahabharata*, which dates much later than *Ramanaya*. Here the younger wife of *Pandu*, *Madri*, died on the funeral pyre of her husband leaving the children to the care of the first wife, *Kunti*.

The custom of sati has been prevalent ever since. The mythical literature of India is scattered with stories of sati. The word sati is also used as an adjective to describe a devoted, virtuous, and loving wife of high moral character. A family from which a widow goes sati, is highly regarded and enjoys enhanced prestige.

Widows usually remarried until the *Mauryan* period (322-200 BC). But when Manu decreed that "nowhere is a second husband permitted to respectable women", upper-caste Hindus soon held that marriage was for life. This meant that women could neither divorce nor remarry, if widowed. *Niyoga,* the forced appropriation of a childless widow by her husband's brother had been practiced, but faded during the *Gupta* period and Emperor *Akbar* banned it in areas under Mughal control.

There are certain aspects of the motivation behind a woman's decision for going sati. This subject is complex. There are some answers to this question as provided by Dr. *Jotsna Kamat* in her book, "The Origins Of The Sati System" (Ref. 9) and are quoted as follows:

- "Burning the wife along with the attendants, horses and carriages of the dead dignitary was a common practice among some Central Asian tribes. India being the melting pot of good and bad social systems of its constituent cultures, the custom of Sati was absorbed.

- In a time, which believed that a woman's path to heaven is through *Sheela* and *Pativritya* – her character, and devotion to her husband, it was perhaps thought that a woman's life served no purpose after the death of her husband.

- It might have come into practice as an evil family conspiracy against the widow to benefit from her assets and gold.

- The life of a widow was so bad (this has continued to this day in India), the woman perhaps favored death to humiliation.

- The women who went Sati were glorified to no avail. The entice of fame and immortality cannot be ruled out on why women committed Sati.

- There is another suicide tradition in the Jain religion called "Sallekhana", where one dedicated one's soul in prayer. Despite of this tradition, numerous instances in Indian history illustrate when a Jain woman has preferred Sati over Sallakhana---especially in the cases of untimely deaths of the husband.

- Some women believed that those who died with the love of their life, were united with the man in heaven in an eternal marriage. Numerous women believed that they have married the same man in several of their lives. There is an interesting instance of a wife who went Sati with another man (not her husband), because of her belief that *he was the one.*

- In Bengal, a system called *Dayabhaga* prevailed entitling a woman equal property along with male members of the departed husband. This may be the reason for the Sati system being more popular in that region, wherin the woman was driven to commit Sati by force.

• There are numerous occasions when the woman experiences a divine calling and decided to commit Sati."

It has been mentioned that the Agni Puran glorifies the Sati but some other scriptures like *Medhati*, say that Sati is like committing a suicide and should be avoided. Sati is practiced in India even today, though it had been banned in the early nineteenth century.

Child Marriages:

Marriages of girls who were only 8 or 10 years old were quite common in medieval India. Girls did not receive any education and they were not allowed to acquire maturity to make their own decisions regarding choosing their life partners. Their parents or elders made these decisions for them. A girl at this age, as can be expected, is going to follow the orders of her parents without questioning. And she has a complete faith in what the parents decide. Moreover, she does not even understand the meaning of marriage. The marriage ceremony, for her, is then a nice party in which she gets to wear nice clothes and eat good food. If her husband is almost her age, she is happy to make friends with him and thinks that she has one more friend to play with. In case her husband is much older than her, which is the case in many instances, she likes the love and affection, which she receives from an elderly person. The seriousness of the commitment, which is associated with the marriage, never crosses her mind.

The law-givers of the medevail times favoured early marriages since they viewed the feminine nature as being essentially perverse and ruled by instinct, and feared, therefore, that a nubile girl would not have the patience to wait the attainment of mature age and performance of marriage before satisfying her desires. She may secretly fall in love with a young man, without caring about his status, reputation etc. and become pregnant as a result. And a girl who looses her virginity is at once not eligible for marriage. Hence the risks of keeping a young girl unmarried untill she acquires maturity was considered to be quite considerable. Another consideration for a girl's early marriage was financial; a girl was completely dependent on her father, which was a financial burden. The boys, on the other hand used to earn some wages. On account of these considerations the lawgivers were in favour of early marriages. The minimum age for marriage has been specified by *Manu's* Codes as eight or twelve; by *Kautlya* as twelve and sixteen by the *Jataka*. The child marriages were far less frequent before the seventh century compared to their occurances later on. This might be partly due to the beginning of the Mughal incursions and lack of protection available for citizens in general and for girls in particular.

The girls during this time period in the history of India were given some education. It was of a different style compared to what the boys were receiving but nevertheless was adequate for preparing them for marriage and to assume the responsibilities of a full-fledged housewife. At home, they were taught the arts of cooking, supervising the domestic servants and other slaves, some rudimentary religious knowledge and in some cases teachers would come home to teach them elementary subjects, which also made them literate. They also learnt some arts such as painting or playing a musical instrument like a *Veena*. The girls were brought up to believe that a woman's fulfillment was in motherhood; she was trained to respect elders, know the hierarchy in a joint family and pay respects accordingly. She knew right from the beginning that she would have to leave her family and go to her would-be husband's family. She was also brought up to understand that after her marriage, her sole duty was to look after the happiness of her husband. Her own happiness would become secondary.

During the Mughal domination of India, it was quite common for the Mughals to pick any girl they wanted for their harams. The exception was that they were not allowed to pick married women. This was an important consideration in marrying the girls very early in order to save them from abduction. In later years, however, the Mughals disregarded their own religious dictum and started abducting married women. The practice of early childhood marriages did protect the women during the Mughal domination but this practice had been in vogue long before the arrival of the Mughals. It is something, which the society had been practicing for centuries. Why was this practiced? Some explain it based on the theory that the Brahmins and their domination of the society is responsible for it.

The explanation given is that when a girl who was married while she was quite young, had to leave her home and go to the bridegroom's home where she was required to work hard right from the early morning till late at night without much rest in a totally new and unfriendly atmosphere. She was also not getting proper nutrition since she was supposed to eat whatever remained after everybody in the family had eaten. In large joint families, there used to be very little left over most of the time. In many instances, there would be guests for dinner. The very young girl whose body had not quite completely developed had to have sex with her husband as soon as she reached puberty. Pregnancy would result. In most cases this would result in miscarriages for the first few times. This would result in her being looked down upon since the bridegroom's family expects her to give them a son. In case she did give birth to a son, she would pick up some respect. But the result of this tremendous pressure and lack of nutrition coupled with little medical help generally resulted in sickness and early death. Such deats were not mourned seriously. The husband would be soon looking for another wife and generally would get married soon after the death of his wife. The same story would repeat again. The Brahmins would again be engaged in performance of the second marriage, in the performance of the last rites of the dead woman and other rituals, which they would dictate. The bridegroom would again receive a dowry. So both the Brahmin and the Bridegroom would benefit. The bride's family would be the losers along with the girl who had been used as though she was an expandable piece of material.

A passage from the most common marriage ceremony is cited here, which is a clear proof of the age of the girl/daughter is the time of her marriage. The age of the bride would not have been mentioned in the marriage procedure unless it was an acceptable practice.

The father of the bride says the following to the bridegroom on the occasion of giving away the daughter:

> *"This daughter who was born in my dynasty, has been brought-up*
> *by me is eight years old and now I have given her to you. May*
> *she give you sons and daughters. Do not violate her in any*
> *aspects of Dharma, artha or kama." (Dharma means all*
> *aspects of duty, religion, and customs and traditions,*
> *Artha means all aspects concerning monitory matters,*
> *and Kama means all aspects of love attachment and affection.)*
> *(Ref: 7)*

From this statement it is quite clear that there was a practice of girls as young as eight years old. And this procedure of marriage has been in vogue for a number of centuries and meets the approval of the traditional Hindu marriage procedure, based on the Vedas. It is really quite doubtful if this is based on the Vedas since the Stotra from the Rigveda quoted in the earlier part directs that no girl should marry before attaining the age of fourteen. If one looks into the Rig Veda, there is clear direction on the recommended age for marriage. One of the stanzas states that a girl should not, in any case, marry below the age of 14, and should marry when she is matured and is able to make her own decision in choosing a life partner.

The tradition of Jauhar:

Jauhar was a tradition, mostly among the *Rajput* women of Rajasthan. This was a tradition in which the wives of the Rajputs and other ladies would end their lives by jumping into a large fire. These ladies used to do this when they received a message from their husbands from the battlefield that they were certainly going to lose the battle and that they would fight till the very end. The message would also say that there is no hope of anybody returning alive from the battlefield. This type of situation mostly occurred during the Mughal period when the *Rajputs* used to fight with a large Mughal army. The *Rajputs* were very proud people and did not believe in running away from the battle. That would be considered dishonorable. Their wives would perform jauhar in order to save their honor and dignity since if they remained alive, the victorious Mughals would capture them and large-scale rape and dishonor would certainly take place. Many ladies would be made slaves or made a part of their harem. This was most certainly unacceptable to the proud *Rajputs*. This would also bring dishonor to the pure *Rajput* dynasty.

Many incidents of jauhar have taken place in Rajasthan. When one visits the old forts in various parts of this province, the history comes alive and one can visualize the fierce battles, which took place. One will also find handprints of the ladies who had given up their lives in jauhar these handprints are on the walls at the entrance to the forts and are in blood of those ladies! One can get a good idea of the cruelty of the Mughals and the bravery of the Rajputs who laid down their lives for the sake of protecting their kingdom, their honor and their ladies from the barbaric Mughals. At the end of the Mughal power, the attacks on Rajput kingdoms stopped and so did the jauhars.

CHAPTER 3.
WOMEN DURING THE MUGHAL PERIOD: (700 TO 1700 AD)

General:

So far the discussion of the subject of women's status has been dominated by the Hindu religious practices and the two important religions, which came into being in the fifth and sixth centuries before Christ, that is, Buddhism and Jainism. These three religions were indiginious to India and were primarily of a tolerant nature. Meaning that there was no forced conversion and intolerance shown to Hinduism. With the dawn of the Mughal period this changed drastically. Many invaders of different sorts have invaded India coming through the northeastern passage. The very earliest were Greek, in 550 B.C.E. who attacked the king of Punjab and defeated him. He was impressed by the high standard of the culture and morality of the king and gave him back his kingdom but left his emissary behind. There was a inter-mixing of the Greek and Indian people, resulting in a change in the Indian society in many ways. These invaders did not come to permanently stay. Neither did they have any intention of converting the population of India. They were open minded, tried to understand the way of life in India and probably took some things from here, which they liked and thought were worth adopting. Local Indian population went through a similar process. The Indian way of life and culture was, therefore, not adversely affected.

It were the Muslim invasions, which started around 700 AD, which were of a much more serious nature and posed the utmost danger to the Indian culture and religion. Prophet Muhammad was born in 571 A.D. and the religion of Islam started just a few years later. It was in 712 AD that Sind was conquered by *Muhammad bin Quasim*. So it may be said that the Muslim invaders started raiding India approximately two centuries after the birth of

Islam. The initial attacks, prior to the conquest of Sindh were intended to carry out raids in which the invader's main objective was to attack places and establishments where they could find valuables such as gold, diamonds, silver, and other rare and precious things. They did not care whether these places were places of worship or private properties. They would invariably plunder and destroy the properties, kill the people guarding them, and if they saw any beautiful women, they would rape them, kill them or in some instances, take them as slaves or take them and make them a part of their *haram*. The Muslim invaders considered women as objects or possessions belonging to their fathers, brothers or husbands.

The start of the purdah system:

The Mughals brought the purdah system to India. This concept was quite new and foreign. Pundit Jawaharlal Nehru writes in his famous book, "The Glimpses of World History" : "….Arab women did not observe purdah in the beginning. Success imitate more and more the customs of the two old empires on either side of them- the Eastern Roman and the Persian. They had defeated the former and put an end to the latter, but they themselves succumbed to many an evil habit of these empires… Gradually the haram system begins, and men and women meet each other less and less socially. Unhappily this seclusion of women became a feature of Islamic society, and India also learnt it from the Muslims when they came here." Both Mahatma Gandhi and Jawaharlal Nehru campaigned vigorously against the system of purdah. "Chastity", Gandhiji said, "is not a hothouse growth….It cannot be protected by the surrounding wall of the *purdah*. It must grow from within….. It must be a very poor thing that can not stand the gaze of men. Men to be men, must be able to trust their womenfolk, even as the latter are compelled to trust them….Let us then tear down the purdah with one mighty effort." Again: "I am of the opinion that the purdah in India is a recent institution and was adopted during the period of Hindu decline. Gargi could not have held her discourses from behind the purdah. Nor is the purdah universal in India. It is unknown in the Deccan, Gujarat, Maharashtra and the Punjab. It is unknown among the peasantry…."

Jawaharlal Nehru wrote in the *Glimpses of World History*: "Whenever I think of women in purdah, cut off from the outside world, I invariably think of a prison or a zoo! How can a nation go ahead if half of its population is kept hidden away in a kind of prison?"

The Muslims also believed in polygamy, which permitted them to marry any number of women as they wished. This implied that a woman's own wish did not matter at all. It is degrading for a woman to belong to a man who has kept many like her in his haram. This also had a terrifying effect on the local women population. The freedom, to which the women had been accustomed to for the past many centuries had to be drastically curtailed in the interest of saving their lives, their chastity, pride and self respect. The women then had to confine themselves inside their dwellings away from the gaze of the barbaric Muslim invaders. The women also started hiding themselves by using "purdah", a cloth worn over their head to hide their face and upper body. This was then the beginning of the purdah system in India and the origin being the invasion of the Muslims and the fear they created in the indigenous population. The areas most affected by the practice of this purdah system were naturally those where the Muslims had the most influence. These areas were the north including the United Provinces, Bihar, Rajasthan, Madhya Pradesh, Bengal and the other northern provinces. Southern India, the Deccan, right from Maharashtra to Kerala , and the Punjab were not affected by this practice. This is evident even today in the way the women of these southern provinces dress.

In the Punjab, a new religion, Sikhism was born, which was against the purdah system.

The purdah practice became more common among women of high class and not so common among the lower caste and the working class women. These women could not do menial work with the purdah. The system of purdah has gradually disappeared in India over the past about fifty years. This is due to the awakening of Indian woman, their education in more numbers, the great efforts of the able leadership of Mahatma Gandhi and Pundit Jawaharlal Nehru. The British Raj also has to be credited for this since they brought a fresh outlook in the country. When the British women came to India, they did not use the purdah since it was not practiced in England and they wondered why the Indian women were hiding themselves inside the so- called "purdah". It, of course, aroused a great amount of curiosity and questions were being asked about the basis for observing such a strange system. This had an impact on the Indian population. The big fear, which the women of India were under during the Mughal rule was no more a factor under the British. The Muslims were not able to pick up girls freely from the roadside under the British.

Purdah is still being practiced in the rural areas of Rajasthan, in small villages where the illiteracy of women is still great. But this is a tiny percentage of the total population. It is expected that this also will disappear in a few years as the education and literacy will spread in these remote areas. This also applies to other remote areas of India. With the wide coverage of Indian communication networks, especially the television and the radio, the villagers are now able to modernize themselves at a much faster pace. The disadvantage here is that the media, especially the television is not necessarily teaching the desired values. There is an emphasis on imitating the Americans. And not everything American is good thing to learn for Indian women.

Recently, Mrs.*Pratibha Patil* had been elected to the highest office of the president of the Indian Republic. A question was immediately asked regarding purdah to her. The lady was only covering her head partially on the back, which is the established practice of public appearance by respectable and cultured women of India. She made it quite clear that it ought not to be confused with the *purdah*. She also mentioned that Purdah was the system started by the Mughals. This statement of hers immediately drew protests from the Islamic groups. Mrs. *Indira Gandhi* and Mrs. *Vijaya Laxumi Pundit* also used to cover their heads in similar fashion.

Child marriages in the Mughal period:

This long- standing practice, which has been in existence over the past many centuries, during the Gupta period and thereafter and consolidated during the Moghul rule, is on the decline in India. In the big cities and other major population centers it has practically vanished. In these places the percentage of educated women have grown substantially and everybody has acquired a good deal of awareness. Not only that the women have become educated, they hold good employment and are independent financially. This has also resulted in them making their own decisions regarding their marriage. But the story in the remote rural areas in certain provinces is quite different. The level of illetracy is high and a woman is totally dependent on the family for her fate. The elder in the family, a patriarch makes decision with regard to when and with whom she is going to marry. Marriages are also carried out to settle old scores such as large debts. A patriarch will marry his very young daughter to an elderly person from whom he has borrowed money and is now unable to pay back. Giving his young girl's hand to him in marriage will relieve him from the debt.

A big change in the mindset of the people also resulted with respect to their treatment of the women in the sense that they started considering women more as a liability. A girl child, therefore became more as a liability rather than a happy addition to the family as it used to be. The system of child marriages also began at this period in the history. An early marriage, prior to attaining puberty, became a preferred option since the family could get rid of the girl early and be free from the worry of keeping her protected till she attained adulthood.

Effect on women's education under Mughal rule:

The Muslim invasion and their effect on the women of India had another big negative impact. This was concerning their education. Education for women had been restricted for women prior to the arrival of Mughals. Women were allowed limited education enough for them to take care of their households. After the arrival of the Mughals, educational restrictions became even more stringent since Mughals did not believe in educating women. According to the Mughal customs the place of a woman was in the haram. Her social exposure was practically absent. A portion of the house was reserved for the women of the haram where no body was allowed to visit except the close relatives of the husband. In addition to this the Mughals used to pick up women from the street as they pleased. So under such new atmosphere the movements of the indigenous women became further restricted and whatever educational opportunities they had were also lost. The only opportunity, which was left for them was to learn something at home from her own relatives. Gradually then it became quite accepted and normal that a girl would not receive any schooling. For a girl to leave the protection of her house and to go to school or any such place of learning became a dangerous and highly risky proposition. Because it implied providing her the necessary protection right from the time she leaves her house till she returns home, most people could not provide such protection. When the girls became of marriageable age, no body expected them to be educated. And the girls used to be married at a very early age anyway. The restriction on the education of girls has been tremendously damaging to the women of India and again the Muslim invasion is partly to blame.

The Muslims ruled India for about five centuries, from about 1200 AD to 1700 AD. But the Muslim invasions started much earlier and these incursions had a very profound effect on the women of India. For all these centuries Hindus and others had to protect their women from the barbaric Muslims and it resulted in imposing more restrictions on the freedom of women. This has had a very deep and lasting effect on the freedom of women in India. The protection and safety of women became the primary concern. Their education was of secondary importance. Things started to change after the arrival of the British and later after when India became independent. But, as can be expected, the centuries of restrictions had taken a lasting and permanent hold on the customs and traditions. Any changes to take place would take a long time to bring about the desired results.

The beginning of women's education started with the arrival of the Christian missionaries and their efforts in establishing schools for girls. The big problem faced by the missionaries was that they did not recognize the existing Brahminical system of education in which, among other things, the medium of instruction was the local varnacular. This posed a considerable challenge for the girls. The British did not recognize the existing Brahminical education since they considered it to be outmoded and the vernaculars to be a "waste of time." The first Western-style girl's school was founded in Calcutta in 1820, by David Hare, a watchmaker, who was influenced by European rationalist philosophy. With an explicit evangelical mission, missionaries for a time drew students from the lower castes. In response, Indian groups opened schools to avoid conversion. The first school to attract high-caste women was established in Calcutta in 1849 by *Ishwar Chandra Vidya Sagar*, with the help of *Bethune*, one of th Governor General's Council. And was called Bethune School (later College). Girl's schools were supported by individuals, reform societies, and, after 1854, by grants from the Indian Government. In 1882 there were eight educational institutions for females in India: most were private schools, and one college, with a total of 127,066 students. The graduates of these schools a tiny fraction of India's women, became the India's next generation of leaders of social reform movements.

After the collapse of the Mughal empire, Muslim reformists blamed the fall on Islam's rigid traditionalism; conservatives considered the military defeat a devine punishment for moral laxity. An important reformer, *Sir Sayaad Ahmed Khan*, held British weapons and the British educational and judicial system responsible for the Mughal defeat and British rule. He admired Western technology and ideas, especially science, and tried to inject them into Muslim intellectual life, while defending Islamic social system from Western criticism. He began reform oriented exegetical studies of the Qur'an and Hadith, and in 1875 founded Aligarh Muslim University to teach Western science in Muslim context. But he was less eager to reform laws governing women. Acknowledging that Qur'an mandated neither the purdah nor denying female education, Khan wanted men to be educated first, especially in Western subjects. He felt female education should emphasize moral and spiritual values, and did what he could to hinder radical reformers who wanted women too to be exposed to Western ideas. Not until the twentieth century were schools founded for Muslim girls, with some Western studies. Since these schools opened over men's opposition, they were especially strict about upholding purdah and stressing family traditions, obedience, and authority. Male students, in contrast, were encouraged to reinterpret tradition.

The Sikh religion advocated that women have equal right to get educated as men. This movement of educating women started much earlier than the collapse of the Mughal Empire. Sikhism also allowed women to participate freely and equally in their religious activities.

At the turn of the century, a mere 725 of India's millions of women worked in the professions. Men who had previously supported reform began to oppose it when a few literate women challenged the authority of men over women. Nevertheless, the percentage of literate women slowly grew— from 0.9 percent in 1901 to 3.4 percent in 1941. By 1936 over 3 milliun Indian women and girls were studying in 38,262 schools, in contrast to approximately 100,000 in 1882. *Rokeya Sakhawat Hossain* (1880-1932) has been called the first and foremost feminist of Muslim society in Bengal. Born to a conservative father who became wealthy as a landlord, then married a supportive man. Hossain gradually liberated herself and went to work in a school for Muslim girls. In 1911 she started the first Muslim girl's school in Calcutta, and introduced adult literacy programs for both Hindu and Muslim women. She also founded the Association of Muslim Women. She wrote a book about the stifling life of girls at one of the schools. Explaining that Muslims did not want girls (who had to travel to school) to be seen, the school devised a special bus, without windows but with two blocks of latticework, three inches wide and eighteen inches long, above the front and back doors. The first time the bus was used, the airless heat and darkness in the metal box made the children ill. The English woman who ran the school opened the lattices and hung colored curtains over the openings. Still it was too hot, and the girls fainted. Parents complained, and many took their daughters out of the school. Muslim men wrote the school letters sighned "Brothers-in-Islam," objecting to the curtains because, they said, breezes blew them open and violated purdah rules. Such were the problems faced by educators so far as the Muslim girls were concerned.

Hindu women targeted by Mughals creating an atmosphere of terror:

The next wave of the Moghul invaders, who came, came with the intention of settling down in the subcontinent. For them the local kings and heads of large or small kingdoms did not present any formidable resistance. It must be mentioned that North India had experienced a relatively peaceful period prior to the arrival of the Moghuls. This period is famous as the golden period in the history of India. The Mauryas and the Guptas who ruled during this period over most of North India were followers of Buddhism and Jainism was also prevalent. Both these religions preached non-violence. The strong emphasis on non-violence had drained the martial elements from the armies of these large empires. This made the armies of these kingdoms unsuitable mentally for defending against the fierce Mughals.. The Mughal armies were also much superior in terms of their armaments and techniques of conducting warfare. Their armies consisted of horsemen and their attacks used to be fierce and fast. The Moghuls also conducted wars on the basis of religion. They considered these wars in the name of Allah and as their religious duty, a jihad because according to Islam they must either kill or convert the non-Muslims, they called "infidels." The Muslims today also consider themselves superior to all others who are not followers of Islam. The Moghuls, therefore, had a very sacred religious purpose in conducting these wars. After a battle, they would most certainly convert the local population to Islam and capture the women and either kill them, enslave them, rape them or make them a part of their harem. This happened on a large scale. The phenomenal increase in the Muslim population, which we see today in India, is a direct result of this conversion. The other important factor to note is that the Hindus would not allow a person who had been converted to Islam by force, to reconvert to Hinduism. That person used to be considered completely outcast.

The invaders have been called Moghuls or Muslims but that term has been loosely applied. In fact a large variety of invaders came, among them were: Arabs, Turks, Afghans, and the Mughals. They brought with them their own religion, customs and traditions. These were quite different from the local traditions, customs and religious beliefs of the Hindu and other religious population. The invaders were generally followers of Islam and they imposed the *Sharia Law* on the locals. In accordance with Islam, all the Hindus were considered "Infidels" and it was considered the holy duty of the Mghals to convert them to Islam or kill them. Islam also permitted every Mughal to marry at least four wives, but they could many more and keep more in their harem. The government of India, even today, allows a Muslim to marry up to four wives, even though, a Muslim country such as Pakistan, does not permit marrying more than one woman. This created chaos in the Hindu population since, in spite of considering the Hindus as infiddles; they did freely marry high-class Hindu women such as Brahmins by force. They would generally kill the relatives of the woman. Their cruelty had no limits since they would kill the husband or father of the woman in front of her family in the most barbaric way. A passage from the book, *The Wonder That Was India*, by S.A.A. Rizvi illustrates this:

" From their earliest settlement, Muslims had married Hindu girls, although from the thirteenth century onwards many immigrants either came with their families or summoned them when they settled down. The Muslims preferred girls from the higher classes as wives. For example, when *Khwaja Muinuddin Chisti* settled at Ajmer he took two wives, although he was then aged sixty-five. One of them was a Hindu raja's daughter who had been seized during a raid on the Hindus by the local Muslim commander. *Sultan Alloudin Khilji* married Kamala Devi, the widow of Raja Karan of Gujarat, who had been taken captive after the Raja's defeat. Alauddin's son, *Khizar Khan*, married Kamala Devi's daughter by Raja Haran, Deval Devi. During Alauddin's reign, *Ghiyasuddin Tughluk*, whom the Sultan had made governor of Dipalpur, had wished to marry his brother, Rajab to one of the Raja of Dipalpur's daughters. Then, upon hearing of the beauty of Rana Mal Bhatti's daughter, he made the Rana's life unbeareable until the girl was married to Rajab. *Firoz Shah Tuglak* was their son. During *Mohmmad bin Tughluk's* reign, Firuz himself married the pretty sister of a Gujar, Saharan.

"It is significant that the Shaykzadas (descendents of the Sufi leaders) married Brahmin girls. In the sixteenth century Miran Sadr-I Jahan and Shaykh Abdur Rahim, who hailed from Avadh, married Brahman wives whom they have obviously chosen themselves."

These examples illustrate clearly that the Muslim invaders and later rulers had no regard for the culture and traditions of the native population and they chose and picked up any woman or girl as they wished in order to satisfy their lusts. They considered women no more than objects of enjoyment. It was, of course, relatively easy to get these women. It no doubt made the life of the local population miserable, to say the least particularly that of the women. The result was that the women had to hide themselves in their homes and their active participation in the society and their education suffered drastically. The Muslim rule in India for a period of about seven hundred years completely destroyed the wonderful social order and culture, the honor and dignity of women.

Certain outstanding examples from the history are worth citing to give the reader an idea of the magnitude of the problem, especially in North India. The following is quoted from the chapter entitled, *Holocast*, from the book *"Status of Indian Women, A Historical Perspective,* by B.R.Sharan: (Ref. 19)

After the death of *Prithvi Raj Chawan, Ala-ud-din* of the *Khilji* tribe came on the Indian scene. In 1296, after his notorious invasion of the Deccan, he returned to Delhi with a lot of booty. The old king *Jalal-ud-din Khilji,* his uncle, went out to welcome his victorious nephew and while he was clasping his hand, Ala-ud-din basely had him murdered by one of his followers. Ala-ud-din advanced upon Delhi with his uncle's head held aloft upon a lance. He then conducted a campain against the Rajput fortress of Chitorgarh where a young prince Lukumsi was on the throne at that time.

Bhimsi was the uncle of the young prince, and protector during his minority. He had espoused the daughter of Hamir Sank (Chohan) of Ceylon. Her name was Pudmani, a title bestowed on account of her being superlatively fair and beautiful. Having failed in the first attempt, Ala-ud-din mustered his strength and attacked again. When success deluded him, he limited his demand to the possession of Pudmani. At length he restricted his demand to a mere sight of this extraordinary beauty, finally reducing it to the proposal of beholding her through the medium of mirrors, which was accepted. Relying on the faith of the Rajput, he entered Chittor, slightly guarded, and having gratified his wish, returned. Bhimsi, unwilling to be outdone in confidence, accompanied the king to the foot of the fortress. Here Ala-ud-din had an ambush; Bhimsi was made prisoner, hurried away to the Tatar camp, and his liberty was made dependent on the surrender of Pudmani. Despair reigned Chitor, when this fatal event was known, and it was debated whether Pudmani should be resigned as a ransom for Bhimsi. When she was informed of this, she expressed her acquiescence and equipped herself with wherewithal to secure her from dishonor. Two chiefs of her own kin and clan of Ceylon, her uncle Gorah, and his nephew Badal, however devised a scheme for the liberation of their prince without hazarding her life or fame. Intimation was dispatched to Ala-ud-din that on the day he withdrew from his trenches the fair Pudmini would be sent, surrounded by her females and handmaids, not only those who would accompany her to Delhi, but many others who desired to pay her their last mark of reverence. Seven hundred covered litters proceeded to the royal camp. In each was placed one of the bravest defenders of Chitor, borne by six armed soldiers disguised as litter porters. When they breached the camp, half an hour was granted for a parting interview between the Hindu prince and his bride. They then placed their prince in a litter and some returned with him. After some time the devoted band issued from their litters; but Ala-ud-din was too well guarded. Pursuit was ordered and those who guarded the return of the prince perished to a man. A fleet horse had been kept ready for Bhimsi but at the outer gate of the fort the host of Ala-ud-din was encountered. The choicest of the heroes of Chiror met the assault. Bhimsi succeded in ascending the fort and for a time Ala-ud-din was defeated in his objective.

Ala-ud-din returned in 1303 AD. Siege was laid and when eleven of his twelve sons had fallen in turn, Bhimsi called his chiefs around him and said, "Now I devote myself to Chittor." But another awful sacrifice was to precede this act of self-devotion, in that horrible rite, the Johar, where females are immolated to preserve them from pollution or captivity. *The funeral pyre was lighted within the great subterranean retreat, in chambers impervious to the light of the day, and the defenders of Chitor beheld in procession the queens, their own wifes and daughters, to the number of several thousands. The fair Pudmini closed the throng, which was augmented by whatever of female beauty or youth could be trained by Tatar lust. They were conveyed to the cavern, and the opening closed upon them, leaving them to find security from dishonor in the devouring element* A contest now arose between the Rana and his surviving son; but the father prevailed, and Ajaisi, in obedience of his commands, with a small band passed through the enemy lines….The Rana, satisfied that his line was not extinct now prepared to follow his brave sons; and calling around him his devoted clans, for whom life had no longer any charms, they open the portals and descended to the plains and with reckless despair, carried death, or met it, in the crowded ranks of Alla. The Tatar conqueror took possession of an inanimate capital, strewed with brave defenders, the smoke yet issuing from the recesses where lay consumed the once fair object of his desire." (Refer to Col. James Tod, *Annals And Antiquities of Rajasthan", Ref. 20*).

Later in history, in the early sixteenth century, Humayun, son of Babar, was on the throne of Delhi. Karnavati, the wife of late Rana Sanga, in the interest of protecting her son, sent a Rakhi (a wrist band, which a sister puts on her brother's wrist as a token of brother/sister bond with the pledge that the brother will always protect her), to Humayun. Humayun accepted the Rakhi and promised to protect her. But it so happened that while Humayun was engaged on the Bengal front. Chittor was besieged by Muslim Sultans of Central India and a message was sent to Humayun from Chittor for help but

Humayun returned too late to help. *A massive jauhar led by Karnawati too place. Karnawati led the procession of willing victims to their doom and thirteen thousand females were thus swept at once into the fires of the jouhar!* A passage from the great sacred book, *Sri Guru Granth Sahib,* of Sikhs condemns the brutalities and rapes committed by the Mughal invador Babar: (Ref. 28)

"Modesty and righteousness both have vanished and falsehood moves about as the leader, O Lalo. The function of the Quazis and the Brahmins is over and the Satan now reads the marriage rites (rape). The Muslim women read the quaran and in suffering call upon God, O Lalo. The Hindu women of high caste and others of low caste, may also be put in the same account, O Lalo." Guru Nanak Dev, Tilang, pg. 772.).

Humayun's son, Akbar (1567) was a very ambitious. His approach with regard to getting the women of the Rajput noble families was different from his predecessors. Instead of demanding a particular woman for his sexual satisfaction and to attack that particular kingdom if they do not yield to his demand and the subsequent jauhar, which follows after the defeat of that kingdom, he devised a festival called *Naroza,* which literally means "a new years' day". He required that women from the Rajput noble families be attending this festival. The festival was only for females, no males were allowed in except that he himself attended disguised and selected a different woman for him to enjoy each night of the festival. The festival lasted for nine days.

Moving on to the seventeenth century, the last most powerful emperor, Aurangzeb of the Mughal dynasty was ruling. He was the worst of the lot, very cruel and anti- Hindu. He was also a very devout Muslim but he did demand the hand of the princess of Roopnaghar, a junior branch of the Mewar house, and with the demand was also a stipulation that two thousand horses also accompany the princess. Denial would of course mean a war. But in this case the brave and proud Rajputani rejected the demand outright. She married the chief of the Rajput race and sought his protection. In response to the demand by the Mughal emperor, the brave princess said " Is the swan to be the mate of the stork: a Rajputni, pure in blood, to be the wife to the monkey faced barbarian!" Concluding with the threat of sels-destruction if not saved from dishonor. Aurangzeb gathered all his sons who were engaged on different fronts, amassed a big army and attacked Chitor. The Rana had come to know of the princesses' determination and fought with the Mughal armies bravely with the result that the Mughals suffered a defeat. In this venture the Mughals suffered great losses, both men and material. (Ref. 20). This is yet another example of the Mughal's desire to have high class Hindu/Rajput women. And they were always prepared to use force if their demands were not met.

There are some high profile cases but the sexual harassment and abduction of ordinary women was taking place. They had no protection from the atrocities of the barbarians. Aurangzeb's reign ended in 1707. The Mughal power in Delhi declined drastically after Aurangzeb and the Rajputs then started gaining their strength. But the Mughal rule had a very lasting and devasting effect on the Rajput clans and communities. A stage had come when no girls were to be found in affected areas. As to the extent to which the female infanticide had reached in many parts of India we read in Lerchenfield's work, "When in the year 1836 the first inquiry into this matter was made by the anglo-Indian authorities, it was shone that, for example, in Western Rajputana in a group of 10,000 of the population there was not one girl ! In Manikpur, the Rajput nobility admitted that in their district for more than 100 years no girl baby had lived longer than one year. A government official ascertained first the practice of murder in 308 districts, which he had visited. In 26 he found not one girl under six years of age, in 28, not one under nubile age. In a few districts no marriage had taken place within the memory of a man, and in one the last marriage dated 80 years back. Marriages were rare and were performed in the very dark of night so as not to let the Mughals know of the event and to protect the bride.

Whatever good the Mughals might have done in India, there is no doubt that their rule brought down the dignified position occupied by Indian women. Education of women was stopped and they became victims of evil customs like very early child marriages with attendant fallouts. Some social scientists have very rightly described the Mughal era as the dark age for women. By the end of this era women no longer enjoyed the freedom of the earlier times, and even within the family as a unit, their importance became nil.

The state in which the women in India are today is, in most part, the direct result of the Muslim invasions and their prolonged rule and sexual exploitation of women of India. It was because of this barbaric Mughal rule that the women of India had to adopt so many evil customs. The Muslim influence had been more prominent in the Northern part of India, since that was the area where they arrived first and that is where the major battles were fought. In South India where the invaders were not able to penetrate, women remained relatively safe. The most striking difference, even today, which one may observe is the custom of "Purdah", which is commonly practiced by women of the North and a complete absence of this practice in the South.

The examples cited here are from the history book and comprise of some of the important high profile cases. Innumerable ordinary cases, which happened, never found a place in the history books. There are of course, innumerable local tales of Moghul atrocities and bravery of local people in saving the honor of their women. This is why in India there is rich history to be found at almost every corner. They are also very important and represent the terrible plight of the Indian woman. Even in providing these examples, some famous and prominent examples, were not reported. The history, which we now know had been written by the Mughals and that was recognized as official. Some of the accounts of history recorded by foreign visitors and witnesses present an entirely different picture.

There is again a difference between women from North verses from the South so far as the level of education, the freedom enjoyed, the equality with their male counterparts and their general social status is concerned. The percentage of literacy in the South is far greater than in the North. The difference is attributable to the Muslim influence in the North. The next paragraph describes the differences.

Status of women in South India in medieval times (10th to 14th Centuries):

As indicated before, the Southern part of India was not as affected by the Mughals as the North, since the Mughal conquest did not penitrate that deep in the South. Dr. Jotsna Kamat has written a on this subject in which she states as follows:

"According to B.P.Mazumbar, Northern India did not have any women administrators of provinces or kingdoms during this period. In contrast, Karnataca had women who administered villages, towns, divisions and heralded social and religious institutions. ….

"Historical sources of the period are abundantly filled with stories of accomplished women of the time. Shantaladevi , the the Hoysala queen was an expert in singing, dancing and instrumental music. She also held durbar with her illustrious husband Vishnuvardhana….

"It is evident from a inscription of 1187 A.D. that the Jain nuns enjoyed the same freedom as their male counterparts.

There were female trustees, priestesses, philanthropists, musicians and scholars. ...."

Restrictions on widow marriage:

The terrible plight of the widows has already been described. It ought to be mentioned that in addition to all the inhuman conditions to which they were subjected, they were not allowed to remarry. At a time when Brahmins were in power, they decreed that a woman can marry once in her lifetime and hence for her to remarry after the death of her husband was out of the question. This placed a widow in a very difficult condition, especially the very young widows, who by a stroke of bad luck became widows, in many cases even without their marriage being consummated. The Hindus also, in many cases, blamed the widow for her husband's death since they believed that she brought bad luck to her husband.

In Sikhism, Guru Amar Das has condemned the cruel custom of sati, female infanticide and advocated widow remarriage. Guru Amar Das also believed that women wearing veils (purdah) was demeaning. (Ref. 28).

The women of Bengal took a hand in improving their lot. R.C.Majumdar cites an example of the new spirit among Bengali women the numerous letters they wrote to the local journals, as early as in 1835, asking for the spread of women's education. They also demanded the removals of the social evils from which they had been suffering for long, such as the prohibition of widow remarriage. Ishwar Chandra Vidyasagar played a leading part in the campaign to legalise remarriage. In order to get proof from the scriptures, he went to Calcutta and studied the scriptures. Finally he found the proof, which he was after. He was overjoyed. His efforts resulted in the enactment of the Hindu Women's Remarriage Act in 1856. The significance of this measure will be evident from the following words of Pundita Ramabai, which written toward the close of the 19th century, continued to be largely true description of the plight of the widow in Hindu society, especially among the so-called higher castes, until 1930s :

"Throughout India widowhood is regarded as the punishment for horrible crimes committed by woman in her former existence. But it is the child widow upon whom in an especial manner falls the abuse and hatred of the community.... Among the Brahmins of the Deccan the heads of all widows must be shaved regularly every fortnight. The widow must wear a single coarse garment. She must eat only one meal during the twenty-four hours of the day. She must never take part in family feasts. A man or woman thinks it unlucky to behold a widow's face before seeing any other object in the morning. In addition to all this, the young widow is always looked upon with suspicion, for fear she may some time bring disgrace upon the family by committing some improper act….. Her life then, destitute as it is of the least literary knowledge, void of hope, empty of every pleasure and social advantage, becomes intolerable, a curse to herself and to society at large."

The usual benediction when a married woman bows respectfully before elders is "Long may you live unwidowed." There is a widely observed tradition of the wife fasting and praying on certain days of the year for the long life and wellbeing of her husband. A prominent reformer, *Raja Ram Mohan Roy*, born on 22nd may, 1772, was greatly opposed to restrictions on widow remarriage. He himself married a widow to set an example for the whole society. Along with *Debandranath Tagore* (1817-1905), father of the famous poet, *Rabindranath Tagore*, he founded the *Braho Samaj* in 1828. The aims and objectives of this institution were to promote remarriage of widows and to restore respect and dignity to them. It also provided necessary shelter and education to widows. In Maharashtra, similar awakening happened. *Mahershi Annasahib Karve* also remarried. Haribalhal Parchure also remarried. They were both discriminated by the society. They were not allowed to dine with everybody. They were asked to seat separately for dinner. *Dhondo Keshav* (popularly known as Mahershi) *Karve* (1858-1962) was a crusader against injustice to women. After his first wife died in 1891 he married a widow, Godubai, in 1893. He founded in the same year the *Vidhva Vivaha Pratibandi Nivarak Mandali* (Society for the removal of obstacles to widow remarriage) to help needy widows and look after their children's education. In 1898 he established a widow's home, and in 1908 the *Nish Kaam Karma Math* to train volunteers for selsless work. His greatest achievement was the establishment of a women's university, for which he collected funds in England, America and east Africa. Established in Pune in 1916, it received a munificent donation of fifteen lakh rupees in 1920 from Sir Vithaldas Thackersay and was named as the *Shrimati Nathibai Damodar Thackersay Women's University* in memory of the donor's mother. A notable feature of the university, which moved to Mumbai in 1936, was the employment of Indian languages for instruction at a time when a foreign language was being used for imparting even elementary knowledge in arts and science. But English was taught as a compulsory subject.

In her essay, *Popular Perceptions of Widow-remarriage in Haryana : Past and Present*, Prem Chowdhry presents a different picture of the widow ermarriage. (Ref.17). According to her remarriage of widows was not a problem in the State of Haryana. The society there was quite open to the widow remarriage and the widow could easily marry the younger brother of her deceased husband, if he was still unmarried. The custom of widow-remarriage as traditionally followed has special features in Haryana. Known as *Karewa,* it is a throwback to the old Rig-Vedic custom of *niyog* (levitate marriage), which was prevalent in the geographical region of Haryana and Punjab associated with early Vedic Aryan settlements. The *karewa* is a white sheet colored at the corners, was thrown by the man, over the widow's head, signifying his acceptance of her as his wife. Symbolically this gesture of protection extended once again to a woman who had become autonomous. The man also bestowed color (red being the auspicious hue associated with matrimony) upon the woman and, through this custom, established social consent for cohabitation. Ther could be certain variations to it. For example, it could take the form of either placing *churris* (glass bangles) on the widow's wrist or sometime even a gold *nuth* (nose-ring) on her nose and a red sheet over her head with a rupee tied in one of the corners, before a full assembly. This would be followed by the distribution of *gur* (molasses) or sweets. This custom is followed to this day. It is important to note that this type of marriage is not accompanied by any religious ceremony, since no woman can customarily go through the marriage ceremony twice

Karewa, as a rule, has always been primarily a levirate marriage in which the widow is accepted as wife by one of the younger brothers of the deceased husband: failing him, the husband's elder brother; failing him, his first cousin, and so on. It is then true that a widow could remarry but with whom she will marry was strictly a decision of her deceased husband's family. In Haryana and the surrounding region, widow remarriage is an accepted thing. Even the higher castes such as the Brahmins and the Kshtrias who were earlier opposed to it, have also accepted it. The popularity of this practice is evident from the numbers estimated: among widows of marriageable age, only one in thousand is found to have remained unmarried. The statical calculations are also not far from this. The 1981 census shows that among the rural women of Haryana between the "marriageable age" of 16 and 44 years only 0.77 percent were widows.

The Mughals were not opposed to widow remarriage since their religion permitted such marriages. The British were also not opposed to the widow remarriage. A widow getting remarried was looked down upon. This restriction applied to all the widows irrespective of their age. In many instances women did become widows while they were quite young. Girls who used to get married at an early age of 8 or 10 used to become widows two or three years after their marriage. This was not so uncommon since sickness and diseases were causing early deaths. In those instances the young girl had to spend her remaining life in terrible condition, which can only be described as unbearable.

The tradition of devdasies:

The word "Devdasi" is composed of two separate words, Dev, meaning god and dasi, meaning servant or slave. The joint word literally means servant of god. The offering of a girl to the temple to become a devdasi had been a very old tradition in India. The system is prevailent all over India. The names of Devdasies are different in different regions: for example, Devarattiyal in Tamil Nadu, Mahris in Kerala, Natis in Assam, Muralis in Maharashtra, Basvis and Muralis in Andhra Pradesh, and Jogatis and Basvis in Karnataka. Presently, according to Dr. I.S. Gilada, the true meaning of the word Devdasi is understood as "prostitute". That is what all Devdasis are, prostitutes. But they are not covered under the "Supression of Immoral Traffic Act", because they function under the guise of blind superstition and religious beliefs and not on the basis of economic gain.

There is a mythological story to which the origin of this tradition may be traced back to. The Devdasi tradition has become extinct in almost all parts of India except Karnataka. Everwhere else it is open prostitution. But in Karnataka and at the border are between Maharashtra/Karnataka it is still perpetuated and carried down to the next generation of girls through the dedication of little girls to goddess, *Yellamma,* on Megha Purnima day at *Saundatti* , in Belgaum district, every year.

The myth behind dedication of girls to the goddess goes something like this: Renuka was the wife of sage Jamadagni. She was extremely pure and dedicated to her husband. Renuka used to make a new pot every day to fetch water from the river. On one occasion, while she was filling her newly made water pot, she happened to see the reflection of the "*Gandharva*" couple in the water. Gandharvas are demi-gods and are very beautiful. Renuka was bewitched by the handsomeness of the male Gandharva, albeit just for a moment. This resulted in cracking her pot. After returning to the Ashram, the sage saw the crack in the pot and through his devine power of perseption knew that she had "sinned" by coveting a man other than her husband. The sage was angered and ordered his twelve year- old son, Parsuram, tobehead his own mother. Parsuram carried out the orders of his father. Happy with his son, the sage asked his son for anything he wished from his father as a boon. The clever son asked his father to bring back his mother to life. The sage saw a *matangi* woman (a low caste woman) passing by and he beheaded her and attached her head to the body of Renuka. Renuka was thus briught back to life. The sage blessed her saying that unmarried girls who would worship her as a goddess, would be dedicated to her for the rest of their lives by marrying her for the physical fulfillment of her son, Parsuram, through her. As Parsuram resides in every man, these girls have to view every man who come to them for sexual satisfaction as the human embodiment of Parsuram and would satisfy the man without asking anything in return. (Ref. 21) These girls would then lose the right to turn back a man even if he was a leper. In addition, these girls would have to go begging for alms on Tuesdays and Fridays in the name of *Yellema* as that would be their source of livelihood.

It is quite a complex story, which dates back to the third century AD but has created a very miserable life for a girl who is given up to be a Devdasi. These girls work under the supervision of the temple high priest and are to obey the orders given. They are given any and all tasks to do in and around the temple. Their subsistence comes out of the donations received by the temple. The girls are, of course, not allowed to marry. They are supposed to be good in arts such as singing, dancing and instrumental music. They perform at the temple in front of the idol and audiences who gather at the temple on certain festive occasions. Dr. Kamat writes the following:

> *"Dedicating girls to temples was an ancient practice and by the tenth century, it had become well established. Some of them were experts of arts including singing, dancing, and acting performances."*

The tradition of Devdasies continues. The families who wish to get rid of their daughter to avoid paying for her marriage, education, and dowry donate their girls to the temple. In plain words, an unwanted girl child is donated to the temple to become a Devdasi. There has been a lot of corruption reported in connection with the devdasies. In many instances the devdasis are used by the priests or other rich or noble persons for the satisfaction of their sexual desires. According to the tradition, these girls are not to refuse any engagement in sex with any man, as stated above. This is the reason why devdasis are a sort of prostitutes under the guise of a ridiculous religious belief or superstition.

Within the large temple establishments, there are a number of devdasies, and a large staff of pujaris (persons who perform the worship), and sub-pujaris and other Brahmins doing minor jobs in the up-keep of the temple. It is a big establishment. There are older devdasis who have been in the service for many years and then there are younger ones who have just recently joined. Girls join when they are quite young, generally around 4 or 5. The older devdasis look after the training and development of the younger girls. They teach them various arts such as vocal music, dance, acting, playing musical instruments depending on their own expertise. The girls learn fast at their young age. The devdasis present a high-class performance on certain important religious events, depicting the stories of the various incarnations of the lord and other mythical themes. These performances are worth watching. Such performances are a regular occurrence in the temples of South India. Large crowds gather in the evenings to watch these performances, which excel in artistry. People donate large sums of money to these temples in order to promote such performances, which are considered a part of devotion to the lord.

Historically, when the *Pallava* and the *Chola* dynasties ruled between the 6th and the 13th century AD, the devdasi system was well established and devdasies were a well- respected class of women. They were also regarded as custodians of the arts. The ancient classical literature describes them as beautiful, accomplished, famous and honorable. There was no hint of ostracism. They were wealthy, being bestowed with grand gifts of land and property and jewellery by their wealthier and royal patrons. There are iscriptions dating back to 1004 AD on the Raja Rajeshwar temple at Tanjore, which maintain that there were 400 devdasis in the temple who were second in importance to the templepriests. The shrine of Someshwar in Gujarat maintained 500 devdasis. According to Vivakanand Manawade, secretary of Vimochana, an organization that helps devdasis, the earliest reference to the system is found in some stone inscriptions in 1113 AD at Ahalli in Karnataka. The word "prostitute" came into being in the year 733 AD according toManawade.

The earliest and reliable explict reference to devdasis system in Pune is found in the copper place inscriptions of the *Rashtrakuta* kings in the 8th and 10th centuries. But the existence of devdasis here predates these inscriptions by many years. The *Yadava* kings of Daulatabad overthrew the *Rashtrakuta* kings in 973 AD. But the devdasis went on with the practice of dancing before temple idols and in the bed -chambers of the new rulers, the *Yadava*.

There is a very interesting true story, which happened in the 12th Centuary, has a devdasi connection and this story has been immortalized on account of a wonderful and beautiful poetic composition, which came about as a result of the love for a devdasi. It so happened that a devdasi who was beautiful and an accomplished dancer, was devoted to lord *Krishna* and used to perform before his idol in a temple in south India and a renouned poet by the name of *Jayadeva,* devotee of lord Vishnu, also was a regular visitor to this temple. The two fell in love with easc other. The poet got inspiration out of this and composed a poem in Sanskrit called *Gita Govinda,* which became very popular and was based on the theme of the love and devotion, which the gopies of Vrindavan had for lord *Krishna.* The poem also had the additional benefit of reviving *Vaishnavism,* (the devotion for lord Vishnu, the most important God in the Hindu panthion). The fame and populariyu of this beautiful composition caught the attention of the British and *Sir William Jones* got it translated into English in 1792. The composition has been subsequently translated into other European languages. The readers will also note that the tradition of devdasis is fairly old.

Pune came under Shahaji Bhonsle in the 17th century and by this time, the peths such as the Shaniwarpeth, Raviwarpeth, and Somwarpeth had already emerged as well as the notorious red-light areas of Budhwar and Shukarwar Peths, and by 1818 the devdasis had deteriorated to the profession of prostitution. Gone was the enormous respect they enjoyed as members of a class next to the priestly class. They became experts in love- making, pleasing men with their bodies. The practice spread all over Belgaon, Gulburga, and Bellary districts of Karnataka and Satara, Kolhapur, Solhapur and Osmanabad districts of Maharashtra. With the passage of time the system degenerated when priests, royalty, rich and powerful men began to use devdasis purely as objects of sexual pleasure.

Chakresh Jain rightly observes in *Devdasis: Maids of God-and Men,* (Express Magazine, June 9, 1985): "Present- day devdasis are not the descendents of courteseans, nor are they proficient in any art. They are not concubines of the rich and are not wealthy. The lives of the devdasis of Maharashtra and Karnataka are dedicated to *Yallamma,* the universal mother. They are married to her and can marry no one else. The only art they are conversant in is the art of submitting to any man who desires them and is willing to pay for their favous."

At one time, devdasis were considered so auspicious that their presence was compulsory at every wedding for the making of the *mangalsutra* (an auspicious neck ornament worn by every married woman till the death of her husband), which would be given to a new bride in a normal marriage. This was based on the belief that a devdasi is an eternally married *suhagan* (an edict for a fortunate woman who has a husband), who can never be widowed, having married to a Goddess and thus, if the mangalsutra is made by her, the bride too, would die a *sumangali*. (The woman who dies while her husband is alive). Those days are now no more because, being exploited by the wealthier and powerful class of men in society, on one hand, and beset with poverty, on the other, the devdasis have been driven to prostitution.

The difference between the commercial system of prostitution as it exists everywhere and the devdasis who are now prostitutes, lies in the fact that the former is purely commercial, based on basic need for survival, whereas the latter is being perpetuated in the name of *Yallamma*, though the motivation is the same, i.e. survival. In the case of commercial prostitutes, they do not have to get their daughters into prostitution, whereas in the case of the devdasis, they dedicate their daughters to Yallamma and make them devdasis, based on the blind belief, superstitution, and illetracy. Illiterate people in Saundatti and Nippani who do not belong to the devdasi cult, are also known to give their gaughters in dedication to the Goddess *Yallamma* to escape her "wrath". Among Banjaras of Ratlam and Mandsu districts, prostitution of the eldest daughter is compulsory. Today the line of demarcation between a commercial prostitute and a devdasi-turned prostitute is rather thin, or almost blurred. In commercial prostitution one is not born in the profession, but enters into it by choice, while in the case of devdasi system one is born in the profession and is groomed for it right from the birth. The commercial prostitution does not have any religious or superstitutios basis, the devdasi system does.

According to the Indian Health Organization, nearly 15 to 20 percent of the total number of prostitutes in Mumbai's red- light district is devdasis. Ninety percent of the devdasis are *Harijans*, the untouchables and lowest caste in the Hindu religion, because *Yallamma* is the Goddess of the *Harijans*. Her head belonged to a Harijan woman, as mentioned earlier.

An effort was made to stop the devdasi tradition by arranging a conference under the auspices of *Mahatma Phule Samta Prathisthan of Pune* along with professor Subash Joshi of Nippani and professor Vithal Banne of Gandhinglaj. It was a first conference of its kind but it had no effect on the devdasi tradition, none at all.

Dr. Gilada estimates that the devdasis constitute about 25 % of the total population of prostitutes in India. Even today about 1,000 young girls are dedicated to the goddess Yallamma on Megha Purnima day at Saundatti. This is the biggest festival of the year in the areas where the temple of goddess Yallamma stands. But apart from this, girls are dedicated on every purnima (a full moon day) day of every month to goddess Yallamma to become devdasi, alias, a prostitute.

Women's education:

The girls in the medieval period, especially Hindu girls were not given any formal education. They were only taught things relevant to domestic work. The famous Indian philosopher, *Vatasyana* wrote that women ought to be well versed in 64 different arts. These included cooking, grinding, decorating, household medicine, recitation of certain basic religious hymns, and so on. The restriction on education as mentioned was particularly harsh on the Hindu girls. Other religions such as Buddhism, Jainism and Chriastanity were much more liberal. In these religions, no distinction was made between men and women. Women were given equal opportunity to educate themselves as men. In Buddhism and Jainism they believed that god is equally graceful to both men and women and both can attain salvation. Women preachers were spreading the teachings of their religions. According to *Huen Tsang*, a famous Chinese traveler during that time and who wrote accounts of his travels, *Rajshri*, the sister of *Harshavardhana*, was a distinguished scholar of her time. Another such example is the daughter of king *Ashka*, *Sanghmitra*. She and her brother, Mahendra, went to Sri Lanka to preach Buddhism.

In South India, the condition of women was better than in the North. As mentioned earlier, many women in South India were administrators and carried heavy responsibilities at local, community and state levels. Women had representations in practically all fields. *Domino Paes*, the famous Portuguese traveler, testifies to this effect. According to him, in the kingdom of Vijayanagar, women were present in each and every field. They could wrestle, blow the trumpet, weild the sword with equal dexterity as men. Another traveler, *Nuntz*, concurs with the accounts of Paes and writes that women were employed in writing expenses, recording the affairs of the kingdom, which confirms that they were educated. There is no evidence of any public school in North India, but according to famous historian, *Ibn Batuta*, there were thirteen schools for girls and twenty-four for the boys in Honavar. The major evil present in South India was that of the Devdasis.

The plight of Indian women in medieval times and at the starting of the modern period in Indian history can be aptly summarized by the following poetic composition of the great Indian poet and Noble laurate, Rabindra Nath Tagore, as follows:

> *"O Lord Why have you not given women the right*
> *to conquer her destiny?*
> *Why does she have to wait head bowed,*
> *By the roadside, waiting with tired patience,*
> *Hoping for a miracle in the morrow?"*

After India got independence, a great change has taken place with regard to women's education. Article 45 of the Indian constitution directs the government to provide "free and compulsory education for all children until they complete the age of 14." The importance of this goal has been emphasized repeatedly in the sixty odd years since Indian independence through the establishment of several governmental and non-governmental schemes directed at increasing educational opportunities and improving literacy. In 1979-1980, the government created the non- formal education (NFE) program, in an effort to reach children who were difficult to draw into the formal educational system, especially girls and working children. Teachers were local people trained to run NFE schools. The National Literacy Mission, established in 1988, extends this initiative to adult literacy. And a pilot project called education for women's equality and socio-economic empowerment. In 1994, the District Primary Education Program (DPEP) was launched specially to target low-literacy districts across India. One of DPEP's aim is to improve girl's access to basic education through an approach based on decentralized teacher training and curriculum development, school building, and community mobilization.

Poverty is a very big factor for quite a few families in deciding how much they can spend on educating their children. A family with limited resources gives priority to educating their son (s)., since he is the one going to support his wife and family. Even though the education is free to a certain level, there are costs involved in school uniforms, books, transportations, stationary, all of which become burdensome for a family of limited resources. Additionally, going to school involves homework, which means little time available for help in the household work. From this point of view, it is better to get the girls stay at home and do the housework, since not only does it satisfy the need of help in the housework but it also trains the girls for their future role as a housewife. Families who have sufficient resources educate *all* their children. In this case they have to make sure that the girls learn housework as well since this will stand them in good stead for their future responsibilities as housewives. Muslim communities had long struggled with the problem of retaining a distinct Islamic identity while acquiring mainstream secular education. They have, therefore, resisted sending the children to school, especially girls. Solutions to such identity concerns have, often been worked out by local groups working in close consultation with religious leaders and other community elders. People's Movement (Lok Jumbish), a prominent NGO, specializing in education, for instance, has been instrumental in developing and implementing educational policy specifically directed at Muslim women of the Rajasthani Meo community with considerable success.

Continued government expansion of education schemes especially directed at girls and women, have resulted in considerable improvement in the literacy of women. Data from 2001 census indicate considerable advancement in the field of literacy. India now has an overall literacy rate of 65 percent with female and male literact stand at 54 and 76 percent, respectively. Regional variations in literacy are quite significant. In Bihar, female and male literacy stand at 34 and 60 percent, in Kerala, the rates are 94 and 88 percent, respectively. Kerala has among the highest literacy rates in the developing world, and literacy programs in that state have served as models for their national counterparts. Literacy rates for women in the rural areas stand at 47 percent and in urban areas at 73 percent. These figures indicate an improvement of between 40 and 50 percent since 1951 for both men and women, with women's literacy in urban areas and men's literacy in the rural areas showing the most dramatic increases. Since 1981, the overall literacy rate has improved by approximately 20 percent and that of women by 25 percent.

CHAPTER 4.
ISSUES CONCERNING WOMEN IN BRITISH RAJ AND MODERN INDIA AFTER INDEPENDENCE:

Let us take stock of the status of Indian woman at the time of the arrival of the British and other Europeans in India. This is important since it gives an idea of the impression, which the foreigners had at the time of their arrival and their first encounter with the civilization of this part of the world. In the preceeding chapters the deteriorating conditions of the Indian women has been outlined over the many centuries. The end of the Moghul Empire in the eighteenth century and the consequent confusion and political disarray, which followed throught the country further added to the miseries of the Indian women. When the British arrived in India, the position of the Indian women was at its lowest ebb in the Indian history. Child marriage was generally practiced in all high class Hindus, and had even spread to some sections of the Muslim population. Sati tradition was prevailent and even Sikhs practiced it though forbidden by their Gurus. Purdah was strictly enforced by Muslims and in certain Hindu communities, especially in the north. In the Hindu society, female litracy was regarded "as a source of moral danger since only dancing girls could normally read and write". And ladies of the orthodox families could have been shocked if a report had spread that they were acquainted with singing and dancing. Polygamy was practiced by all those who could afford it. Prostitution was rampant, and every city and town teemed with singing and dancing girls, and no social function was complete without a "Nautch" as the performance by professional dancers was called. All Hindu temples openly and surreptiously harboured Devdasis.

As against this position, when the British left the country in 1947, most of this had changed. Some good legislation, which was inacted during the

British rule has already been enumerated. That streak of progressive legislation continued in post-independent India. Child- marriage and widow burning had been effectively stopped throughout the country, and widow remarriage legally permitted. Female education was introduced and encouraged to such an extent that literacy, far from being reconed as a moral lapse, came to be considered as desirable accomplishment for girls. Polygamy, though not abolished, was looked down upon as old fashioned, and not in keeping with the dignity and restraint expected of an educated, cultured gentleman. Prostitution was recognized as a social evil and association with prostitutes, a mark of depravity. Political equality of sexes was accepted in principle and many women held responsible positions under the Government and sone were elected or nominated to the legislatures. The advancement made in the improvement of the status of women in post-independent India was more rapid but was possible by the sound foundation laid during the British rule.

Several factors contributed towards the uplift of Indian women during the British rule. First and most important was the exposure of the Indians to the British society. The British were wellknown for their chivalerous attitude towards women. The second factor was the general awakening of the Indians to the developments of the twentith century. Lastly, the freedom fight in which Indians engaged gave good impetus to the uplift of women since the struggle for freedom was combined with many such issues of improvement in the Indian society, empowerment of women was one of them. This was also the time during which some great Indian leaders had a good look at the condition of Indian society from the "outside". One of the most important acomplishment of the British conquest of India was that it brought together the vast south Asian sub-continent into one united country. The sub-continent was otherwise sub-divided into some larger and some smaller kingdoms and territories operating quite independently. It was only during the British rule that the Indians, for the first time, in their recent history felt that they belonged to a one country, India.

Before discussing the good changes, which happened during the British Raj, some consideration ought to be given to the conditions in the beginning when the East India Company had started making inroads into Indian territory and started expanding their hold on areas, which they could acquire on account of local chaos and careless administration and disunity. At first when the East India Company started its business in India, it avoided the expense of sending the women with them and encouraged the employees to take Indian wives or concubines. During those times a voyage to India was an adventure and living in India was also not without risks especially since the British were not completely secure. In their bid to conquer India, the British were always moving and fighting, which was not suitable for peaceful and secure living of British women. In addition, the added responsibility of protecting and caring for women would weaken the soldiers in their effort for conquest. Pran Nevile, in his book, *Beyond the Veil, Indian Women in the Raj*, has presented the status of Indian women during the British Raj. The book describes various categories of women: the women of aristocracy, of village, mistresses, entertainers, working women, women in marriage and women's dresses, ornaments and costumes. The author is fascinated with women of India. The main theme of the book is the relationship of the British soldiers with the women of India and this is most importantly covered in the chapters on *Bibis and Mistresses and Public Entertainers*. The following excerpts from these chapters will provide an idea of what were the conditions of Indian women under British protection/custody:

"Towards the end of the 18th century, there were only 250 European women in Calcutta, while there were 4000 men. The civilians and soldiers were, therefore, encouraged and even subsidized by the Company to take native wives and mistresses. It was a common practice for the sahibs to set up zananas or to keep Indian bibis. The bibi was an Indian mistress, a common law wife, or long- term consort of the Englishman, who could afford to set up even a modest establishment. At times they got married but there were insurmountable difficulties in the way of a Christain marriage with a pagan.

Captain Thomas Williamson, who spent twenty years in the Company's service in India, in his famous guide book, *East India Vade Mecum,* justified the practice of keeping Indian mistresses as they were far more economical than maintaining European wives. According to him, "The attachment of many European gentlemen to their native mistresses is not to be described. An infatuation beyond all comparison prevails, causing every confidence, of whatever description, to be reposed in the sable queen of the harem"

To continue: "Englishmen preferred native girls to the white English women. Samuel Brown, a Company official, noted: "the native women were so amazingly playful, so anxious to please, that a person, accustomed to their society, shrinks from the idea of encouraging the whims, or yielding to the furies of an English woman." There are a number of examples cited by the author in which an English man states his personal experience of having sexual relationships with Indian women: Innes Monroe (1780-84), Dr. John Scott, a physician in Madras, Samuel Brown, a Company official, Sir Garnet Wolseley, and so on all praising the beauty and loyality of the women in their haram. An English Editor of a local newspaper went to the extent of advising the "sahibs" to sleep with the Indian women to keep themselves cool in the beastely summer of Calcutta. In fact the Portugese obtained a *firman* (a royal decree), from the Mughal Emperor, *Shahjahan*, to keep Bengali women during summer to protect themselves from the heat of the Delta." Such was the way in which the women of India were treated. This amounts to treating the women of India as mere objects of desire. The only solace was that the women received protection and lived comfortably but they had sacrificed their tradition, religious requirements etc.

Further, "there was no shame about these liaisons. Even the Governor General, *Sir John Shore,* and the Governor of Bombay and members of his Council, publicly had native women as their mistresses. These irregular unions attracted no censure. They were seldom a secret, as can be gathered from the account of the birth of Qui Hi's son, in the satiric poem, "The Grand Master".

> *Poor Gulab was in that way,*
> *That those who" love their lords" should be;*
> *And in a week, to Qui Hi's joy,*
> *Produced our youth a chopping boy,*
> *Our hero now, without pretence,*
> *Thought himself of some consequence,*
> *A child he had got, and what was curious,*
> *He knew the infant was not spurious;*
> *For Qui Hi was never tied*
> *By licence to his Indian bride,*
> *Yet he was confident that she*
> *Had acted with fidelity."*

The classic case is that of Job Charmock, founder of the city of Calcutta, who married a beautiful Brahmin girl, Leela, after resquing her from a funeral pyre where she was going to perform "sati". The legend has it that the great English sahib was greatly in love with her and she persuaded him to live like a Hindu.

"By the third decade of the 19th century, with the introduction of the overland route as well as steamships, English girls started to come to India in large numbers to hunt for husbands. The practice of keeping bibis and native mistresses came to be frowned upon; Englishmen were advised to distance themselves from native connections. The memsahibs launched a full-scale campaign against "bibidom". They spared no effort in abolishing the "bibi" system, as they considered it a threat to their position and scandalous for the ruling class. Thus, thousands of connected bibis, loving and good mothers, were driven out of their homes. After the mutiny of 1857, the institution of keeping Indian women as bibis nearly disappeared."

This sums up the treatment of Indian women by the Europeans, especially Englishmen. They used them when they needed to satisfy their sexual needs and discarded them when their own women arrived. They also worked on a policy of looking down upon the Indians and the women after completing their conquest of India.

"The relationships, which the Englishmen had with the Indian women, resulted in producing a number of what are known as "Anglo-Indians".

It was the policy of the British to maintain a distance between them and the Indians and they would not allow any Indians to attend their parties and other functions. They would have Indian servants to dance attendance on them. The ladies were instructed not to mix with the local ladies. Most of the English women did not like this colonial attitude but mostly all toed the official line. Some independent-minded women did venture into the Indian society, studied their culture and understood their way of life. "Fanny Parks", the wife of the collector of customs at Allahabad came in 1822 and immediately plunged into the rich texture of Indian life. She celebrated Hindu festivals, learned Persian, played the sitar and made a vast collection of Indian insects, fossils, religious icons, and animal skulls." (Ref.16).

During the Raj the British introduced a number of new policies, which were intended to benefit the British. For example, they disallowed the manufacture of cloth and many small cottage industry products, which harmed the women engaged in this industry, especially the textile industry. The case of the British government ordering to cut the hands of the laborers who were the master craftsmen making the world's finest muslin is a well-known example of British atrocities in India. This action was taken by the British to eliminate this fine product from the market and have no product to compete with their own.

In the area of social reforms, the British had studied the famous *Manusmriti* and based their legislation on the basis of the laws prescribed in that ancient text, for all the Hindus, all across India without caring to understand the regional differences within the Hindu society and having no idea about the correct interpretation of this old text. The result was that the women in the

South, where matrilineal tradition existed, could ask for maintenance from separated husbands according to joint family ownership of private land, the British law invested absolute ownership of private property in male heads of households, which ended the rights of women there. The British imposed ancient Hindu law on groups, which were previously not governed by it, annulling the rights of women possessed even in patriarchal and patrilineal regions. British administrators also overrode the Muslim women's inheritance rights disregarding Muslim law and harming lower-caste women. Restoration of Muslim law became a nationalistic issue later for urban Muslims.

The British colonial officers made the Indian woman's degradation as a major ideological foundation for British rule in India. They passed laws expected to benefit women, but also set in stone the *Brahminic Laws of Manu,* which before the *Gentoo Code* of 1772 had been applied flexiably. In ignorance of Indian customs and the complexity of competing legal systems in India, they reduced the flexibility inherent in the customary law. Ironically, they created an extensive system to enforce a legal code, which further restricted women's independence, right to property and control over their children.

Not much is known about women's economic activities during the Raj, but Ramusack writes that some elite women in Bengal were *zamindars* (land lords) with varying degrees of authority over their estates. Most women who worked for pay were in professions that catered to women. Some common women became wealthy, especially in Lucknow. They maintained the traditional elite culture and earned enough to buy property and pay taxes. Vast majority of women worked in agriculture some in manufacturing making matches, jute, and textiles. The most visible were the women who worked in the tea and coffee plantations. Some women also worked as maids and attendants in the *zananas* (women's quarters) of the rich people.

Status of education and literacy:

As mentioned earlier, there were few opportunities for women to get educated in the medieval period, which includes the Mughal period. This situation continued after the arrival of the British. With the British also came the missionaries with the primary intention of converting the local population to Christianity. The British did not recognize the existing system of education and forced the western style of education on the local male as well as female population. This was a difficult task, especially to make the girls to get out of their homes to go to schools. The Hindus were concerned about the violation of the purity and the Muslims were concerned about the observation of the purdah.

Missionaries and philanthropists built western style schools for girls. The first one of these schools was built in Calcutta in 1820, by David Hare, a watch-maker, who was influenced by European rationalist philosophy. The first lot of students came from the lower castes only since they were afraid that education in this school was intended for conversion to Christianity. The first school to attract the high-caste women was established by a well-known reformist, *Ishwar Chandra Vidyasagar* in 1849. This school was opened with the help of *J.E.D. Bethune*, one of the Governor General's Council, and was called Bethune School (later College). In 1882 there were 2697 educational institutions for females in India: most were primary schools, but there were also eighty-two secondary schools, fifteen normal schools, and one college, with a total of 127,066 students. (Ref. 14) The graduates of these schools, a tiny minority of India's women, became the next generation of leaders of social reform movements.

Sir Sayyad Ahmed Khan, a Muslim reformer, acknowledged that the Quaran mandated neither purdah nor denying female education. He founded the Aligarh Muslim University, with the intention of teaching Muslims the western subjects of science and technology but within the Islamic context. He was a liberal thinker but yet he did not believe in educating females to the same extent as men. He wanted the female education to be limited to the moral and spiritual aspects. He was against completely exposing Muslim females to the western ideas. It was not until the twentieth century that the Muslim girls were got exposed to Western studies.

The percentage of literate women grew: from 0.9 % in 1901 to 3.4 % in 1941. By 1936 over three million Indian girls and women were studying in 38,262 schools, in contrast to approximately 100,000 in 1882. (Ref.5).

"There have been many prominent reformers who have contributed substantially in promoting education. Their contributions have been described in a later section, "Prominent Social Reformers."

With the British government taking charge of the Indian sub-continent in 1857, many elite Indian families, which included successful professionals, rich feudal lords, (Jagirdars), princesses, and businessmen learnt the Western lifestyle, learnt English to win favors from the rulers. These families were given prominent appointments by the British. These families got their sons and daughters educated in Western style, both in India and later in foreign countries, mostly in England. A prominent example in this category is the family of Pt. Jawaharlal Nehru. His father was a very successful lawyer in Allahabad. He made his fortune through his legal practice and quickly adopted the British lifestyle. He discarded his "Kashmiri Brahmin" clothes and life style, donned expensive British clothes, dined in western style, rode horses, spoke English at home and in short lived like a British lord. Living like this had been the dream of most Indians. And those who had the money and the patronage of the British did adopt this life-style. He wanted his son, Jawaharlal to be educated in England, learn the English manners and after returning to India follow in his footsteps. Things did not turn out that way. The independence movement was very strong and Jawaharlal got involved in it and under the strong influence of Mahatma Gandhi, he discarded his expensive British suits and got into the *desi* , the home spun clothes, which were promoted by Mahatma Gandhi in retaliation to the British imposition of restriction on the manifacture of cloth in India. There are a number of other examples of rich Indians getting educated in England and switching swiftly to the British life-style.

Motilal Nehru also educated his daughter, *Mrs. Vijays Laxumi Pundit* in the Western style. The British appreciated this a great deal. The average Indian looked at them with awe and respect since what this family had achieved was rare and practically impossible for them to achieve, even though they would very much like to enjoy the life-style, which the Nehru family was enjoying. The maharajas of the princely states followed the same path. The young princes and princesses were put in charge of British nannies and were asked to teach them English and British etiquette. The princesses who were kept in purdah were initiated into British clothing, hairstyles and other things like driving etc. The result was that they grew up to be British in every way except their names and in some cases the color of their skin. They also traveled abroad and visited Europe and England where they played polo, did sight-seeing, ate in expensive restaurants and best of all expanded their outlook. All this made them desirable company for the British rulers. They would get invitations to prominent parties. They would, in turn throw lavish parties for the rulers.

There was another class of people who were neither rich nor powerful but were very intelligent. They made their mark in studies, acquired a great deal of command of English. These people were successful in obtaining good positions within the government. The British government had started a scheme to employ the Indians in the administration of the country. The service was called Indian Civil Service (ICS) and it was open to all, Indians as well as the British. To be accepted, one had to pass a competitive examination and also score well in a interview. The scholarly Indians did very well in these competitions. Candidates from the South Indian states generally did much better than the ones from North India on account of their better command of English. Having secured employment in this manner, they educated their children in the Western style. The level of education of females in South India had always been much higher than elsewhere else in India but now the emphasis was placed on English. The important point about the South Indian population generally had been that even though they learnt English very well, they did not discard their culture. The girls received traditional education in addition to the Western education. The traditional education generally consisted of music, which may include vocal or instrumental, dance, domestic chores like cooking, decorating, etc. A combination of good Western education and traditional arts along with the traditional culture was considered desirable qualities.

The situation with regard to education of women was and still is quite different in cities as opposed to the rural areas. This has been discussed previously. The rural areas have been quite backward and are still stuck in the antiquated traditions denying females opportunities for getting educated. The following table illustrates the disparity between the rural and urban litracy within each Indian state (Ref. 22):

FEMALE LITERACY RATES IN RURAL AND URBAN AREAS, 1971

States	rural	urban	total	
All India		13.2	42.3	18.7
Andhra Pradesh	10.9	36.3	15.8	
Assam	16.5	50.9	19.3	
Bihar	6.4	31.9	8.7	
Gujarat	17.2	44.8	24.3	
Haryana		9.2	41.5	14.9
Himachal Pradesh	18.2	52.2	20.2	
Jammu and Kashmir	5.0	28.4	9.3	
Kerala	53.1	60.6	54.3	
Madhya Pradesh	6.1	37.0	10.9	
Maharashtra		17.8	47.3	26.4
Manipur		16.4	40.4	19.5
Meghalaya		18.9	59.7	24.6
Karnataka		14.5	41.6	21.0

Nagaland		16.4	49.5	18.7
Orrisa	12.1	36.1	13.9	
Punjab	19.9	45.4	25.9	
Rajasthan		4.0	29.7	8.5
Tamil Nadu		19.0	45.4	26.9
Tripura	17.3	55.0	21.2	
Uttar Pradesh		7.0	34.4	10.7
West Bengal		15.0	47.8	22.4

In most villages in North India, child marriages are still practiced. The family does not see any point in educating the girls beyond third or fourth grade since she is going to be married at age 8 or 10. They think that the girl should work at home and help in the household work. This help in domestic work is a bit of compensation for the amount the family would be spending in her marriage, especially the dowry. Once the girl gets married her chances of continuing any education are finished. The girls in the city are in a different environment. There are many schools for girls and the families are not so conservative in their outlook. The elite and other Indians in high positions become role models for the average. To educate girls is encouraged. The middle-class and upper middle-class families generally send their girls to the university. These girls earn degrees. The subjects they study are generally arts. But some do very well in science and mathematics. Many become medical professionals and engineers. The very recent trend is for the girls learning skills in computer technology and they have very well in this field. There are a large number of women presently employed in the "information technology". And the number of women entering this field is on the increase. This field is very much suited to women since it does not require physical exertion and in many cases they are able to work from home.

Getting back to the elite of India, the women of this class had the advantage over the poor and the middle class. The women who were the first batch of educated women in the western style easily assumed the leadership in India. Some outstanding examples are : Mrs. Vijaya Laxumi Pandit, Mrs. Indira Gandhi, Sarojani Naidu, Padma Naidu. Mrs. Pandit was Jawaharlal's sister, Indira was his daughter, Padma was Sarojani Naidu's daughter. It is good that these women got into leadership but it is apparent that their rise to the top positions was on account of their belonging to the elite families. Unfortunately, to rise to the leadership position in India it is not important to have capability and quality. One must belong to a famous elite family. This is illustrated in Sonia Gandhi, an Italian woman, who is in power only because she was the wife of Rajeev Gandhi, the ex prime minister of India and grand son of Jawaharlal Nehru. Indian people feel that they are so much indebted to the Nehru family that they wish to keep the offsprings of Jawaharlal Nehru in power for the next many generations!

"Educational opportunities for women created after independence: The constitution of India directs the government to provide "free and compulsory education for all children until they complete the
age of 14."

The importance of this goal has been repeatedly emphasized in the fifty odd years since Indian independence through the establishment of several government and non-governmental schemes directed at increasing educational opportunities and improving literacy." Continued efforts by the government in expanding the educational schemes especially directed at girls and women have produced very encouraging results: data from the 2001 census indicate considerable advancement in the field of literacy. India now has an overall literacy rate of 65 %, with the male and female literacy rates of 76 and 54 % respectively. Regional differences in literacy rates are quite significant. For example, in Bihar, the female and male literacy rates are 34 and 60 percent whereas in keral, the rates are 94 and 88 percent respectively. Kerala has the highest literacy rates in all of the developing countries, and literacy programs in Kerala are considered as models for other countries. The literacy rate for women in the rural areas is 47 % whereas the rate in the cities is 73 %. For men the literacy rate in the rural areas is 71 % and the rate in the urban areas is 87 %. These figures indicate an improvement of 40 and 50 percent since 1951, for both men and women, with women's literacy in urban areas and men's literacy in the rural areas showing the most dramatic increases. Since 1981, the overall literacy rate has improved by approximately 20 %, and that of women by nearly 25 percent.

There had been a general dissatisfaction and rejection of the British policy of harsh taxation and persecution in the Indian population. This ultimately resulted in the famous mutiny of 1857. The introduction of English in India resulted in many Indians becoming very proficient in English and some acquired high qualifications from England, especially becoming lawyers. Rich and privileged Indians were in an advantaged position and were able to become educated in the British style. They probably thought that the British would be staying in India for a long time and British style education will stand them in good stead for obtaining high positions in the administration and generally gaining respect and favors from the ruling British. During this period, the women belonging to the rich and powerful families, in many instances, also got educated either in India or in England for further studies. A man or woman who had earned a foreign qualification, mostly from England, got preferential treatment from the British. To gain favors from the British one had to not only obtain the right qualification but also adopt a British/western life style.

The set-up of the Indian society in terms of its traditions, practices and treatment of women did not change on account of the arrival of the British. The same old problems, which had haunted the Indian society for the past many centuries continued. The sati tradition, child marriages, restrictions on widow marriage, the prevention of women from getting educated, the purdah system all continued, albeit now there was a foreign power, entirely different from the Muslims and with a completely different culture and, which was life style having an impact on the local population. A completely new language was being imposed. The British had little understanding of the local culture, which they misunderstood and whatever they learnt through translations was misinterpreted. Having recognized all this, it must be said that the arrival of the British and with them the missionaries brought a modern, western style system of education to India. The British also encouraged women's education as mentioned earlier. Apart from the administrators and the British official policy, there were many individuals who were genuinely interested in the welfare of the Indian women. Their contributions are covered under the section, "Prominent Social Reformers." Please also refer to Appendix II for some of the statements made by prominent Indian educational thinkers and philosophers.

The Muslim women of India have always lagged behind their Hindu or Christian sisters because of the ever present fear in the minds of the Muslims of exposure of their womem/daughters to ideas "other than Islamic". So even the secular education provided in normal Indian schools based on the curriculams designed and approved by the States is not acceptable to the Muslims. The fundamentalist stance adopted by the Mulim community presents the biggest impedement tn the path of a Muslim girl in getting educated. The objections of the Muslim community to allow their daughters to go to a regular school have been there for the past at least two centuries but the conditions have not vastly improved even after independence and even after efforts by the Government of India to make conditions more acceptable to the Muslim community. A recent case in this context is of interest: (Ref.24)

It is a case in which Saifa Iqbal, the principal of a school, who wished to run the school for girls on the basis of a secular curriculum was opposed in her attempts by the fundamentalists. The school, which provides secular education to children living in the Muslim dominated Jamia Nagar area of the city, received support from the *Darul-Uloom* (House of knowledge) school located at Deoband in Utter Pradesh to let the principal run the school as she saw fit and not as a *Madarsa*. *Darul-Uloom* also issued a religious edict against one Mohammed Shafi Moonis, a trustee of the school who was attempting to seize control of the school and to stop the teaching according to the secular curriculum rather than the *madarsa* system. This was quite a scary situation for Iqbal since Moonis happened to be a very influencial person in the community.

Iqbal, herself a member of the All-India Muslim personal Law Board and author of the book: *Women and Islamic Law*, said the fatwa against Moonis "upheld the dignity of women" and was a landmark at a time when the status of women in Islamic society is low. At a press conference Iqbal blamed institutions like *Jamaat-e-Islam Hind* for women's subservient condition, which, she said was far removed from that originally envisioned by Islam. "They exercise a Mafia-like grip over Muslims in the name of the religion", "she said.

This is an instance, which happened in 2002 and clearly illustrates the state of Muslim women and the struggle of Muslim women to release themselves from the age old male domination and outdated and regressive thinking, which still prevails in the Muslim community. The sad part is that the "mullahs" who hold power in the Muslim community, being the religious leaders, are the ones instrumental in perpetuating this suppression of women under religious pretext. Well, one knows very well that nowadays all kinds of things are being done by the Muslims of the world today under the banner of "Jihad" and Islam. But this explains why the Muslim women are unable to get the desired education in India. The condition of Muslim women in certain other countries is much worse.

A recent book by Zoya Hasan and Ritu Menon entitled, "*Unequal Citizens: Muslim Women in India*" (Ref. 25), presents the results of a national survey covering around 10,000 Muslim and Hindu women and is a good study of the status of Muslim women in India. It provides a broad- spectrum investigation into the socio-economic status of Muslim women in India, and delves into the roots of their disadvantaged condition of life. The study's findings pertaining to the levels of literacy and education levels are as follows:

"The low socio-economic status of Muslims is now well- known; like the scheduled Castes, they are disproportionately represented among the poor and have the lowest per capita income indicators. This is ascribed not only to the lack of access to asset ownership, but also to poor educational attainment and occupational patterns, which show clustering in low- paid activities, as well as the concentration of the Muslim population in the economically backward regions of the country."

Further: "One of the standard assumptions about Muslim women is that religion prevents them from getting more equal access to education. It is certainly true that Muslim women are more likely to be illeterate than Hindu women (in the survey, 59 per cent never attended school and less than 10 per cent had completed school). However, the study shows that it is essentially the result of low socio-economic status, rather than religion. Across the survey, among all communities and caste groups, financial constraints and gender bias dominate over other factors in determining levels of education. In those regions where Muslims are better off (as in the south and to a lesser degree in the west), Muslim women also have higher levels of education."

"Two other features that are more specific to Muslim community may have operated to devalue education for girls. The first is that Muslim men also have very low educational attainment in general. The study found that 26 per cent of educated Muslim women had illetrate husbands. This low male education level would create further pressures to impose ceilings on girl's education, so as not to render them "unmarriageable". In addition, the low age of marriage is a major inhibiting factor. At the national level, the mean age of marriage of Muslim girls is very low at 15.6 years, and in the rural north it falls to an appalling 13.9 years."

The study also attributes a strong patriarchal structure with complete control pf women by men in the Muslim households, preventing women from making decisions for themselves. The cause for lack of education among Muslim men might be their religious beliefs regarding education, that is, "what is appropriate for studying". Muslims in India and else where in the countries where the population is predominantly Muslim, only send their boys to Madrasas and after their completion of the study in the Madrasa, their education is deemed to be complete. Girls do not even attend Madrasas.

The Sati Tradition:

There is a widespread misapprehension that this evil custom is peculiar to India. Anthropologists have found that it has been prevalent in many primitive communities including some Red Indian tribes of North America; in Dahomey and among the Bafiote of Africa; and in many Pacific Islands. Jawaharlal Nehru says in *The Discovery of India:* "Probably the practice was brought to India originally by the Scytho-Tartars, among whom the custom prevailed of vassals and liegemen killing themselves on the death of their lord. In early Sanskrit Literature the sati custom is denounced. Akbar tried to stop it and the Marathas also were opposed to it." The writer of a scholarly work on the Hindu sacraments cites the *Rig Veda* (X 18.7), the *Athara Veda* (XVIII 3.1.2) and other texts to show that they only indicate a "ritualistic" survival of the sati custom. During the earlier period, gifts to the dead were buried or burnt with the corpse; including sometimes slaves and even wife. Atherva calls it "the ancient custom". This inhuman practice was discontinued in the Rigvedic times though the formality of the widow lying on the funeral pyre was retained. Thus the *Grhyasutras,* which deal with domestic rites, prescribe ritualistic substitution for the real burning of the widow. The chief mourner, or who was to set fire to the pyre, should then address the dead, saying:

> *"O mortal! This woman (your wife), wishing to be joined to you*
> *in a future world, is lying by the corpse. She has always observerd*
> *the duties of a faithful wife. Grant her permission to abide in this*
> *world, and relinquish your wealth to your descendants."*

A younger brother of the dead, or a disciple, or a servant, should then should proceed to the pyre, hold the left hand of the woman, and ask her to come away: "Rise up, woman, you lie by the side of the lifeless; come to the world of the living, away from the husband, and become the wife of him who holds your hand and is willing to marry you."

But the sati system never entirely ceased, and later on it was revived in certain tribes and families. It was mostly prevalent among the Rajputs." The British were opposed to the sati tradition. They abolished it in 1829. The Indians exalted it even more. Widows who expressed even the slightest inclination to commit it, but later wavered, were dragged to the flames kicking and screaming. A new twist was given to the situation by a belief that the death of a man was the fault of his wife. This line of thinking was quite common and is still quite common. Anything which happened, which was not considered good for the family or not in accordance with the family's expectations, were dumped on the bride or the wife, who was quickly blamed for the bad luck *she* brought to the family. If a boy was born to her, she was considered auspicious, bringing good luck but if a girl was born, she would be cursed and considered inauspicious. This is just one example of how the woman was blamed and her life would then be made a hell.

"In the eighteenth-century Bengal, sati took hold with a vengeance. Families drugged widows, tied them to the bodies of their dead husbands, and forced them to the fire with bamboo sticks. They devised an elaborate rite invoking Kali, in which a widow dressed as a bride entered the flames with fanfare acclaiming her for conferring glory on her natal and conjugal families. Of the women burned, 55 percent came from the upper classes, and the rest from the upwardly mobile lower castes. For many families sati led to social status and a reputation for virtue, but male fear and hatred of women was an important factor in it"

In the eradication of the Sati system, there was also a great deal of contribution from many reformists of India. *Raja Ram Mohan Roy*, (born on 22 May, 1772), was prominent amongst them. He was the flag-bearer of social reforms for women. He was vehemently opposed to the evils prevalent in the society at that time. It was on account of his efforts that led to *Lord William Bentinik* banning the Sati in 1829. He also did great work in the field of education for women banning child marriages, and promoted remarriages of widows. To set an example, he himself married a widow. He also founded *Brahmo Samaj* in cooperation with *Dwarka Nath Tagore*.

Sikhism condems the *Sati Tradition*. The following passage from the sacred religious book of the Sikhs, *Sri Guru Granth Sahib* is noteworthy:

"They cannot be called satis, who burn themselves with their dead husbands. They can only be called satis, if they bear the shock of separation. They may also be known as satis, who live with character and contentment and always show veneration to their husbands by remembering them." (Guru Amar Das, Var Suhi, pg. 787).

The purdah system:

As it got introduced in the Indian social system, it became quite popular among the Rajput princesses, the rich, powerful and noble households. The poorer, unprivileged and lower caste could not afford to hide their women in the purdah just sitting in the zananas of their homes. The simple reason was that women of such social standing had to go and work to earn wages. Working in the industry such as textile or on the construction site or in on the farms, which was the common place of work, was not possible with the purdah. So the purdah became the life style of the elite. With the coming of the British, who did not like the purdah and brought their own "superior" standards and life style and culture with them and the Indian princesses, women from the rich and elite households who came in closer contact with them, were highly influenced by this new culture. This resulted in a change in the women from this elite group and since they were sold on the idea that this new foreign culture was "superior", they decided to give up the purdah and started emulating the British women. Some of them went a long ways to adapt to this change. They had their traditional long hair cut short and styled in western style and started wearing western dresses and discarded sarees or other traditional Indian dresses, which they reserved for special occasions. They also came out of their secluded zananas and began mingling with men and women of their equivalent status freely, especially the British. They learnt English. Some of them were sent to England to get educated and excelled in English, acquired British manners and accents, which made them acceptable into the exclusive British gatherings, quite popular and very desirable places to be at that time. These ladies also learnt driving an automobile, riding a horse and in many cases learnt playing polo, all this earned them an admiration from the ruling Britons. This change in the women of the upper class assured the British that these families, especially the women, were really paying the due respect to their culture and the rest of the population will certainly follow their example. In the meantime, the lower caste, working woman remained where they were because they could not undergo this kind of transformation. The middle class, which included the white coller workers and the Christians did try to become anglicized to the best of their ability but they were limited by their resources and their traditions. An important thing to note is that nobody criticized these elite women for rejecting their traditional life-style and adopting the western. In contrast, the women belonging to the middle class were not allowed to give up the purdah and were subject to heavy criticism if they started to emulate the women of the upper class and elite. It took a long time, mainly after India got independence that the women of the middle class started enjoying more freedom, especially in the urban centers. This was also the beginning of the urban woman acquiring education and employment. And this has had a profound effect on the demise of the purdah.

The purdah has been practically wiped out from the urban areas but it is well entranched and thriving in the villages of northern India where the rate of literacy is very low. Women of poor and lower caste still practice purdah in the states of Rajasthan, Uttar Pradesh, Madhya Pradesh and other northern states. Daughters-in-laws observe purdah in front of their fathers-in-laws and other elders as a gesture of showing respect. They also live in the inner portion of the house away from the area generally lived in by the elders. But they go to work in the field where they do not observe purdah in the company of women of their own age. If a stranger approaches them they would immediately pull over the cloth and hide their face. This behavior is typical in the rural areas where women are illitrate.

Purdah system had never found a foothold in South India. The area starting from the State of Maharashtra, going south right up to Kerala was never affected by the purdah system, primarily because this area was not as moch influenced by the Mualim conquerors. The exception is the State of Hydrabad where there was a Muslim rule. There is, therefore, a Muslim cultural influence in this area such as the use of *Urdu* but the predominant population is still under the influence of the southern culture. The women of Suoth India wear a longer saree worn quite differently from the northern women. There are a large proportion of women who work in the farm or on construction sites who wear their sarees tightly making them freer for doing manual work. Women with a young child carry the child on their backs and move about freely with their heads uncovered. During my engineering course, I took training on a dam construction site in Utter Pradesh. The Rihand dam project was being constructed by Hindustan Construction Company based in Maharashtra. This company had its own construction labor force, which it transported to every site. It had erected a temporary housing colony for its construction crew. They stayed in this colony with their families. In most cases, both the husband and wife worked on the construction. The women in their long Marathi sarees, worn tightly, worked on the site either sprinkling water on the concrete or transporting construction materials. I have seen these women spending all day on a two feet wide catwalk in the sweltering heat. In many cases the women carried an infant on her back. They had to move on the catwalk high up on the side of the dam. On a one hundred and fifty feet high dam the women were working fearlessly at heights of eighty or ninety feet. Depending on the timing of the shifts, some women used to bring lunches, which they had cooked earlier, and ate right on the site, with their husbands, if possible.

The purdah system created a big impediment in the process of getting the girls to go to the school. The British were quite enthusiastic about educating the women and schools for girls were started. Buses, which picked up girls from door to door were arranged. To keep the purdah, the windows were covered with specially made bamboo partitions, which created lack of ventilation. This was improved by covering the windows with thick cloth curtains. This made the inside hot and stuffy to the extent that the girls started fainting and tired. Parents of girls, especially the Muslim, threatened to withdraw their daughters from the program. In the early nineteenth century, Christian nuns came to India to start educating Indian women. Missionaries and philanthropists built Western-style girl's schools. In 1857, the East India Company was dissolved and the British government took over governing India. At this time the wives of the British serving in India were permitted to go to India to join their husbands. Other women, not belonging to the upper class, such as doctors and prostitutes also arrived in search for men. Female missionaries pioneered zanana education, teaching upper-caste Indian women at home, others at school.

Child Marriages:

Marriages of girls who were about 8 or ten years of age were quite common in medieval India. They were not allowed to educate themselves and were treated as objects rather than human beings with any rights or having any personality. A quotation from the famous work by Sant Tulsidas, the *Ramcharit Manas* states: *"Dhol, gawar, pashu aru nari, ye sab tadan ke adhikari."* Meaning: the drum, an illiterate, an animal and a woman, all can be beaten. Women were, as mentioned, placed in the same category as animals. Child marriages, due to a longer married life, which increased the birth rate.

In independent India, one finds male domination, dowry system, arranged marriages without the consent of either the girl or the boy or both, early childhood marriages, illiterate women not knowing their rights, exploitation and oppression of women under the guise of religion, corruption rampant in all sectors and all levels of the society, system of bribery and breakdown of the law and order. A woman in such conditions has nowhere to turn to for help. If her family does not or cannot provide her the necessary protection or support, she has nowhere else where her independence and rights can be protected. Teenaged girls are bought in Nepal from their parents and brought in Bombay to satisfy the increasing demand for prostitutes there. A young bride is burnt alive because the groom's family did not receive enough money in dowry. No body wants a girl any more since her birth entails spending a large amount of money in her marriage as well a hefty sum to be offered to the groom in dowry. Girls are, therefore, killed moments after their birth. Now with the advancement of technology, it has become possible to determine the sex of the child in the womb. Ultra sound is used to do this. Parents are now using this technology and perform an abortion if it is a girl. This is against the law but the practice is rampant. Some doctors do this and accept bribes. Complaints to police do not help because they are corrupt and accept bribes as well.

Not all women in India are subject to the conditions described here. A large percentage of young get married in the traditional manner. In most of these cases a bride is expected to perform as follows:

> "*The housewife is the first to get up in the morning; she then has to clean the house, light the fire, prepare the early morning meal. She has to work throught the day to provide food for the family, serve everybody's needs. She was not to indulge in games*
> *and plays. At mealtime she had to serve everyone first and had to eat what was left over, all by herself. The metaphors, which Vyasa employs are telling: a wife has to follow her husband everywhere like a shadow, she has to support him like a companion, has to execute his orders like a servant or slave. Such good behaviour, the sastras say, will be rewarded in this life by well-being, and after this life by heaven; contrary behavior*
> *will be punished by lengthy sojourns in hell and a bad rebirth.*"—Taken from "A Survey Of Hinduism", by Klaus K. Klostermaier.

These standards set by the *Sastras* (religious texts), are quite demanding and departure from these are thought of as sin. These expectations from a woman might perhaps be appropriate in the ancient times but are not applicable in the modern setting. But in a joint family the newlywed is pressured and controlled by citing these high ideals. The poor woman is never able to satisfy these expectations and is subjected to constant ridicule and sharp taunts. Her married life is not a pleasant one. If she is not the subject of this kind of harassment, she can be made to feel sad and unworthy on account of giving birth to a girl. Those women who are unable to give birth to a boy are considered to be the most unfortunate. They are told that they have brought bad luck and misfortune to the family. It is, however known that it is not within the power of a woman to produce a boy. The conception of a boy depends on the success of the husband's sperm, as is well known. The punishment is, of course, dished out to the woman. The well-known case is that of King Henry the VIII. In his case he killed his wives but in India the woman is looked down upon and is not respected in the society.

After independence, women have made a lot of progress. This progress is in many fields. In academics, literature, sciences, politics, law, journalism and so on. While recognizing this progress, it must be mentioned that the progress is not evenly distributed in all sectors of the society. Women of privileged families made good progress because they had the means and right connections. Prominent examples of such success stories are women of the Nehru family. Indira Gandhi, Mr. Nehru's daughter, was accompanying him everywhere and used to play host at parties held in his residence where all kinds of influential people used to be received. She, therefore, got the right grooming for a political position. She also got educated in France where she learned European manners and etiquette. But her appointment as the president of the congress party was not because she was considered eminently suited for the job but it was thought that she could be easily manipulated. Mrs. Vijay Laxumi Pandit, who became the general secretary of the United Nations, is yet another example from the Nehru family. The Nehrus were rich to start with and Jawaharlal had the blessings of Mahatma Gandhi. In India, of course, there is a great tendency for hero worship and after the demise of the Maharajas, the Nehrus are considered to be the only family suitable for the top job. Right now Sonia Gandhi is the leader of the ruling congress party and should have become the prime minister of India. But since she is an Italian by birth, it did not sit well with the electorate. She still holds the reins of power.

There are many more examples of this sort but in terms of the total population this represents a very tiny minority. The bulk of the women population, which has made progress, comes from the large middle class of India. There is more than three hundred million middle class and their number is growing very fast. The middle class families, who are mostly city dwellers, believe strongly in educating their daughters. Depending upon individual family circumstances, the girls get very well educated. The level of education differs depending on specific circumstances. If the girl is beautiful she does not require a high level of education to be valuable in the "Marriage Market". The parents generally also do not have to pay a dowry or may be just a small dowry. If the girl is average in looks, she has to make up by acquiring a higher level of education and in addition, good amount of dowry to become desirable in the marriage market. The girl who is not so good looking requires a hefty sum of money in dowry and very high educational qualifications. In this case she has a limited number of eligible males interested. These are the conditions of the marriage market and apply to those girls who wish to get married. And the majority of girls in India do want to marry. If a girl wishes to acquire higher education, she can do so after getting married if her husband's family permits. In many cases this can be discussed prior to marriage. In many cases the grooms family likes the girl who is educated enough to be able to get a job and earn money. This additional income is very welcome and is a great help to the family in times when greater family income means higher standard of living and better living conditions. In many cases, the family does not favor their daughter-in-law to go out and work because they think the dignity and prestige of their family is then compromised. In their opinion, if the wife works, the people think that the husband is unable to provide enough, that is, not successful enough.

This discussion again points to the fact that the status of the woman is like a commodity and her value in the marriage market is determined by a combination of several factors such as her youth, beauty, level of education, her earning capacity, and the capacity of her parents to pay dowry. The very recent trend is for a girl to acquire some skills in the operation of the computers. She is now able to earn decent salary doing computer related jobs. These jobs are not necessarily highly skilled ones such as software design or systems administration but may involve data entry or working in a call center. But these jobs pay enough for the girl to be able to live independently or relieve her parents from her personal expenses. Many girls while living at home have been able to accumulate enough money to pay for their marriage and dowry.

Tragedies have taken place and are still taking place in terms of harassment of the brides, constant taunts and in many cases "burning the bride", as they call it, on account of not receiving satisfactory money in dowry. Dowry is illegal in India but it is widely and openly practiced. This whole situation has robbed the woman of her dignity and honor and her rightful place in the society. The situation is a far cry from the *Vedic* ideal of equality between sexes and marriage taking place by mutual choice and compatibility considerations.

All parents consider a daughter to be a big liability since they have to spend money to raise her, provide her education, and pay for her marriage and dowry. All of this is of no use to them in the end. This is a very narrow way of looking at the situation but most of the people have this narrow vision. This is the main reason why people are getting abortions performed if the fetus is diagnosed to be a female. Surprisingly, the percentage of such abortions is greater in the cities where the people are better educated rather than the rural areas. The number of females lost in this manner and other causes such as bride burning is estimated in millions. Some estimate this number to be about twenty fife million each year. The problem has now become quite acute. In many areas there are many eligible bachelors but there are no girls available. Some people are so desperate that they are abducting girls from distant locations and are using force to take the girl away. Police and other law enforcing agencies are primarily of little help in protecting the girl or her family, especially when something like this happens suddenly without notice.

Indians who have left India and migrated to first world countries like Canada or United Kingdom have not left the practice of condemning their female child. Abortion of a female child is not legal in these countries and the medical professionals in these countries are not corrupt, like in India, to perform abortions illegally. The Indians, therefore go to India to get this illegal abortions done. In India it is easy to bribe a medical practitioner and get an abortion done.

In India there is a lot stacked against a widow. To become a widow is a very unfortunate thing for a woman in India. Earlier, a widow was not allowed to marry. She had to live extremely simply. She could only wear a cheap white sari, cut all her hair, wear no ornaments, attend no auspicious ceremonies and if by any chance if one confronted her on his/her way to do any important task, it was considered a bad omen. If she remained in her husband's house, she would be expected to do most of the housework. Her living quarters would have bare minimum furniture. In short she was made to feel that she was an unwanted person. This imposition applied to all widows, no matter what her age. In many cases a widow would be sent to a special "hostel", where widows live. These conditions have improved in the past fifty years or so by the efforts of some outstanding social reformers. The most outstanding example is the effort of Maharashi Karve of Pune, Maharashtra, who spread the word for giving a proper place in the society to the widow. He has opened residences for widows where they can get proper protection, a school where they can get education of their liking, marriage arrangements for those willing, and above all no stigma attached for just being a widow. They can wear normal clothes and live normal life. Those who are educated and qualified are allowed to work and earn to support themselves, whereas those who are not qualified are given the opportunity to educate themselves and once they become able to find employment, can get a job and become self-supporting. This restores dignity and self-respect to the widow. This is one of the best institutions of this type in India. Facilities such as this are not available everywhere and majority of widows still suffer the stigma and do not enjoy the normal life. Many widows commit suicides, many give up their life by going "Sati". Sati is an old cult in which a widow joins her husband in his funeral pyre and burns herself alive. This had been outlawed in India for the past many years, even before India became independent, that is, during the British times but the practice continues. It is practiced in the rural areas where the law is not applied strictly and in many cases the police turn a blind eye. A very good depiction of widow life has been done in a recent film called, "Water". The conditions belong to a period during the 1930s in Bengal where the society was very conservative. The conditions have changed there since then.

There is another practice in some parts of India, where a young unwanted girl is given to a temple establishment. This girl becomes unwanted if she becomes an orphan or her birth is from an unmarried mother or if she was born to a prostitute or for some such reason. In this case a ceremony is performed in which the girl is married to God and then remains in the temple under the custody of the priest. Girls such as these perform and dance in the temple, do work as ordered and in many instances the priest has sex with her if he wishes or she is ordered to have sex with a donor to the temple if he desires. Her life is really limited and ruined. She becomes, in effect, a prostitute. And this is cleverly done under the guise of the religion. In fact the religion does not recommend or remotely suggest anything like this. There are a lot of things done in India under the guise of the religion, which are not true and are legitimatised under religious pretext. The religion, of course, gets the bad publicity.

After having discussed some of the ways in which a woman is persecuted in India it is important to point out the various success stories. A vast number of women have made a tremendous progress in practically all fields. These women have made a break from the traditional rigidity, which has gripped Indian society for the past many centuries. These rigidities, which the Indian society imposed upon itself on account of various circumstances, the main one being the invasion by Mughals and their domination for a period of about seven centuries. In any case, the basic elements of indigenous culture survived in many areas and while the British ruled India or after India got Independence, the woman was able to free herself from the chains of rigid traditions and make progress. Women from practically all classes of the society made progress but the majority came from the educated middle class. The result has been very impressive. In India today the women excel in the fields of education, politics, music, social affairs, medicine, business management, sciences, teaching, sales, commerce and business, computers, architecture, literature, and other fine arts. As mentioned before, these women are primarily from the urban areas. The woman from the rural areas is still miles behind. The illiteracy in rural women is quite common and contributes to the overall illiteracy, which is estimated at over 50%.

There are some outstanding examples of women doing top jobs in a variety of fields. Women have actively participated in the struggle for independence. After gaining independence, many women remained politically active. Indira Gandhi became the first prime minister of India. In her getting that position, a couple of factors were at play besides her merit. Firstly, being the daughter of the first prime- minister, Jawahar Lal Nehru, India wanted to show their gratitude to him and voting Indira was one way of doing it. Secondly, India wanted to show to the world that in India we treat women on an equal basis as men and a woman can occupy the top job. Just recently, Mrs. Pratibha Patil has been elected the first president of India. In this case, she is a really meritorious lady. There were of course other candidates, all male and all equally capable, but her being a woman, made her case much stronger. In interviewing women from rural India, they said the election of a woman president would not make any difference to their lot. Similar comments were made when Mrs. Indira Gandhi was elected. This illustrates that the lives of women in the rural and poor strata of the Indian society keeps going as usual and the elite enjoy power sharing and other privileges. There is practically no regard for the plight pf the woman toiling hard to meet the both ends meet and to care for her family. It is almost similar to the North American problem where the poor remain poor and the rich get richer. The poor cannot break the cycle of poverty.

An outstanding example of bravery and struggle for independence is Maharani *Laxumi Bai* of *Zhashi*, who fought the British, riding on the horse, with her infant son tied to her back. She died in that battle, which took place around the middle of the nineteenth century when the great mutiny against the British, took place.

Problem of female infanticide/feticide:

As women were supposed to be and are still considered very much unwanted, the birth of a female child in the family is still considered an unfortunate thing. The reasons behind this mind set is that the family gets burdened with the paying of the dowry and the high costs of performing an elaborate marriage ceremony, the cost of educating and bringing up the child. In addition, the girl's in-laws would be constantly demanding money and threatening to mistreat the girl if payments were not made. In view of this, the families, now-a- days make use of the new technology to identify the sex of the conceived child and if it is found to be a girl, get an abortion performed. This is "nipping the problem in the bud", so to say. This method of getting rid of the girl child is widely used in India, not only by less educated people but surprisingly by educated people with good standard of living. The rate of female feticides is greater in the cities than in the villages. In the villages where the people do not have ready access to the modern ultrasound technology, the girl child is killed immediately after delivery. To identify the sex of the conceived child and to let the parents know this information is illegal in India, so also the abortion of the girl child without any medical reason. The mother of the conceived child, generally the daughter-in-law, has no say in this matter, which is again a matter of mistreatment of women, a serious matter of not allowing the basic human right to the mother. The unborn girl child or the freshly delivered one, of course, has no rights at all. The number of female infanticides and foeticides in India are alarmingly high. The number of such cases per year has been estimated in millions. It is, however, difficult to accurately determine these numbers since quite a few cases are not reported or get unnoticed. The result of this is that it has had an impact on the demography of India. The ratio of female to male population has been skewed. There are fewer females than males on an overall basis, with variations in different regions.

In many parts of India, it has been reported, that young men, who wish to get married, cannot find *any* girls with whom they can marry. It has also been reported that the situation has become so desperate that men who wish to get married have organized gangs to abduct girls from different regions and then get married to them.

The government of India has now recognized the problem of female infanticide and consider it to be a serious one. Not only that it is serious but to have such a problem is quite embarrassing internationally. Developed countries, to which category India wants to belong, ask questions about it. The Indians who have migrated to foreign countries feel very ashamed and embarrassed when confronted with questions concerning dowry and infanticides. The prime minister of India, Mr. Manmohan Singh expressed his deep concern recently and was reported as follows:

" It was a plea not from the prime minister of India but from a proud father of three daughters: "SAVE THE GIRL CHILD". Launching the country's biggest ever campaign against the "inhuman and uncivilized practice" of female infanticide. PM *Manmohan Singh* said "no nation, society or community could hold its head high and claim to be a part of a civilized world if it condoned the practice of discriminating against women. Hitting out at progressive, wealthy and educated states like Gujarat, Punjab and Delhi for their dwindling sex ratio." Singh said it indicated that growing economic prosperity and education levels had not led to a corresponding mitigation as far as reducing female foeticide was concerned. The 2001 census figures showed Punjab had only 798 girls per 1,000 boys, Haryana 819, Delhi 868 and Gujarat 883. According to Singh, the child sex ratio in the 0 to 6 age group had been showing continuous decline in the past four decades. The decline in number of girls per 1,000 boys from 962 in 1981 to 927 in the year 2001 was alarming, he said, "I urge every citizen to step forward and help in empowering the girl child. The action must begin at home, in our families. I do not say this as the prime minister of India. I say this as the proud father of three daughters. I wish for every girl in our country what I wish for my own daughters." Singh said, " Societal discrimination against women begins in our homes and even before the girl is child is born. One of the most inhuman, uncivilized and reprehensible practices is the practice of female foeticide. The patriarchal mindset and preference for male children is compounded with unethical conduct on the part of some medical practitioners who illegally offer sex determination services. We must overcome this great problem through social awareness and strict enforcement of the Pre-Conception and Pre-Natal Diagnostics Techniques Act." He added. Pointing to social ills like female illiteracy, obscurantist social practices like child marriage, dowry, poor nutritional entitlements and taboos on women in public places making the Indian women and especially the Indian girl child extremely vulnerable, Singh said. The National Literacy Mission should be reoriented to improve female literacy and challenge the adverse sex ratio in the country." (From Weekly Times of India, Toronto, Canada. It can be accessed @ www. weeklytimesof india.com).

Status of marriage:

The vast majority of Indian marriages are arranged by parents or by other relatives. The concept of "arranged" marriage, which the westerners have is that the girl is asked by her parents to marry a certain man of their choice and she has no say in this matter. This might only be true in a few cases but the reality is different. In most cases, the parents or other relatives search for a suitable match for their daughter of marriageable age and only when she has decided to get married. The daughter is initially consulted as to what type of husband she would like. The search is then focused on that basis. The relatives or parents try to contact their friends or look into other sources such as special newspapers, which advertise personal information regarding males and females willing to get married. A preliminary selection is made based on the available information and detailed information is then obtained by direct contact with the other party or by indirect means, used discretely to verify the information and a background check of the eligible bachelor. This is made to ensure the authenticity of the information about the would- be bridegroom to avoid forgery and embarrassment. Once the list is narrowed down, a meeting is generally arranged between the girl and the boy at either the girl's or the boy's residence. Elders from both sides are present at this meeting. The purpose of this meeting is to have the opportunity for both parties to see each other, not only the girl and the boy but also the elders who have better perception and judgment. In India, the concept is that the marriage is not just between the boy and the girl, but between the two families and hence the presence of the elders. If things look good up to this point, the girl and the boy are allowed to meet in private to get to know each other and exchange their ideas about the family life, which each one of them is seeking. If after this meeting both the parties give their approval, that is to say that they like each other and would like to marry, then the marriage is performed at a suitable date.

For both the girl and the boy there are many proposals for consideration and no marriage plans are finalized unless the girl and the boy have had a chance to properly consider these proposals. A marriage is finalized by eliminating one proposal at a time till the best one is chosen and approved by all parties concerned. So the marriages are still arranged by parents for the most part, but what individual parleying goes into the process of "arranging" marriages is itself negotiated to suit the needs of all individuals and families involved.

This process of "arranged" marriage is used by majority of the population but there are exceptions. Conservative and traditional people in the remote villages of Rajasthan and elsewhere where the population is still illiterate and uneducated, the marriages are decided by the parents only. Neither the girl nor the boy have any say in the matter. Parental authority, particularly that of the father, is supreme. The same sort of thing happens in the Muslim community where the wishes of the girl take a back seat to all sorts of other considerations. In the Muslim communities, the practice is also to marry the daughter to her cousin. This is done even if the girl is opposed to it. In South India there is a tradition of endogamous within the caste group) or cross-cousin marriage. The positive aspect of this type of marriage is that the girl does not move into an unknown household and thereby is not subject to the stress of moving into an entirely new environment where she does not know anybody and is not familiar with their style of living. She has to also find her right place in the new family and establish her reputation. All this is not required in the cross-cousin style of marriage. It is now reported that this practice is gradually diminishing. The Vedas recommend boy/girl unions to be from distant locations. The cross-cousin marriage practice is not in keeping with this recommendation. It is also observed that if the marriage is from a distant location, the resulting offsprings are healthier and more intelligent.

Brids after marriage generally move into the house of the bridegroom. In most cases in India, there still are extended family systems where many families live in the same house. Under the older parents there may be several brothers and sisters, some brothers who are married, live with their wives and children. The sisters of the groom are not married. The household has a hierarchy of power and authority to make decisions and to pay proper respects as necessary. The new bride has to learn the ladder of hierarchy and tailor her behavior accordingly. The extended family system is now breaking down, especially in the cities where the new brides are educated and have jobs and both the husband and wife are working. Now-a-days couples want independence and want to live separately. They do come and visit their parents but do not stay with them like the old traditional way. It is also observed that in most cases the bride is generally more educated than the mother-in-law and it is difficult for her to obey her unconditionally. On the other hand, the mother-in-law also respects the education of the bride and hesitates imposing her authority on her just like in the olden days. The following article, which appeared in *India Journal* on December 21, 2007, entitled, *In Modern India Tradition Shackles Love, Marriage*, is interesting and noteworthy:

"In drama and intrigue, the story is straight out of a film script---she a fabulously rich girl, he an IT engineer, and both dare to marry despite her family's arch- resistance

Changing cars to throw off their pursuers, the two traveled hundreds of miles to knock on the doors of a New Delhi court to seek protection. The love affair of Konedela Srija, the daughter of a top Indian film star, Chiranjeevi, briefly gripped India, where a deeply conservative society is still resisting social change that economics progress brings. Sonia's story is the latest in a spate of high profile cases of defiance of conservative parents by children trying to become more independent and assertive----sometimes at a terrible price.

In several cases the runaway couples have sought protection from courts and even landed up at television studios, hoping that media coverage would win them a pardon from their families. But what has sparked a public outcry and a debate on urban India's make-up is the fate of a Muslim man who married a rich Hindu girl against the wishes of her family and turned up dead on the railroad tracks of an eastern city several monts ago. Sociologists say economic progress and growing contact with western values are influencing India's cultural traditions and leading to increased confrontation between the old and the young. Transition from joint to unit families, agrarian to industrial society and emancipation and empowerment of women have influenced of not only the cultural moorings of the society, but also the nature and character of marriages," A.K.Verma of the Center of Developing Societies said. In India, where dating, let alone pre-marital sex is frowned on, 95 percent of all marriages are still arranged---alliances that are almost always determined by religion caste and class considerations. India's divorce rate is below 5 percent. Inter-caste couples, which defy their parent's wishes are often banished from families or villages. In some cases, families have ordered "honor killings". In the fight between tradition and modernism, Payal Thakur, a 31- year old hospitality industry professional, says she paid dearly. "We tried everything we could to convince his parents, but they wouldn't even allow me inside their house," said Thakur, who ended her 8-year old relationship because of caste differences. "Finally, he married someone his parents chose."

Experts point to India's patriarchal family as an enduring social institution that sets the marriage rules. It is a space where power relationships of gender, age, caste and class are played out, in ways that sustain larger social structure of authority.", says Anjali Monteiro, a professor at the India's Tata Institute of Social Sciences. Modernity and education are seen as trappings necessary for social and material success, useful as long as they do not destabilize traditions. Winds of liberation have, however, blowing in educated middle-class families in the cities, due in part with increased contact with western culture and education. Television shows talk openly of gay rights and single parenthood. Social norms have loosened. Live-in couples now flaunt their relationships and a previously unthinkable level of boldness is evident in fashion and lifestyles. But for the winds of change, Nadia Pillai, a Muslim, could never have married her Hindu lover of 8 years, a union eventually accepted by their families after vehement protests. "My mother stopped talking to me and went into depression for 7-8 months", Pillai, now a mother of a girl, told Reuters. "But we just put our foot down. They were not insensible people."

But the change is slow.

"A girl's freedom of choice depends entirely on whether she is financially independent or not," said Anshika Mishra, a media professional who at 29 has resisted parental pressure to marry according to their choice

Indeed, India's conservative ethos is so ingrained that surveys show that a majority of young are inclined towards arranged marriages. A survey by India Today showed more than 70 percent of youngsters favored arranged marriages. "Materialism and a willingness to permit women in the workplace have also not translated into an upheaval of old patriarchal attitudes," commentator Amrita Shah wrote in the Indian Express newspaper. Verma said that love follows marriage in India in contrast to the West where love culminates in marriage. There as soon as the love is lost, the marriage is broken," said Verma, from the center for the Study of Developing Societies. "In India, since marriage is a finished and a closing thing, love has to slowly germinate as a seedling and has to be nurtured."

In most Indian families, the girl is prepared for marriage right from the time she is born. This preparation is aimed at making her suitable for a groom, a groom whose picture the parents have in their mind. The girl is, therefore, given the type of education, religious indoctrination, cultural immersion, a cultivation of liking for her own family's traditions and values right from the early age so that she turns out to be a very desirable bride for "that" groom, which the family wishes for her. The total preparation of the girl may vary depending on certain factors: how beautiful is she?, How good is she in studies?, Generally, if a girl is homely, she is given more education to enhance her ability to obtain employment and earn. Some eligible men would prefer her if their own capacity to earn is not very good. On the other hand, a beautiful girl does not require too much education since she would have no difficulty in finding a high earning groom. The basic thing the parents do is to keep their daughter protected from the modern winds of female liberalism, which may make her defy her parents.

The divorce rate in India is very small compared to the western countries. This does not imply that the marriages in India are more successful. The provisions in law regarding divorce vary depending on to which religion one belongs. For example, a Muslim man can divorce his wife by just repeating the word, *talaq* (literally meaning divorce), three times. A Muslim woman is powerless to do anything in a situation like this. Recently, Muslim law Board has given right of divorce to women. When it comes to divorce in a Hindu family, the laws are different from those for the Muslims. If a Hindu man or a woman wishes to seek a divorce, the matter has to be resolved in the court of law. A divorce is looked down upon in the Indian society. It is regarded as the sign of failure of marriage and people generally blame the woman for the failure. The stigma attached to a divorced woman is such that it would be difficult, if not impossible, for her to get married again. She is treated as if she has committed a crime. The law grants daughters the right to live in their birth family's dwelling, so long as they are unmarried, widowed, or legally separated. Married daughters have no claim at all, not even the right to stay in their father's house if they need to flee their in-law's house because they are being harassed, tortured, or threatened with murder. A father may choose to take his daughter, but is not bound to do so. It is extremely difficult for woman to get out of oppressive marriages because they often have no place to go. And fathers usually get the custody of children. In addition, the mothers have hard time supporting their children.

The condition of Muslim women who are a minority within India is different from the Hindu brides. The marriage in a Muslim family is governed by the antiquated "Sharia" law, which is ruled by the "mullahas", the religious leaders in the Muslim communities. Cases of marital disputes are referred to the Mullahas for resolution and their verdict is the final word. In this context the Muslim women are fed up with this system and demand freedom and enjoyment of fundamental human rights. The Muslim system under which a husband can divorce his wife by just pronouncing the word "*talaaq*" (meaning divorce) three times and that is acceptable even when the pronouncement is done in the absence of the wife! Muslim women are against this system. A recent court case, which was presented in the Bombay High Court in May, 2002, is of interest in this context. The case consisted of a Muslim woman who had been divorced by her husband by uttering the word "talaaq" three times and the woman, Rahim Bi, filed an appeal in the Bombay High Court asking for declaring the divorce by her husband illegal. The court gave its ruling in favour of Rahim Bi, a mother of three children. In ruling on Bi's petition asking for financial assistance from her former husband for herself and their three daughters, the court declared that Muslim men can only seek divorce through the courts, and left it up to the judges to decide matters of support. Importantly, the court also said that the woman had to be present in the court.

Under divorces based on Islamic sharia law, reasons for seeking a divorce can be trivial. As a result the dreaded talaaq has been responsible for the destitution of many Muslim women across all social classes and educational levels in India. "The ruling helps to ensure transparency in divorce cases and puts an end to the capricious use of the talaaq and the denial of maintenance." Sais Anees Ahmed, a prominent legal advocate.

Seventeen years ago another Muslim woman, Shah Bano, asked a court to ensure support from her husband, who had divorced her after 43 years of marriage and thrown her out on the street. In that case the Supreme Court ruled that it could not accept the plea by Bono's husband, which was that he was only bound by the Islamic law. The court ruled that a husband must assist his wife financially after a divorce if she has no other means. But such was the uproar by the fundamentalist Muslims against the ruling in the Bano case that the Rajiv Gandhi's government in 1986 diluted it through legislation in parliament. The result was that in several Indian states a divorced woman could not claim maintenance beyond the "iddat" (three menstrual cycles) period. Attempts by women's rights groups to have it extended have been strongly opposed by fundamental groups like *Jamaat-e-Islami Hind* and even the *All India Muslim Personal Law Board*. But other groups such as the *Muslim Women's Forum*, led by Syeeda Hameed, have been working quietly to ensure that Muslim women in India get equal benefits to those of those of other Islamic societies like Turkey.

It is evident from these cases in which the women have shone extraordinary courage in going to the courts to seek justice. Under normal circumstances a Muslim woman would not venture such an action because of the fear of reprisals from the community in which she has to live. These cases also throw light on the precarious conditions under which a Muslim woman has to live since her husband can give her a divorce any time any where without any legitimate basis. A lot of improvement is reuired in this matter to improve the cause of the Muslim woman.

Marriages in Christian society are quite stable and separation of husband and wife or divorces are settled in the normal courts of law. The Christian communities treat their women with respect and therefore the condition of Christian women is far better than either Hindu or Muslim. There are no child marriages and girls get educated without restrictions.

The concept of good marriage in Sikhism is described in the holy bkkok of the Sikh religion, *Sri Guru Granth Sahib* as follows:

"They are not said to be husband and wife, who merely sit together. Rather they alone are called husband and wife, who have one soul in two bodies." (Guru Amar Das, Pauri, pg. 788).(Ref. 28).

The tradition of dowry:

The tradition of giving and accepting dowry is an old and established one. This topic is related to marriage. In the Hindu marriage, the scriptures have laid down the procedures to be followed for performing a marriage. The idea of the marriage is that the bride is conceived as Goddess Laxumi and the bridegroom is conceived as Lord Vishnu. In the marriage procedure a puja is performed for both, separately. A puja consists of presenting a set of new clothes to the bridegroom and a *varadakshina* (a donation of money). The set of new clothes and the amount of money given to the bridegroom can be just a token or it can be any thing depending on the desire and capacity of the bride's parents. This has been made an important issue of prestige in the marriages. Normally, and according to the scriptures, the groom should accept whatever is given to him in the form of "*varadakshina*". As a matter of fact the primary objective of the marriage ceremony is the "*Kanyadan*", i.e. "the giving away of the daughter". The ceremony, therefore, consists of the father of the bride "gives his daughter's hand" to the bridegroom, in the Hindu tradition it id literally called "he donates his daughter" to the groom. This is important to bring out because the "daughter" or "*kanya*" is the main gift the groom is receiving, not the new set of clothes or the money. But people have either forgotten this true meaning or they have decided to ignore it. The result has been that much emphasis has been placed on what the groom is going to receive in gifts, i.e. dowry. The love and emotional attachment, which the couple have for each other becomes entirely secondary and the dowry is of primary importance.

As mentioned earlier, the bride, conceived in the form of Goddess Lakshmi is also worshipped and "*dakshina*" is also offered to her from the groom's side. She has also to receive a set of new clothes and certain basic ornaments, necessary for a wedded wife. These ornaments consist of a "*mangalsutra*", a set of bangles and earrings. The total cost of all these items is not much and for an average earner is easy to afford. But here again, it depends on the desire of the groom. He may decide to give expensive dresses and set or sets of ornaments the total cost of them could be as high as one wants it to be. What a groom is giving to the bride is not considered of much importance in the Hindu society.

The driving force behind the dowry is greed. Marriage, therefore, is not a joining of two loving souls but a purely commercial transaction in which the father of the groom is the main player and has the upper hand. The bride's parents are the under dogs and are trying to strike a deal acceptable to all concerned. The groom and the bride are reduced to the status of "pawns" in the marriage game. There was a time when the families of the groom and bride would conduct open negotiations concerning what would the groom receive in dowry, but after the government's declaration that the dowry taking/giving is illegal, no body now openly demands a dowry. It is simply expected that the father is going to give "something" to the groom. And that "something" must be in keeping with the expectations of the groom's father and suitable for the groom, i.e. the groom's educational qualifications and his earning capacity, his social status and family reputation. The parents of the bride have to think hard before making a decision to establish a relationship with the family of the groom, since if the status of the groom's family is high, the relationship could be very expensive. Expensive, initially in terms of the dowry at the time of the marriage and later in terms of the gifts to be given at various religious and family occasions. This may prove to be a heavy load the bride's parents may not be able to carry, especially if they are not rich and/or they have other daughters also waiting to get married.

If the family of the groom is educated and sensible and has good values, a jump from a lower clas to a higher class can be successful and the married couple can enjoy a happy life. But in other cases the family life of the newly married couple can be a living nightmare. The consequences of having not received enough dowry are very serious. They may consist of harrasment of the newly wedded bride: daily taunts, to make her do enormous house work, physical harrasment such as beatings, restrictions on her movements and contacts, restructions on her entertainment, and in many cases murder, which is called "bride burning". These murders are conducted in such a manner as to appear as though they were accidents. The widowed husband, in most cases, remarries and gets a new gift of dowry from the parents of his new bride!

A stop to this can be put by the couple themselves by standing up to their parents and leave them and live in a separate place of their own and organize their life free from these threats and harassments. In some cases this is now happening with the girls getting good education and are able to support themselves. Shoma Chatterjee has the following to say about the dowry: (Ref. 21)

"Dowry is love-neutral and negotiation-neutral in our society. It does not matter whether it is a love marriage or an arranged one, the giving of dowry is considered as much a status symbol for the father of the bride as it is for the groom's father to receive it. If the boy's father does not receive a dowry, whther he has asked for it or not, he feels that his son has been "insulted", as if dowry is the measuring stick of a man's dignity not status."

Money is a universal language. It is the medium of exchange that helps to bring in gold, furniture, jewellery, and everything else that goes to make a dowry. I have seen myself that if a girl comes from a more affluent background, and if her parents continue to shower her in-laws and her husband with gifts, then they can be kept happy. This gift giving must be voluntary, and without being asked for. The girl herself is often eager that her parents make such gifts so that her "happiness" is assured. Love, therefore, is no substitute for dowry-ridden marriages. Dowry is in fact, no longer a word in the dictionary. It is no longer a custom. It is an institution by itself, which all of us have nutured and encouraged, directly or indirectly, actively and passively, so that it is now so deeply ingrained into our society and our social life that those who submit to it often get burnt at the stake and those who try to avoid it, end up like the three Kanpur sisters who hanged themselves. When dowry is the basic foundation of the social system in the country, it does not matter whether the marriage is based on "love" or "arrangement", the password is the same: *dowry!*

My opinion is that material wellbeing and happiness are closely related. If one is materially well off, his (her) day-to-day life will be comfortable and happy. The happiness one enjoys from a loving relationship is of a different sort altogether. Both kinds of happinesses are required in life. But for a person of pride and self- respect, he must be completely self-reliant and create his material wellbeing by his own hard earned money; not by receiving dowry from his father-in-law. Take pride in your own achievements, buy your own car and take pleasure and pride in driving it. If you cannot afford to buy a car, drive a bicycle and be satisfied in what you have. If your rich father-in-law offers you gifts, do not accept them because you would be compromising your pride and self-respect. In a situation where a girl from an effluent family marries into a not-so-well-to-do family, it is natural for her loving father to feel for her and to give her presents from time to time with the intention of making her life more enjoyable. There is love and affection in this type of gift giving. It would break the heart of the girl's father if her husband refused to accept such a wel- intended gift(s). A person with pride ought to explain to his wife that such gifts are not a good idea. It puts the husband in a difficult situation. It is, as far as possible, better to establish relationships through marriage with families of equal status to avoid worries and problems associated with dowry and "gify" giving/taking.

The problem of dowry taking/giving is confined to the Hindus. Other religious communities such as Christians, Sikks, Jains, Buddhists, etc. do not suffer from this tradition. However, marriages in Jains and Sikhs are celebrated in an elaborate fashion, the cost is, in many instances, quite considerable. "Gifts" are exchanged and again, the costs of these gifts are a matter of prestige.

The following passage from the *Sri Guru Granth Sahib* states the position of Sikhism on the subject of dowry:

"Any other dowry, which the perverse place for show, that is false pride and worthless gilding, O' my Father! Give me the Name of Lord God as gift and dowry." (Guru Amar Das, Sri Rag, pg. 79).

Violence against women:

Domestic violence is a very common and serious problem in India. Women in India have been subjected to violence, both physical as well as mental, for a long time. The occurrence of domestic violence has not decreased with the modernization and increase in the percentage of women and men getting educated. The root causes of domestic violence are, generally speaking: greed, poverty, poor and difficult mother-in-law/daughter-in-law relationships, problems within a joint family system, lack of freedom available to the daughter-in-law, and so on.

In India, taking or giving a dowry is illegal but the practice of dowry is still quite alive. To file a complaint in the court by somebody against a prospective proponent for marriage regarding dowry is a rare thing. While negotiating and finalizing the marriage, the matter of dowry is discussed, in confidence, and it is in most cases, a matter of utmost importance, which can make or break the deal. It has been observed that in quite a few instances after having accepted a dowry from the parents of the bride, when the new daughter-in-law tries to settle down in her new home, (the groom's home), the parents of the groom demand more money from the parents of the bride and threaten that they will make the life of the daughter miserable if the required payments are not made. If the parents of the daughter are unable to make payments, it results in the harassment of the girl. This harassment may take several forms out of which the most serious is the murder of the new bride by dousing her with kerosene and setting her on fire. This is called "bride burning." The murder is so arranged that it has the appearance of a suicide and in most cases no action is taken against the criminals. Soon after the death of the young bride, the groom gets married again and now he is in for accepting a new dowry. Cases like this happen in a joint family, especially when the girl is completely dependent on the groom's family and has no place to go, not even her own family. If she returned to her own family, she would never be allowed to return to her husband's family again and no body would consider marrying her. This would be a great burden on her own family since they would have to take care of her for the rest of her life.

Statistics on 'dowry deaths" vary enormously: the National Crime Bureau of the Government of India puts the number of dowry deaths at about 6,000 a year (in 1997), whereas unofficial estimates stand as high as 25,000. Because dowry murders come to attention of the activists, because of suspiciously high "suicide" rates among young, lower to middle-class, married women—research done by the women's organization Vimochana (Bangalore) indicates that most cases of dowry murder are still categorized as either "suicides" or "accidents"—they are notoriously hard to investigate and prosecute as murders. Approximately one-third of all reported cases are not investigated; as a result, the majority of others languish in the courts and still more are not reported because *both* the bride's in-laws (who are responsible for the crime and for accepting dowry) *and* the bride's family (who als agreed to give dowry) would be culpable under existing laws.

The custom of giving/taking dowry is not uniformly practiced throughout India, although studies suggest that it is growing increasingly popular, even among tribal communities as they make the shift from more agrarian and rural to urban economies. Such trends have observers to conclude that dowry is a phenomenon with specific links to (lower) middle class lifestyles and desires for class mobility in general, in plain words, greed. Instances of dowry related violence have, therefore, increased.

The situation concerning dowry in South India is different from North. In the South, where the family structure is matriarchal, it is the groom who may be required to pay the dowry. In marriage negotiations, it is the bride's side, which has the upper hand. In these areas, the incidence of violence against women on account of dowry or any other reason is practically absent. The very high percentage of education in female as well as male population is also a factor in reduced or no violence against women.

Rape is among the most common crimes against women in India and continued to be grossly underreported. The first feminist campaigns in the mid- to late- 1970s against rape focused on cases of police rape and have since broadened ti include all forms of "custodial rape", or cases in which a woman was raped by a custodian (landlord, policeman, employer, and the like), as well as other kinds of rapes, including married rape and the rape of prostitutes. It was largely the efforts of the women's groups that publicized the issue of custodial rape to such an extent that legislators were eventually compelled to change existing rape laws, most importantly shifting the burden of proof to the accused. This legal provision notwithstanding, those accused of custodial rape are often easily acquitted on the basis of their social stature, which makes their claims to innocence more "believable" than the woman's charges. In addition, maritial rape and rape of prostitutes are still not socially viewed as deserving of legal protection. The women involved often face humiliation in the courts, in addition to social dishonor and tremendous public scrutiny of their lives. Women's groups have found that women rape victims are often unwilling participants in campaigns against rape, making the task of pressing charges and any further legislative reforms even more difficult.

In addition to the above, wife battering is also prevalent in some parts of India. In those communities, which are located in some areas of Rajasthan, UP, Madhya Pradesh, and Haryana, the husband's beating of his wife is an acceptable practice and is a part of their culture. The beating of wife may precipitate if the husband gets upset, and the reason for him to get upset might be quite minor. Surprisingly, the wife accepts it as a part of her "normal" relationship with her husband. I have personally herd this from a maidservant who had bruises on her body and when my friend's mother, who was a medical doctor, enquired, she told her that she received a beating last night from her husband. Then after a pause she asked, "Doesn't sahib beat you once in a while?". When she was told that sahib never beat me, she was surprised and said, "Every *man* beats his wife once in a while. Isn't sahib man enough to beat you? *Our men* beat us once in a while." From this brief exchange it was clear that beating the wife was considered a "manly" act. Apart from this practice in these communities, which are basically backward and at the lower social strata, wives are receiving beatings in other well-to-do homes. These cases are not reported to the authorities since it becomes a matter of saving the good name of the family and the consequences of such a report would result in the breakdown of the marriage. The husband would never beat his wife if she is educated and employed and capable of living on her own. And there lies the key to put a stop to this violence.

The sati tradition is an act of gross violence against women and this matter has been dealt with in a separate section. The sati and the bride burning are the two acts of violence, which are unique to India and the world wonders about them and is quick to categorize Indian society as uncivilized. The fact is that the sati tradition, which was practiced in the past centuries, is now practically vanished. The other types of violence do exist but are no more normal or abnormal than routine violence in the United States, where a woman is said to be battered every fifteen seconds, usually by a spouse or a boy friend. The National Crime Records Bureau (NCRB) has reported the following statistics pertaining to crimes committed against women in India, 1999-2000. :

Female foeticide:

- In India increased by 49.2% between 1999-2000.

- Rape: 16,373 women were raped during the year;

- 45 women were raped every day; 1 every 32 minutes;

- An increase of 6.7% in the incidents of rape was between 1997-2002.

Incest:

- 2.25% of the total rape cases were cases of incest.

Sexual Harassment:

- 44,098 incidents of sexual harassment were reported;

- 121 women were sexually harassed every day; 1every day:

- An increase of 20.6% was seen in incidents of sexual harassment between 1997-2002.

Importation of girls/trafficking:

- 11,332 women and girls and women were trafficked;

- 31 women and girls were trafficked every day, 1 every 46 minutes.

Kidnapping and Abductions:

- 14,630 women and minor girls were kidnapped or abducted;

- 40 women and minor girls were kidnapped every day; 1 every 66 minutes.

Dowry Related Murders:

- 7,895 women were murdered due to dowry; 21 every day.

Domestic Violence:

- 49,273 women faced domestic violence in their marital homes;

- 135 women were tortured by their husbands and in-laws every day; 1woman every 11 minutes.

- Domestic violence constitutes 33.3% of the total crimes committed against women.

- A steep rise of 34.5% in domestic violence cases was witnessed between 1997-2002.

- Over 40% of married women face physical abuse by their husband; 1 in every 2 women faces domestic violence in any of its forms—physical, sexual, psychological, and or economical.

Suicides committed by women:

- 12,134 women were driven to commit suicide due to dowry;

- 110,424 housewives committed suicide between 1997-2001 and accounted for 52% of the total female victims.

Sexual abuse of women:

- Out of 600 women respondents, 76% had been sexually abused in childhood or adolescence;

- Of the abusers, 42% were "uncle" or "cousin"; 4% were "father" or "brother".

Maternal death rate:

- India's maternal mortality rate stands at 450 per 100,000 live births, against 540 in 1998-1999. The figures are way behind India's Millennium Development Goals, which call for a reduction to 109 by 2015, according to UNICEF.

NOTE: The data reported here is is only a partial reflection of the extent of crimes against women as most incidents go unreported. NCRB predicted that the growth rate of crime against women would be higher than the population growth rate by 2010.

A Comparison Of Statistics Between India And World Pertaining To Crimes Against Women:

Social Indicator	India	World
Infant mortality rate, per 1,000 live births	73	60
Maternal mortality rate, per 100,000 live births	570	430
Female literacy, %	58	77.6
Female school enrolment	47	62
Earned income by females %	26	58
Underweight children %	53	30
Total fertility rate	3.2	2.9
Women in government, %	6	7
Contraception usage, %	44	56
Low birth weight babies, %	33	17

Source: Google, www.mapsofindia.com

Prostitution, AIDs, trafficking in women and children:

Approximately two million women, about 5 percent out of them are Napalese and Bangladesi, have been estimated to be engaged in the commercial sex trade in India. A quarter of these women are under the age of eighteen, and 25,000 children are engaged in prostitution in major cities. (UNIFEM *south-Asia Regional Anti-Traffiking Program,* 2001, www.unifemantitrafficking.org/main.html.) Several of these women have been sold into sex trade as bonded labor to pay of bosses who have purchased them. Violence is a routine element of their lives, and the women typically suffer from a wide range of sexually transmitted diseases, includind AIDs. The life expectancy of such women is only 30 years. Those women who have tried to return to their families, have not been accepted by their families, which puts them in an extremely desperate situation. Organizations such as *Apne-Aap* in Mumbai and action Aid in Hydrabad, have attempted to provide for women to sleep and bathe, ration cards, vocational training, and educational facilities for workers and their children. There have been excellent documentaries made to show the lives of prostitutes in the brothels of Mumbai. The prostitutes, who were from Khatmandu, Nepal, and were very young and were interviewed and the reporter went to see her parents in Nepal. The father was not shy to admit that he had "sold" his daughter since he had a large family and they were very poor.

The prostitutes of Calcutta are probably the most organized of the lot. They have themselves taken the situation under their own hands for their own protection and to make sure they are provided for things like the ration cards etc, which were taken away from them by the "bosses" or pimps.

The spread of a dangerous disease such as AIDs is on the increase in India. In a recent documentary, a truck driver was interviewed at a stop mid-way between Delhi and Jaipur. This is a stop where prostitutes are available for $ 1 to 2, and generally no protection is used. The truck driver admitted having not used any protection, knowing well that it put his health, his wife's and the prostitute;\'s at risk. His argument was that he "prefers" it this way.

Approximately four million adult Indians are estimated to be HIV positive; one in four AIDs patients in India is a woman. (The World Bank Group and UNGASS, *Regional Update on India,* www.worldbank.org/ungass/India.htm) These numbers are considerably higher for women working in the commercial sex industry. Women are also vulnerable because they are poorly informed about the spread of the disease and not always in a position to insist on the use of condoms. Several studies also indicate that the rate of HIV infection among middle class Indians and housewives is growing at an alarming rate fueled to a large extent by the misconception that AIDs risks are greatest only among poorer commercial sex workers. The reason for this spread can be attributed to the fact that hundreds may see prostitutes and/or have extra marital affairs. The numbers cited here may only represent the lower figures since many victims of AIDs would not report the disease on account of family reputation and it could go on undetected in its early stages.

Legislation for the protection and empowerment of women:

India has had a long history of suppression and mistreatment of women, over the past many centuries on account of moral degradation and a mind set of treating women as unequal and lower grade of human beings as has been discussed under many headings. But fortunately, India also had a very able leadership during the time of independence and immediately preceding it, who had a clear vision for what sort of country they wanted India to be. They were able to draft a very beautiful and forward- looking constitution. All Indian laws derive their authority from the Indian Constitution, which guarantees justice, liberty and equality to all the citizens of India. The preamble speaks of equality of status and of opportunity for all citizens. Article 14 states that "The State shall not deny to any person equality before the law within the territory of India." It not only prohibits discrimination but makes various provisions for the protection of women. Articles 14, 15, especially 15(3), 16, 39 and 51A(e) deserve special mention in this regard. Rights guaranteed under 14,15 and 16 are fundamental rights and if they are violated by the State, a citizen can move the High Court. There have, however, been relatively few cases in which women have asserted their right to equality by moving the courts.

Fundamental rights and constitutional directives
:

Women constitute 330.78 million, representing the 48.3 % of the total population as per the 1981 census. The population has since increased. To attain national objectives, the constitution guarantees Fundamental Rights and Freedoms, such as freedom of speech, protection of life, and personal liberty.

Legislative measures:

Pre-independence Legislation:

1. Regulation No. XXI of 1795 and Regulation No. III of 1804.
These regulations declare the practice of infanticide illegal.

2. Bengal Sati Regulation XVII of 1829
This regulation declares the practice of sati or self-immolation of widows as illegal and punishable by the criminal courts as culpable homicide.

3. The Hindu Widows Remarriage Act 1959 (15 of 1959)
This Act legislates the marriage of Hindu widows.

4. Indian Penal Code, 1960 (45 of 1980)
It provides for punishment for various offences against women like abduction, rape, adultery, bigamy, remarriage during the lifetime of a wife, cruelty and cheating against women and so on.

5. The Converts Marriage Dissolution Act, 1866.
This Act provides for dissolution of a marriage where one of the parties has deserted or been repudiated by other on grounds of conversion to Christanity.

6. Indian Divorce Act 1869 (4 of 1890)
This Act empowers a wife to give petition for dissolution on the grounds of (a) remarriage of husband, (b) change in husband's religion, (c) where the husband is guilty of incestuous adultery, bigamy with adultery, rape, sodomy, or bestiality, adultery coupled with cruelty.

7. The Married Women's Property Act, 1874 (3 of 1874).
It declares that the wages and earnings of any married woman and any property acquired by her oen self through the employment of her arts and skills and all savings and investments thereof shall be her separate property. The Act further guarantees that a married woman may maintain a suite in her own name in respect of her own property.

8. The Power of Attorny Act 1882 (7 of 1882).
According to this Act the woman is empowered to appoint an attorney on her behalf.

9. Civil Procedure Code, 1908 (5 of 1908).
It prohibits arrest or detention of women in civil prison in execution of a decree for the payment of money.

10. Indian Succession Act, 1925 (39 of 1925).
Under this Act the woman has the same right to the property as the husband has on the death of his wife.

11. The Child Marriage Restraint Act, 1929 (19 of 1929)
It fixes the minimum age of marriage at 18 for boys and 15 for girls.

Post-independence legislations:

1. The Special Marriage Act, 1954

This Act permits marriage of, (a) people from different religious faiths without changing their religions, (b) stipulates the minimum age of marriage as 18 years for girls and 21 years for boys.

2. Hindu Marriage Act, 1955

This Act fixes the minimum age of marriage as 18 years for girls and 21 years for boys. The salient feature of this Act is that it makes monogamy as universal.
The Hindu Marriage Act, 1955 and special marriage Act, 1954 were amended in 1976 to provide for the right for the girl to repudiate before attaining maturity, marrying as child, whether the marriage has been consummated or not. Crualty and desertion were added as grounds for divorce and mutual consent were recognized.

3. Hindu Succession Act, 1956.

The Act confers the right to absolute ownership over property and the woman can make a "WILL" leaving her share of property of an intestate being divided among the heirs in accordance with certain prescribed rules for the benefit of women. Rule 1 states that intestate widow or if there were more widows, shall take one share. Rule 2 states that surviving son and daughter and the mothers of intestate shall take one share. Rule 3 states that the heirs in the branch of each deceased son or each pre-deceased daughter of the intestate are also entitled to get one share of the property.

4. The Suppression of Immoral Trafficking of Women and Girls Act, 1956.

This Act prohibits the trafficking of women and girls for purposes of prostitution as an organized means of living. The Act was amended in 1978 and further amended in 1986 with the objective of making the penal provisions in the Act more stringent and effective. The amended Act is entitled, "The Immoral Traffic (Prevention) Act, 1986, and "the salient features of this Act are—widening the scope of this Act to cover all persons whether male or female, who are sexually exploited for commercial purposes, enhancement of period of imprisonment where offences are committed against minors and children, appointment of trafficking police officers, who will have the powers to investigate inter-state offences, prescribing punishment as laid down for rape under the Indian Penal Code or the seduction of victims of trafficking while in custody, interrogation of women and girls removed from the brothels to be held by women police officers or in their absence in the presence of women social workers and setting up of special courts.

5. The Dowry Prohibition Act, 1961:

The dowry prohibition act was first inacted in 1961. The Act was amended in1984 to take the offence cognizable to enhance the penalty, both the fine and the impresement and to widen the scope of the Act to make it more effective. The Act was further amended in 1986 to make the penal provisions more effective and stringent. The minimum punishment for taking or abating dowry has been raised to 5 years and a fine of rupees 15,000. The advertisement in the newspapers, periodicals, etc, offering a share of property as consideration for marriage is punishable. The amendment proposes the appointment of Dowry Prohibition Officers by the state governments. Offences under the Act have been made non-billable. A new offence of "Dowry Death" has been included in the Indian Penal Code consequential to the amendment in this Act.

6. The Commission of Sati (Prevention) Act, 1987:
.

Under this Act commission of sati and its glorification and for matters connected therewith are incidental to such an abatement is punishable by the maximum penalty, that is, death or imprisonment of life. This Act provides more effective prevention for a woman (widow) being sacrificed as Sati.

Although these new regulations have gone a long way in bringing some legal remedy to women victims of domestic violence in their marital homes, it has been found that the women can be victims in their personal homes as well. One study of women and girls who die of burns shows that in greater Bombay 61.3 percent of women who die of burns were in the age group of 15 to 19 years and were never married.

In many cities special police cells have been set-up to deal with complaints under the new provisions. While this is an important step, experience shows that these police cells are not aware of the changes in the law and are operating, more or less, like counseling units. The police are not trained in counseling and they do not have the right attitude either. The result is that the woman victim is generally advised to adjust to her new conditions. The Committee on the Status of Women in India had pointed out that "certain penal provisions in the law are definitely influenced by the established patriarchal system, the dominant position of the husband and the social and economical backwardness of the women."

The legal provisions, as stated are excellent in providing the protection for women, which they require. These provisions are also very helpful in making sure that women are not discriminated in any fields of endeavor including employment, property rights, inheritance and equal participation in the political processes. The big problem in India is not the provisions of the law but its effective implementation, which is very much lacking on account of widespread corruption at all levels of government. Lack of education among women makes things all the more difficult for them since they do not know what the law is. In India bribery and nepotism is rampant and things get done on these basis. The result is that people who are wealthy and have connections get things done to their liking. For the rest, life is very difficult and the old heavy-handed patriarchal way of doing things still continues.

CHAPTER 5.
STEPS TAKEN TO IMPROVE THE STATUS Of WOMEN AFTER INDEPENDENCE

The problems affecting the women of India have been described right from the post- Vedic period when the decay in the Indian society began. This decay continued unabated until the seventeenth century when some awakining started. There have been some remarkable people of strong conviction who were motivated by the idea of improving the status of women who have contributed a lot for the women's cause. The awakening, which began was influenced to a large extent by the exposure of the Indians to a foreign culture, the culture of England and Europe. Some Indians had visited England and had seen first hand the freedoms enjoyed by people there and how much emphasis they placed on individual life. In India there was not much valu for anybody's life unless one was quite rich or powerful. Under the Moghul rule, the Hindus were worth much less than the Moghuls and the women were, of course, of not much valu. They treated women as objects not as human beings.

Changes had started happening even under the British Raj as is evidenced by some good legislation having been enacted prior to independence. This is detailed in Chapter 4. After independence, a legislative assembly was formed consisting of eminent constitutional lawers, thinkers and those who were motivated by the desire to reform the Indian society. The constitution was assembled in 1950 and was adopted the same year when India was declared a republic. The constitution is a social document. It has made important provisions for the protection of the rights of women. They

consist of guaranteeing women equality in all spheres of
life and activity, protection from harrasment, declaring the
dowry system illegal, and so on. Provisions have also been
made to ensure women get opportunites for education.
Women also can take part in the democracy by voting,
standing for any office and to hold any other administrative
positions just as men.

The Government of India had also embarked on five- year plan scheme,
on Russian model, in which certain goals were set, which were to be achieved
at the end of each five- year period. An important part of these plans was
the eradication of illiteracy of women. These goals were quite ambitious
and intended to end the illiteracy among women as soon as possible.
Unfortunately, these goals were not met. Illitracy in women has been reduced
but not to the extent to which it should have been since close to 50% women
are still illitrate, mostly in the villages. The villages occupy most of the India's
area as well as population. So even though it appears that India has made
tremendoud progress, a progress, which has now been well recognized in
the world. This progress is in the technical field of information technology,
engineering and an achievement of self-sufficiency in agricultural products.
And women are a part of this progress. These women are mostly urban
dwellers who have easy access to schools, colleges and technical schools where
they acquire the necessary qualifications. These qualifications get the women
gainful employment just like in the western countries. The opportunities are
not available to women who live in villages and the communities in the rural
areas are still thinking in old ways, i. e.. do not believe in educating women.
According to their thinking, the place of the woman is in the home so what
is the use of wasting money on her edycation? She can learn the housework at
home under the guidance of her mother or any other elderly woman.

Remaining at home also avoids her exposure to the urban "toxic" culture,
which will make her disobedient. In any case, the progress of eliminating
illiteracy in the rural India has been poor. The problem had not been dealt
with as seriously as other areas of the plans such as industrial development,
agriculture, atomic energy and such. Some of the government energy ha
been missdirected. For example, the big project of reorganization the states
based on linguistic basis. This created enormous problems including large-
scale demonstrations, hunger strikes etc. and the remainents of that project
still survives in the form of Sikhs demanding "Khalisthan". This has a large
support in Canada in the west coast of British Columbia. These problems
have kept the government pre-occupied resulting in the neglect of women's

education, which was not of any benefit to the politicians in the short term in winning votes to get re-elected.

Illitracy has prevented women from knowing their rights. It has prevented them from enjoying the freedom to which they have been entitled for quite some time. They have not herd of the legislative changes made so they continue in the same mode as they have been for the past many centuries. Their situation is further complicated by the fact that India is rampant with corruption at all levels. The police who are supposed to uphold the law are one of the most corrupt. Therefore, las have been enscted to protect women under custody.

Legislative measures are not enough to improve the condition of women. Women's literacy needs to be enhanced. India needs more women teachers, better physical facilities such as female washrooms etc. and the government needs to take this matter seriously. Just lip sympathy should not be accepted as an excuse. The government had been interested in keeping the rural population illiterate because this made it easy for them in gaining their votes by keeping them in the dark about the "truth". And an illiterate woman would easily vote according to her husband or family's wishes. The disparity between the rural and urban illiteracy rates has been presented in a tabular form in chapter 4. This table also gives a state wise breakdown of the rates.

A National Committee on the Status of Women in India was appointed under the auspices of the Ministry of Education and Social Welfare in September 1971. The committee submitted its report in 1974. This committee, in essence, is saying that: "there are a number of provisions made in the constitution relating to the rights and status of women in the country. Various enactments and development programs aimed at enabling women to play their role in our national life in an effective manner have supplemented these provisions. These programs have brought about considerable changes in the urban areas, but the problems continue to remain virtually unchanged in most of the rural areas. Further with the changing social and economic conditions in the country a variety of new problems relating to the advancement of women have also emerged. The Government of India feels that a comprehensive examination of all the questions relating to the rights and status of women in this country would provide useful guidelines for the formulation of our social policies."

The Committee felt that: "With the recognition of the need to direct the process of social change and development towards certain desired goals, education has come to be increasingly recognized as a major instrument of social change. The Committee quotes the Education Commission (1964-66): "The realization of the country's aspirations involves changes in the knowledge, skills, interests and values of the people as a whole. This is basic to every program of social and economic betterment of which India stands in need...If this change is to be achieved on a grand scale without violent revolution, there is one instrument and one instrument only that can be used: "Education."

The Committee stated: "One of the expectations from this directive of the use of education is that it will bring about reduction of inequalities in society, on the assumption that education leads to equalization of status between individuals coming from unequal socio-economic strata of society. It was on this argument that the Universal Declaration of Human Rights included education as one of the basic rights of every human being. The constitution of the UNESCO directs its efforts to achieve "equality of educational opportunity without regard to race, sex or distinctions, economical or social."

"The history of the movement for improving women's status all over the world shows emphasis from the beginning on education as the most significant instrument for changing women's subjugated position in society. Increase of educational facilities and opportunities, and the removal of traditional bars of entry of women to particular branches and levels of education, came to be supported by all champions of women's emancipation from the nineteenth century onwards. Social reformers in India, whether they were modernizing liberals, or revivalists, also emphasized the importance of education of women to improve their status in society." In this context it is fitting to compare the data on women's educational status before independence and after independence, since this is a good yardstick for measuring the success of the efforts of Government of India in educating women.

Education Of Girls And Women In Pre-Independence Period:

Year	Percentage Of Literacy For women	Enrolment of Girls in Primary Schools	Secondary Schools	Colleges	Other Institutions	Total
1881-82	0.2	124,291	2,054	6	515	127,066
1901-02	0.7	344,712	9,075	256	2,370	365,413
1921-22	1.8	1,186,224	26,163	905	10,836	1,224,128
1946-47	6.0	3,475,165	602,280	23,207	56,090	4,156,742
No. of girls Enrolled per 100 boys		36 and 14 for Secondary Schools	22 for middle general education 7 for vocational	12 for	12	30

Education Of Girls And Women In The Post-Independence Period:

Enrollment of Girls Year	Primary School Classes	Middle School Classes	Secondary School Classes	Colleges and Universities
1946-47	34.75	3.22	2.81	0.20
1950-51	53.85	5.34	1.61	0.04
1955-56	76.39	8.67	3.18	0.84
1960-61	113.47	16.70	5.41	1.50
1965-66	182.93	28.46	11.72	3.24
1968-69	199.36	34.93	15.60	4.30
1973-74	244.01	45.37	23.40	9.00
1978-79	318.90	72.50	31.70	16.00

The expansion of women's education began at the primary level and mostly got stuck there for quite a few years. In1947, 83% of all girls enrolled were in primary schools (about half of them in grade one only). Expansion at the secondary level was slow to start and slow to expand. In 1947, of all girls enrolled were in secondary schools.

In recognition of the fact that women's education in the rural areas was crusal to the enhancement of the women's status, the National Committee for Women's Education endorsed the suggestion made by the Union Education Minister that a small committee be appointed to look into the causes for lack of public support, particularly in rural areas, for girl's education and to gather public cooperation. This suggestion was made in view of the serious shortfalls in the enrolment of girls. The committee was to suggest, therefore, ways and means of achieving substantial progress in this area.

"The Committee is convinced that it is only through a willing, educated and informed public that any progress can be made at all. Not only is the need urgent, but the ground is also ready for a comprehensive program for mobilizing public cooperation to promote girl's education and giving it constructive channels of expression….."

The work of the National Committee is a good attempt on part of the Government in eradicating illiteracy among women but even after six decades of independence the status of literacy among women has not improved, especially in the rural areas of the country. The lack of progress in this is partly due to lack of aggressive efforts by governments at all levels and partly because of the centuries old culture of not educating the women among the rural population. The old culture of keeping girls at home is based on keeping them safe from the "undesirable" exposure to the "outside" environment on which the family does not have any control but the ill effects of that exposure might create problems for the family. In other words, the "purity" of the girl can be easily maintained by keeping her at home. Under pressure to educate their daughters, the rural families did send their daughters to the schools but did not let them continue after the primary level, i.e. withdrew them prior to the age of puberty. This is the clear observation made by the committee. Another important point, which the people in the rural areas think is that the mothers of the girls did not go to the schools and yet they havesuccessfully managed the affairs of the family. What then is it necessity of educating the daughters if they are going to do the same role as their mothers?

It may be concluded that even though India has made some progress in educating women, especially after gaining independence, a large percentage of female population (approximately 50%) still remains illiterate. A comparison with other countries, which also gained independence around the same time as India, would indicate that India lagges behind them in the area of literacy, especially female literacy. It is hoped that better efforts on part of the Government and greater contacts between the rural and urban populations will, in future, produce positive results in changing the mindset of the rural population.

CHAPTER 6.
SOME PROMINENT SOCIAL REFORMERS

There have been a number of social activists and reformers within the past two centuries. Their great contributions in the improvement of the conditions of Indian women have resulted in good legislation during the British Raj and after independence, the general awakening of women and their empowerment, formation of organizations for promoting women's education and the creation of betterment in their living conditions. Some of these reformers were also activists in the freedom movement within the time frame under consideration. The activists in most cases were both social reformers as well as freedom fighters. Some of these activists such as Sir Sayd Ahmed Khan, Raja Ram Mohan Roy have been already mentioned.

Rokheya Sakhawat Hossain (1880-1932):

She has been called the first and foremost "feminist" of Muslim society in Bengal. (At that time Bengal was not partitioned). Born to a conservative father who became wealthy as a landlord, she was taught secretly by her brother to read and write, then married to a man who was quite supportive of her. Hossain gradually liberated herself and went to work in a school for Muslim girls in Calcutta, and introduced adult literacy programs for both Hindu and Muslim women She also founded the Association of Muslim Women. She also wrote a book about the stifling life at the school for girls (who had to travel to reach school) to be seen, the school devised a special bus, without windows but with two blocks of latticework, three inches wide and eighteen inches long, above the front and back doors. The first time the bus was used, the stuffy hot and dark metal box made the children ill. The English woman who ran the school opened the lattices and hung colored curtains over the openings. It was still quite hot and the girls fainted, had headaches all day and vomited. Parents complained, and many took their girls out of the school. Muslim men wrote the school letters signed "Brothers-in-Islam", objecting to the curtains because, they said, breezes blew them open and violated purdah rules. They threatened to close the school if this problem was not solved.

Raja Ram Mohan Roy (1772-1883):

He was a pioneer in the movement for the uplift of women in India. He was one of the first Indians who believed in Indians learning English language. At a time when the British had not even decided to formally teach English in India, Ram Mohan Roy learnt English privately on his own. He has been rightly described as the father of India's modern enlightenment. He saw the need to revitalize the Indian society by getting rid of the certain traditional evil practices, such as the denial of education to women, polygamy, sati and discrimination against the lower castes. He was not a nationalist in the 20th century sense but he was confident that India would be able to achieve political independence by the acquisition of modern knowledge through the English education. He was right since knowledge of English would provide the Indians the access to western thinking and the importance, which the western countries place on independence. Some of the prominent Indians like Pundit Jawaharlal Nehru, Mahatma Gandhi, Bal Gangadhar Tilak, etc were greatly influenced by the freedom and independence the British were enjoying while denying the same to Indians. Roy's protest against the ways of the early missionaries was with the policemen who were at their back ridiculing the religions of India at the street corner meetings. "It is true that the apostles of Jesus Christ used to preach the superiority of Christianity to the natives of different countries. If the missionaries had distributed and preached the gospel in the nearby countries such as Turkey, Persia, etc., they would be praised but to do this in a place such as Bengal where people were just frightened by the name British, an encroachment upon the rights of her poor, timid and humble inhabitants and upon their religion cannot be viewed in the eyes of God or the public as a justifiable act."

The introduction of English education in India in the first half of the 19th century owes mainly to the vigorous efforts of Ram Mohan Roy. He believed that modern English education would open the doors to scientific knowledge of the kind that had enabled Europe to make rapid strides in industrial civilization, and to contemporary ideas of rational thinking, freedom, democracy and equality of sexes. As mentioned earlier, it was through the medium of English that successive generations of Indians including Gandhiji, Jawaharlal Nehru and others became acquainted with the progressive ideas of the best minds of the West: Thomas Jefferson, Abram Lincoln, Voltaire, Rousseau, Marx, Ruskin and Thoreau, and such stimulating thinkers such as George Bernard Shaw and Bertrand Russell. This intellectual interaction with the west helped to enrich the thinking of educated Indian people and helped a great deal in the independence movement.

In the field of social reform, Ram Mohan Roy is best known for his successful campaign against sati tradition.

Following Ram Mohan's campaign, law abolished sati in 1829. Though prohibited, the practice did not cease completely. Sporadic instances of sati still occur. There is thus a gap between the law and the reality.

The big revolt in 1857 against the British occupation of India did not adversely affect the process of intellectual awakening and social reform initiated by Ram Mohan Roy. Persons nurtured in the Brahmo Samaj, which was founded by Ram Mohan in 1828, carried it forward in Bengal. Debendranath Tagore (1817-1905), father of Rabindranath Tagore, led the Brahmo Samaj after Ram Mohan Roy.

Ananda Charlu (1843-1908):

He was from Madras and was another pioneer who fought for the right of women to education and property and supported the remarriage of widows.

Kandukuri Veeresalingam Pantulu (1848-1919):

He was a renowned Telgu writer, and social reformer who worked tirelessly to overcome the prejudice against widow marriage.

C. Vijaraghacharia (1852-1944);

He was a prominent lawyer, who campaigned against pre-puberty marriage and against untouchability, and advocated a share for the daughter in the father's property.

Venkamamba:

She was a well-known Telgu poet born early in the 19th century in an orthodox Brahmin family who refused to have her head shaved when she became a widow. She was a pioneer in women's movement in South India.

Jotirao Govindrao Phule (1827-90):

He was popularly known as Mahatma Phule and was one of the earliest social reformers in western India. He was o Born in a family of humble caste whose occupation was gardening, he took up, after his own schooling, the cause of education of women and poor. Since women teachers were not available those days, he taught his wife, Savitribai, and made her teacher in a school he opened in 1948 for the women of the lower castes. He went on to start a night school for adults, a widow's home and an orphanage. Phule received encouragement both from the local authorities, who made a grant of land, and from the enlightened Maharaja of Baroda. "Nobody", Jotirao Phule held, "is sacred by birth. Everybody has virtues and vices as a human being."

Gopal Ganesh Agarkar (1856-95):

Agarkar was yet another reformer who did great work in promoting women's education and widow marriage. After he graduated from Deccan College Pune, he led a frugal life and applied himself to social work along with the very famous Bal Gangadhar Tilak. After Agarkar quit as editor of the weekly, *kesari,* he started his own bilingual journal called *Sudharak,* meaning "reformer". For this journal he had Mr. Gopal Krishna Gokhle, a very prominent independence fighter, a lawyer of great repute and mentor of Mahatma Gandhi, contribute to the English portion og this journal.

Baal Gangadhar Tilak (1856-1920):

One of the greatest Indian patriot and a freedom fighter, was yet another great reformer. He started a nationalist weekly, *Kesari,* in Marathi. Mr. Agarkar relinquished the editorship of this weekly because of his difference of opinion with Tilak with regard to the issue of child marriages. Tilak was a radical nationalist but a conservative in social matters. On 24 March 1918 he attended and spoke at an all India Depressed Classes Conference under the presidentship of the progressive Maharaja of Baroda but could not bring himself to sign a personal pledge against observing untouchability in day-to-day life.

Gopal Krishna Gokhle (1866-1915):

Gokhle was the founder of the *Servants of India Society,* which he founded in 1905. Gohkle was also the mentor of Mohandas Karamchand Gandhi, later known as Mahatma Gandhi. Both Agarkar and Gokhle campaigned against the inequalities of the caste system and in favor of women's education and widow remarriage. They used the publication, *Sudharak,* to promote their ideas, which proved to be an effective tool. Both Tilak and Agarkar were excellent journalists of their time.

Pundita Rama Bai (1858-1922):

Quoted earlier, she was the daughter of Anant Padmanabha Dongre, a Vedantic scholar who was persecuted by his Brahmin kinsmen because he had educated his wife, Lakshmibai and made her a "pundita", (meaning learned). Dongre left his village of Malheranjee near Mangalore, and setup an ashram in the hills of Gangamul where Ramabai was born. After her parents died in poverty during the famine of 1874, Rama along with her sister Krishna and brother Srinivasa Shastri went on a pilgrimage, walking several thousand miles. She learnt Sanskrit from her brother and after reaching Calcutta in 1878 she was honored with the titles of *Pundita* and *Saraswati* for her mastery of the language. Ramabai earned a little money by telling *Purana* stories. She began to lose her faith in her ancestral religion when she saw the corruption in the system. After her brother's death Ramabai married Bipin Behari Das Medhavi, a lawyer, who was a *Sudra,* the lowest caste in Hinduism, by birth. He died within two years, and Ramabai went with her baby daughter to Poona. She was welcomed there by the progressive group including justice Mahadev Govond Ranade and Ramkrishna Gopal Bhandarkar. They were members of the Prarthana Samaj, which propagated women's education and campaigned against caste oppression and child marriage. Pundita Ramabai founded the Arya Mahila Samaj, which worked for the freedom of women from the cruel practices imposed by tradition. The Samaj was active in many centers including Ahmednagar, Sholapur, Thane and Bombay.

In 1883, some Christian missionary friends helped Ramabai, who wanted to improve her knowledge of English, to go with her daughter Manorama to England. She stayed with the St. Mary the Virgin at Wangate and was greatly impressed by the Christian missionary's attitude to "fallen women". (The term signified the victims of the male sexual hunger). Ramabai embraced Christianity in September 1883. She visited the USA in 1886, learnt Foible's kindergarten system and prepared a series of lessons for children in Marathi. Pandita Ramabai was the earliest woman to participate in the Indian National Congress. She died in 1922. Sarojani Naidu described Ramabai as a foremost Christian, worthy to be enrolled in the calendar of saints. Pundita Ramabai exemplifies the conversion of some upper-caste Hindus, in Bengal and elsewhere, who were attracted by the intellectual and spiritual appeal of Christianity.

Ramabai Ranade (1862-1924):

She bears the same first name as Pundita Ramabai. Being the wife wife of Justice Mahadev Govind Ranade, (1842-1901), a leading social reformer, she had contributed considerably to the cause of the women herself. Barely 12 when she married the considerably older widower, she took pains to educate herself and worked alongside her husband for women's education. She was active in the *Seva Sadan* (house of service) at Bombay, which trained women workers for educational and medical relief work. Branches of the organization were soon established at Ahmedabad, Surat and Poona. Ramabai's autography in Marathi is a well-known literary work.

Dhondo Keshav Karve (1858-1962):

Popularly known as Maharshi Karve, was a crusader against justice for women. After his first wife died in 1891, he married a widow, Godubai, in 1893. He founded the *Vidhva Viivaha Pratibandhi Niwarak Mandali* (Society for the Removal of Obstacles to Widow Marriage), in 1893, to help needy widows and look after their children's education. In 1828 he established a widow's home, and in 1908 the *Nishkama Karma Math,* (an organization for doing selfless work), to train volunteers for selfless work. His greatest achievement was the establishment of a women's university, for which he collected funds in England, America and East Africa. Established at Poona in 1916, it received a munificent donation of fifteen lakh rupees in 1920 from Sir Vithaldas Thackersey and was named as the Shreemati Nathibai Thackersey Women's University in memory of the donor's mother. A notable feature of the university, which moved to Bombay in 1936, was the employment of Indian languages for instruction at a time when a foreign language was being used for imparting even elementary knowledge in arts and science. But English was taught as a compulsory subject.

Vithalbhai Patel (1873-1933);

Vitthalbhai was the elder brother of Sardar Vallabhbhai Patel, a prominent patriot and freedom fighter fron the state of Gujarat,and was a pioneer social reformer. As a member of the Baroda Municipality and subsequently member and president of the Bombay Municipal Corporation, Vitthalbhai Patel promoted free and compulsory education and gave special encouragement to education to among the so-called untouchable castes. Subsequently as an elected member of the Imperial Legislative Council he introduced a bill to validate marriages between Hindus of different castes. It was opposed by orthodox members of the council led by Pundit Madan Mohan Malvia, but was supported by Tej Bahadur Shastri among others. The bill lapsed with the dissolution of the council. The reform had to wait till 1949 when the provisional parliament of free India passes the *Hindu Marriages Validity Act.* This was an early installment of the legislation for reform and codification of Hindu law, which Jawaharlal Nehru sponsored as Prime Minister.

Vidyagauri Nilkanth (1876-1958):

Nilkhanth was a woman pioneer from Gujarat who educated herself after marriage and became one of the first women graduates. She formed the *Mahila Mandal* (women's group) at Ahmedabad in 1914, and helped to found the Lalshanker Umashankar College for Women. Awarded the *Kaisar-I-Hind* medal by the British authorities in 1926, she returned it during the Civil Disobedience movement of 1930.

Dayanand Saraswati (1824-83):

A Gujarati by birth who came to be popularly known as Maharshi Dayanand Saraswati later, initiated a comprehensive reform movement. He denounced the belief in short cuts to salvation through fasts and pilgrimages, or through listening to medieval texts. Taking his stand on the very Vedas, which were invoked by Hindus, Dayanand campaigned against idol worship, untouchability, child marriages and the relegation of women to inferior status. He advocated women's education, and the freedom of choice for women in selecting their husbands, and the right of every person to study the Vedas. Dayanand founded the *Arya Samaj* in 1875, which did much good work in and around the Punjab in the spread of education, especially among girls, and in improving the conditions of women and the lower castes.

Munshi Raam (1857-1926):

Munshi Raam was one of the followers of Maharashi Dayanand. He later became a sanayasi and was known as Swami Shradhananda. He did a lot of work in promoting Hindu-Muslim unity and consistently opposed child marriage, promoted women's education, widow remarriage, and improvement of the conditions of the lower caste.

Sir Syed Ahmed Khan (1817-98):

His name has already been mentioned earlier. He was a pioneer in the reform movement of the Muslim community. The Muslim community was slow in taking to modern education through English. Khan urged his community to get out of their isolation, which was keeping them backward and to acquire scientific knowledge. "The acquisition of modern knowledge does not mean renunciation of Islam. The Prophet said that knowledge is the heritage of the believer, and that he should acquire it wherever he can find it. He also said that the Muslims should seek knowledge even if they have to go to China to find it. It is obvious that the prophet was not referring to theological knowledge in these sayings. China was at that time the most civilized country in the world, but it was a non-Muslim country and could not teach the Muslims anything about their religion. Islam and Islamic culture prospered as long as the prophet was followed in respect of these teachings; when we ceased to take interest in the knowledge of others, we began to decline in every respect. Did the early Muslims not take to Greek learning avidly? Did this in any respect undermine their loyalty to Islam?"

Sayd Ahmed Khan founded the *Muhammadan Anglo-Oriental College* in 1875, which was raised to the status of a university in 1921 and was named the *Muslim University of Aligarh*. He attacked the purdah system, and the tendency to attribute supernatural powers and miracles to the Prophet and to saints.

The Committee on the Status of Women in India notes in its report that "the emancipation of Indian Muslim women was delayed partly because modern education entered the Muslim community much later, and partly because the seclusion of women was defended by leaders of the community more persistently."

Mohandas Karamchand Gandhi (1869-1948):

He was later popularly known as Mahatma Gandhi. He is also the "father" of the Indian nation. An extremely dedicated independence fighter, a firm believer in the principle of non-violence and was primarily responsible for uniting the country to oust the British rule. In addition to his work as a freedom fighter, he was also a great social reformer and did great work in eradicating the discrimination based on caste and religion. He strongly believed in creating a society where women would be treated equally and they would be empowered both at home and in the society at large.

Born in a middle class family in Porbandar, Gujarat, he was keen on going to England for studies. He obtained a law degree from the University of London in 1891 and was admitted to the bar. He tried to set up a law practice in Bombay but his conscience did not allow taking up cases to defend anybody who was guilty. He said, "I am a lawyer not a liar." Gandhiji also practiced law in South Africa where he was discriminated against by the white government. He returned to India after staging a non-violent protest against the government of South Africa. After his return he was mentored by Gopal Krishna Gokhle and shed his British attire and started wearing simple clothes similar to those worn by a poor peasant to signify his identity with them.

When Gandhiji assumed the leadership the average life span of an Indian woman was only twenty-seven years. Babies and the pregnant women ran a high risk of dying young. Child marriage was very common and widows were in very large numbers (Kasturba was also a child when she married Gandhiji so he was himself a victim of chills marriage). Only 2% of women had any kind of education and women did not have an identity of their own. In North India they practiced the purdah system. Women could not go out of the house unless accompanied by men and their face covered with cloth. (This, of course, was the measure taken to protect women from abduction by Muslims.). The fortunate ones who could go to school had to commute in covered carts. (in north India only).

It is in this context that we have to recognize the enormity of Gandhiji's work. Gandhiji claimed that a woman is completely equal to a man and practiced this in his own life. He learnt to practice it after the incident in South Africa when he ordered Kasturba to clean the latrines and she refused with the result that Gandhiji ordered her to get out of his house. He later repented and apologized to Kasturba.

Thousands and million of women, from all walks of life, educated or uneducated, participated in the independence movement under Gandhiji's leadership, but Gandhiji's independence movement also included social and economic reforms for the whole nation. After a couple of decades this equality became natural. After India's independence in 1947 and adoption of the Constitution in 1950, equality of women was recognized and emphasized and the Hindu Code was formulated. The population was not impressed. They said, "Of course it had to be done." His ideas and thinking was not something new to India. The Vedas had already pronounced them. They seemed new because those ancient principles had been completely forgotten and the society had become corrupt and women had been mistreated since the mediaeval times. Gandhiji promoted equal sharing of domestic work by men and women, which he practiced himself. He advocated respect for women and their contribution in home as well as to the society. He believed in granting liberty to women to provide them equal opportunities for getting educated and participate in the job market as well as in the political process, opportunity to hold political and other offices without prejudice or inequality. A large number of people of various background came in contact with him during his lifetime and were influenced by his personal integrity, honesty, liberal and forward looking thinking, transparency of character, and adherence to truth. Some of the important leaders during the time India got independence were, in fact, his followers. The single most prominent example is that of Pundit Jawaharlal Nehru who after becoming the first prime minister of India was able to pass important legislation in the parliament for the betterment and protection of women. Another prominent follower was Sarojani Naidu who did a lot of work with Gandhiji and turned out to be a very effective politician. She is also an example of a woman of India who contributed enormously during the independence struggle and afterwards thus setting up an example for other women to follow.

Gandhiji thus transformed the conditions of women substantially from what it used to be before his time. His wife, Kasturba's great sacrifices and cooperation which she always gave to her husband, just as most women in India do, without giving any importance to their own wishes, must be recognized and appreciated.

Pundit Jawaharlal Nehru (1889-1964):

A Son of a wealthy lawyer, Pt. Motilal Nehru, he was brought in luxury like the son of an English lord, with an English governess. He was educated in Harrow and Cambridge in England and was admitted to bar in 1912. He developed a great sense of patriotism after the massacre of Jaliaonwalla Bagh. He soon joined with Mahatma Gandhi in the independence movement and through his work and sacrifices, was elected the president of the Indian National Congress and ultimately the first prime minister of India after India became independent.

Jawaharlal Nehru was deeply sympathetic with the cause of the women of India and wanted to set the women of India free from the centuries of evil and mistreatment. He was instrumental in passing many Acts in the parliament for the protection and restoration of equality of women in the Indian society.

Most of the Acts cited earlier were passed under his watch of and initiatives. He had promised women that he would reform Hindu personal law. He faced opposition from the orthodox group until 1954-55 when he was able to enact the laws known collectively as the Hindu Marriage Code. His decision to let the Muslims follow their personal law (he was trying to appease Muslims) disappointed women activists, who felt it was made at the expense of women. There was resistance to reforms prohibiting child marriage and polygamy, but Nehru encountered the greatest opposition when he tried to guarantee women equal inheritance rights. Not until 1956 was he able to push through the Hindu Succession Act, granting equal and absolute inheritance rights to the widow, mother, sons, daughters, (and their immediate heirs), of men who died intestate. Men granted this right with certain conditions; that male heirs could inherit their own and part of their father's shares; that men who made formal wills could bar women from inheriting; and that agricultural tenancies were to be exempt. Thus powerful male groups in some states prevented widows and daughters from inheriting.

Pundit Jawaharlal Nehru had also set an excellent example in terms of Indira Gandhi, his only daughter, whom he brought up with lots of love as a single parent after the death of his wife, Kamala, who died immaturely on account of illness. Pundit Jawaharlal Nehru also cared for Mrs. Indira Gandhi's sons, Rajeev and Sanjeev

CHAPTER 7.
SOME PROMINENT WOMEN OF INDIA

In spite of a general suppression and a treatment of denying basic equality rights and to bind the women into rigid religious customs and traditions, some women have emerged to be quite extraordinary. They had achieved remarkable success during all the periods of Indian history. They are famous and their names shine with glory in the long history of India. They shine like bright stars in an infinite dark night of women's suppression. This essay would not be complete without briefly mentioning the achievements of some of these glorious women. Mention has been made of a number of women of the Vedic and ancient times who had distinguished themselves in the field of education and philosophy. Their achievements have been described in Chapters I, II and the Appendices. Following are the lives and achievements of some of the more recent outstanding women. They did have to overcome a tremendous handicap of the social and religious traditional envirinment.

Panchali, or Draupadi, though regarded as legally the property of her five husbands, virtually ruled over them. Similarly, there have been Hindu queens throughout the historic period, who have influenced their husbands and the names of them appear jointly with those of their husbands on coins and charters. For example, the name of Chandragupta Maurya, wife, Kumaradevi, was termed "Mahadevi", that is great queen and coins were printed in her name. Chandragupta Maurya was the founder of the great Gupta Empire and to have the name on the coin is a privilege, which is accorded to the kings only. The mother of the great Sidharaj Jaysingh, Minaldevi, ruled over Gujarat at the end of the 17th century. Rani Durgavati, the Rathore queen of Jodhpur, did not only rule the state of Marwar for her infant son but had to defend it against the Muhgal Emperor, Aurangazeb. In the more recent history, Ahalyabai Holkar of Indore was an illustrious woman who ruled on behalf of her adopted son. Rani of Jhansi took part in the great mutiny of 1856 against the British and in opposition to the injustice the British did in depriving her of her state. Her story is covered in more detail later.

In another field, in the philosophical dispute between the Adi Sankara and Mandan Mishra and the discussion, which took place, the wife of Mandan Mishra had presided over that famous discussion. Not only that she presided but gave the final judgment in favour of Adi Sankara!

Some of the great women in the ancient Indian history and in Indian epics are:

Kunti:

She was the elder of the two wives of king Pandu of the kingdom of Hastinapur. She raised her three sons and the two sons of the other wife of Pandu, Madri, on her own after the death of Pandu who died on account of a curse. Madri committed sati with Pandu. Kunti was an absolute devotee of lord Krishna. Her devotion to the lord saved her from a number of disasters and insurmountable difficulties, which she faced throughout her life. In the end when the great battle of Mahabharata was over and the sinners were all killed, lord Krishna wanted to give a boon to her and asked, "What would you like have?" To this she gave an unexpected and remarkable response: "Give me misery, O lord". Lord Krishna was stunned. He asked, "Why Kunti? Haven't you had enough in your life?" To this she responded, "It will be easy for me to remember you if I am in misery." Such was the depth of her devotion to the lord and she never faltered in remembering *him*.

Andal:

Andal (725-755) was among the Alvars (poet mystics) of South India. She was so overwhelmed with love for lord Vishnu that she refused to marry anyone else. According to tradition she merged into the deity of Vishnu after being formally married to him.

Akka Mahadevi:

She was a medieval woman of the 12th centuary, a saint and was a devotee of lord Shiva. She is venerated as a symbol of equality of genders and as an early exponent of women's emancipation.

Mira Bai: (1498-1547)

Mira bai was born at Merta in Nagaur District of Rajasthan in a Rathore clan of Rajputs. She was given a very beautiful idol of Krishna by a traveling mendicant. (A religious beggar.) It is said that the mendicant arrived at her house and he had this idol of Krishna with him. Mira bai fell in love with this idol and cried for it after the mendicant had gone. The mendicant was told in a vision to return to her house and give the idol to the little girl, which he did. From that day she kept on worshipping lord Krishna. She was in so much love with that idol that she used to play, dance and sing songs with the idol, assuming that it was alive. Her father's elder brother Vikram Deo who succeeded to the throne arranged her marriage at the age of sixteen with prince Bhoj Raj, the eldest son of Rana Sanga of Chittor. This marriage raised Mira to a very high social status as the ruler of Chittor was considered to be the leader of the Hindu princes of Rajputana. However, her great devotion to lord Krishna did not always endear her to her husband and family. Her love of Krishna was so absorbing that she neglected her social and regal responsibilities. She sang and danced in public temples in praise of lord Krishna and mingled with members of all castes. Because of this she suffered great hardship throughout her life. Her husband died a few years after her marriage and she refused to commit sati, a practice common with the Rajput families of high status at that time.

In order to save the reputation and honor of the royal family attempts were made to kill her many times. In one attempt a pot with a cobra inside was sent to her but when she put her hand inside the pot it turned out into a garland of flowers. In yet another attempt a pot of poison was sent to her as offering to her lord. She drank the poison but the poison had no effect on her. In the end she entered in the inner sanctum of the Krishna temple in Dwarka, when, it is said that the doors of the temple closed by themselves and after a while when the doors opened, Mira was not found. Only her clothes were found wrapped around the deity. Thus she became one with her beloved lord Krishna with whom she got united.

Mira bai was a great poet who composed songs in praise of lord Krishna. She had composed about 1300 songs, each one full of deep devotion, which are extremely popular even today. All famous vocalists have sung her songs. There are dance compositions, movies and other programs incorporating her poetry. Her poetry also forms a part of Hindi literature and is studied at the university level. Those who belong to the *Bhakti* or devotional school of worship sing her poetry. Mira Bai's name is immortalized in her poetry and the remarkable story of her life. She has a unique place in India.

The beauty of Mirabai's poetry cannot be truly appreciated by people who do not know the language, which was a local dialect of Hindi, spoken in that area of Rajasthan. Following is a crude translation of one of the couplets of one of her numerous compositions:

For her love and devotion for lord Krishna she says:

" *With my tears I have cultivated a vine, that is love;*
Now that this vine has matured,
It is going to bear a fruit, that will be bliss. "

After hundreds of years after her death practically all of India sings her devotional songs, which have been sung in many ways, in classical Hindustani music, in semi- classical or other styles in almost all the major languages of India. The reason for their popularity is their depth of devotion, and they appeal to the conscience of an Indian in a way no other devotional poet has done before.

Some of the great women in the recent history and modern India are:

Rani Laxumibai of Jhansi (1828-1858):

The queen of the Maratha ruled princely state of Jhansi in North India, was one of the leading figures of the Indian mutiny or fight for freedom from the British in 1857, and a brave symbol of resistance In no time in the history anywhere has a young woman fought so bravely with her infant son tied on her back with a sword in her hand riding on a horse. Even the British, against whom she was fighting, had a great praise for her courage and bravery.

Originally named Manikamikka at birth, she was born to a Maharashtrian Brahmin family in 1828 in the holy city of Varanashi. Her father, Moropant Tambey looked after her after the death of her mother when Manukamikka or Manu as she was affectionately called, when she was only four. Moropant traveled to the court of Raja Gangadhar Rao Newalkar, the Maharaja of Jhashi, when Manu was thirteen. Manu got married to Gangadhar Rao. She then became the maharani of Jhashi in 1842. She was given the name Laxumibai. Laxumibai gave birth to a son in 1851 but the child died when he was about four months old.

In 1853 Gangadhar Rao fell ill and he was persuaded to adopt a child. He adopted a boy shortly before his death in his distant relationship by the name of Damodar Rao. To ensure that the British would not be able to contest the adoption, the Rani had it witnessed by the local British representatives. Maharaja Gangadhar Rao died the next day, 21 December, 1853. At that time the Governor General of India was lord Dalhousie and he rejected Rani's claim that Damodar Rao was their legal heir. Dalhousie decided to annex the state of Jhanshi under the Doctrine of Lapse. The Rani then did the unprecedented: she sought the advice of a British lawyer and an officer of the East India Company, Robert Ellis, and appealed her case in London. Although these petitions were well argued, they were ultimately rejected because the British were not as much concerned with the justice or what was right or wrong but were most interested in grabbing the territory. They confiscated the state jewels and she was required to leave the fort and the Rani Mahal (the palace of the queen) and leave the town as well. But Rani Laxumi Bai was determined to defend Jhanshi. She proclaimed in her famous words, "Mi Maghi Jhanshi Nahi Denar" (This is in Marathi and means: I will not give up my Jhanshi.)

Jhanshi became a center of the rebellion upon the outbreak of the Indian freedom fight in 1857. Rani Laxumi Bai started strengthening her defense for Jhanshi and assembled a voluntary army. In January of 1858, the British army started its advance on Jhanshi, and in March laid a siege to the city. After two weeks of fighting the British captured the city but the Rani escaped in the guise of a man, strapping her adopted son Damodar Rao closely on her back. She fled to Kalpi where she joined Tantya Topey, another famous Maratha general and freedom fighter of the 1857 mutiny. The British later hanged him. The Rani met her death on June 17 during the battle for Gwalior. The Rani donned warrior's clothes and rode into battle to save Gwalior Fort. A stray bullet mortally wounded her. The British captured Gwalior three days later. General Rose commented that the Rani had been "the bravest and the best."Rani's father, Moropant Tambey was captured and hanged a few days after the fall of Jhanshi.

The story of Rani of Jhanshi is that of courage, bravery and dedication and loyalty to her country. Her glory is immortal and she also proved what an Indian woman could achieve. Her story also brings to light the brutality and unjust behavior of the British. Her bravery has been praised by the famous Indian poet Subhadra Kumari Chauhan in her poetic composition, which is famous, not only as a high quality literary work but as a nationalistic heroic poem proudly read and sung by all Indians.

Sarojani Naidu (1879-1949):

Sarojani Naidu is famous as a poet, a politician and as a feminist. Her maiden name was Sarojani Chattopadhya. She was also called the Nightingale of India. Sarojani was born into a very learned family: her father, Angonath Chattopadhya was a scientist and founder and administrator of Hydrabad College, later Nizam's College. Her mother, Barada Sundari Devi was a poet. Sarojani became Naidu when she married Govindrajulu Naidu, a medical doctor by profession. She had two daughters and two sons.

Sarojani had been a brilliant student, passing her matriculation in a very young age of 12. She studied at the King's College, London, from 1895 to 1898 and then at Grifton College, Cambridge, England. When she attended college in London she became involved in some of the women's suffrage activities. After her return to India she joined the National Congress and the non-cooperation movement. She helped found the Women's India Association with Annie Besant. Being from a Brahmin family, she married a person from a lower caste. Sarojani Naidu was elected the first woman president of the Indian National Congress in 1925. She traveled to Africa and North America lecturing on the Congress Movement. Her independence activities brought down prison sentences in 1930, 1932 and 1942. After India became independent she was appointed Governor of the province of Utter Pradesh. She had many publications to her credit, which included: *The Golden Threshold, (1905), The Bird of Time (1912), The Broken Wing (The Scepter Flute (1928),* and *The Feather of the Dawn (1961).* The dates of these publications clearly indicate that Sarojani was continually engaged in her literary work in spite of her heavy engagement in political work.

Indira Gandhi (1917-1984):

Indira Gandhi was the daughter of Pundit Jawaharlal Nehru and was not related to Mahatma Gandhi. People generally assume that she must be the daughter of the very famous Mahatma Gandhi since the surname is the same. She got the surname Gandhi because of her marriage to Feeroz Gandhi.

Indira was very fortunate to have been born in an elite Nehru family and was very dearly loved by her father whose only child she was. Pundit Nehru used to write to her from his jail cell and used to address her," *Priya*

Darhshani", meaning "the one very lovely to look at". A collection of these letters had been published. The book is a very interesting reading, providing good general information. Indira's mother, Mrs. Kamala Nehru died early on account of illness and was brought up by her father. On account of Pundit Jawaharlal Nehru's life long political activity, the Nehru family was always in the political limelight and Indira got the best possible grooming in political matters. As prime minister of India, Jawaharlal Nehru used to invite and entertain all sorts of dignitaries from the world and Indira used to play the hostess. She also traveled with her father internationally and visited many capitals and world leaders. Thus she came to know many people in high positions in the world. After the death of her father in 1964 she was elected to the parliament and became the minister of information and broadcasting under the prime ministership of Lal Bahadur Shastri who died of heart attack after two years in office. Indira was chosen as the leader of the Congress party as a compromise candidate on account of divisions in the party and they thought that she could be manipulated. But she proved them wrong. She was, as they found out, was an independent minded person, played the game of politics very well and handled the affairs of the country extremely well after becoming the prime minister when the Congress got the majority. Indira was the prime minister from 1966 to 1977.

Indira Gandhi, in her second term as prime minister, had to deal with the Sikh movement of asking for a separate state of their own, which they would call "Khalistan. The Sikh separatist group leaders barricaded themselves in the Sikh shrine of Amritsar and conducted their attacks on Hindus and others. Indira Gandhi, having warned the group to come out and surrender, had to attack the temple to clear out the temple and put an end to their unlawful and criminal acts in the interest of protecting the public. This action enraged the Sikhs and Indira's own Sikh bodyguards assassinated her in her residence as an act of retaliation for ordering an attack on their sacred temple. Indira died in! 984. She was the only female Prime Minister India had in the 20th century. Her popularity exceeded that of queen Elizabeth and she did many good things for India but many of her actions are considered controversial. She had acquired a formidable reputation as a "statesman" internationally. She was extraordinarily skilled in politics but her allowing her son Sanjeev to interfere in National politics and ordering senior ministers and officers was a grave mistake. Her getting elected and becoming the prime minister had much to do with the fact that she was the daughter of Pundit Jawaharlal Nehru and people wanted to express their gratitude to him by voting her in. Many people of India still feel so grateful to her father that they decided to make Rajeev Gandhi their next prime minister and after his death, his Italian born widow, Sonia Gandhi is the president of the Congress party and let Man Mohan Singh become the prime minister since people would not have liked a foreigner in that position. Her son, Rahul Gandhi is now being groomed for the highest post. Such is the state of Indian politics.

M.S. Subbhalakshmi (1916-2004):

An accomplished vocalist in the Karnatic style of music of South India, who had a very melodious voice and was highly decorated for her achievements as an exponent of classical as well as semi-classical music. She was born in Maduri, in Tamil Nadu, in a family of music, her father being a veena player. She had been exposed to music from a very age.

She gave her first public performance during the Mahamaham festival at Kumbhakonam at the age of eight and released her first recording at the age of ten. She began her classical Karnatic music training under Sammangudi Srinivasa Iyer and then Hindustani classical music under Pandit Narayan Rao Vyas. By the age of 17 M.S. was giving concerts on her own, including major performances at the Madras Music Academy, a prestigious center for the study and promotion of Carnatic music. Performance of Carnatic music was until then a domain, traditionally reserved for men. She performed a vast variety of musical forms in different languages including, Telugu, Sanskrit, Hindi, Malayalam, Kannada, Bengali, Gujarati and Marathi.

M.S.Subbalakshmi traveled to London, New York, Canada, the Far East, and other places as India's cultural ambassador. Her concerts at the prestigious Carnegie Hall, New York, the UN General Assembly on UN day in 1966; the Royal Albert Hall, London in 1982; and the Festival of India in Moscow in 1987 were significant landmarks in her carrier. M.S. had also acted in some films: Her first movie, "Sevasadanam", was released in 1938; she played the male role of "Narada" in "Savitri", in 1941 to raise money for launching Kalki, her husband's Tamil weekly. Her title role of the Rajasthani saint-poetess Meera in the eponymous film 1945) gave her national prominence. This movie was remade in Hindi in 1947. The movie had M.S. sing the Meera bhajans with Dilipkumar Roy as the director.

M.S. was widely honored, praised and awarded. Some of the more popular ones include *Padma Bhushan* in 1954, *Sangeet Natak Academy Award* in 1056, *Sangeetha Kalanidhi* in 1968, (literally, treasure chest of music. She was the first woman to receive this title.) Ramon Magasaysay award in 1974, the *Padma Vibhushan* in 1988, the Indira Gandhi Award for National

Integration in 1990, and the *Bharat Ratna* in 1998. She was also honored as the court singer of Tirumala Tirupati Devasthanams. She had been awarded many honorary doctorate degrees. She also received enormous prize money, which she donated to charities.

M.S.Subbalakhmi's rendering of the bhajans composed by Sant Tulsidas and Meera are very popular and so are her recitations of the *Vishnusahastranama Stotra* (thousand names of lord Vishnu in Sanskrit), *Bhaj Govindam Moodha Mate,* composed by Adi Sankaracharya.

Lata Mangeshkar (1929-)

Lata Mangeshkar, a living legend, was born on September 28, 1929 at Indore, Central India. She is the best playback singer in the Indian film industry. She has sung in 980 movies and 25,000 solo, duet, chorus-backed songs to her credit in twenty Indian languages. She has held the Guinness Book of world records from 1974 to 1991 and a record of 30,000 songs from 1948 to 1987. She has been a music director, an actor, and a movie producer.

Lata was awarded *Padma Bhushan* in 1969, *Padma Vibhushan* in 1999, *Dada Sahib Palke Award* in 1989, *Bharat Ratna* in 2001, three *National Film Awards.* 12 *Bengal Film Journalist's Awards,* to name the most important honors received by her. She is, no doubt the most accomplished vocalist in India. Lata is a very modest and unassuming lady who believes in leading a very simple life. Her specialty is that she can sing songs in so many different regional languages of India without any accent as if it was her mother tongue.

Lata was born in a musical family; her father was a renowned vocalist and all her siblings are accomplished musicians, her younger sister, Asha Bhsle is almost as famous as Lata herself.

Mahadevi Verma:

A writer and a poet *par excellence.* Mahadevi Verma is regarded as the best literary figure in India. She had a very difficult life. Married at an early age, she was not liked by her husband who based his dislike on her lack of education. Mahadevi left the family of her husband, Dr. Swarup Narayan Verma and returned to her parent's home. She was from a family of lawyers in Farrukahabad. Living with her family, she got herself educated: She went to Allahabad University and received a Master's Degree in Sanskrit. In addition to being a renowned poet and a writer she was a painter She sketched for her two works, *Deepshika* and *Yatra.* Mahadevi was regarded as one of the four pillars of *Chhayavadi School* of Hindi literature. Her most famous works include: *Ateeit Ke Chalchitra* (The moving frames of the past), *Smriti Ki Rekhayen* (The lines of memory). Her famous poetic publications are: *Nihar, Rashmi, Neerja,* and *Sandhya Geet.* Her work *Shrinkhla Ki Kadiyan* (Links of a chain) reflects the plight of Indian women. Another one of her famous work is: *Sahityakar Ki Astha.* (The faith of literati).

Mahadevi Verma was greatly influenced by Buddhism. She was also deeply aesthetic. Her poetry conveys a pain, the pain of separation from her beloved, in her case the beloved being the Supreme Being. There is also an element of mysticism in her poetry. With her work *Deepshikha,* which contains 52 poems, she ventured into a new field of Hindi literature called *Rahsayavad* (meaning mystery) Mahadevi Verma was also a social reformer and strongly advocated the cause of women of India. Many of her writings reflect her views on the plight of Indian women. She was appointed the first principal of Prayag Mahila Vidyapeeth, started to impart education to girls through Hindi medium. Later she became the chancellor of the institute. In 1956, Indian Government honored her with Padma Bhushan. She was also the first woman to be a fellow of the Sahitya Academy (Literary Academy).

Mrs. Vijaya Lakhsmi Pandit (1900-1990):

She was an outstanding politician, nationalist, independence fighter and an excellent diplomat. Vijaya Lakshmi, sister of Pundit Jawaharlal Nehru, got the same upbringing as Jawaharlal Nehru himself. Brought up in the same luxury, she married Ranjit Sitaram Pandit in 1921. Pandit died in 1944. She was the first Indian woman to hold a cabinet post. In 1937 she was elected to the provincial legislature of the United Provinces (now called Utter Pradesh) and was designated minister of local self-government and public health. She held this post until 1939 and again from 1946 to 1947. In 1946 she was elected to the Constituent Assembly, representing the United Provinces.

When India became independent in 1947, she entered the diplomatic service and became India's ambassador to several countries; the Soviet Union from 1947 to 1949, the United States and Mexico from 1949 to 1951, Ireland from 1955 to 1961, during which time she was also the Indian High Commissioner to the United Kingdom, Spain from 1958 to 1961. She also headed the Indian delegation to the United Nations from 1946 to 1968. In 1953 she became the first woman President of the UN General Assembly.

In India she served as governor of Maharashtra State from 1962 to 1964, after which she was elected to the Lok Sabha (Lower house of the Indian parliament), from Phulpur, her brother's former constituency. Pandit was a harsh critic of her niece; Indira Gandhi after the latter became the prime minister. In 1979 she was appointed the Indian representative to the UN Human Rights Commission, after which she retired from public life. She has written two books: *The Evolution of India (1958), The Scope of Happiness: A Personal Memoir (1979)* .Her belonging to the Nehru family has helped her initially in her success as a politician but she could not have discharged the heavy responsibilities of the high offices she had held if she was not capable. She certainly was an excellent diplomat, politician and an administrator.

Arundhiti Roy (1961-):

Susama Arundhiti Roy the first Indian woman to have won Britain's prestigious Booker Prize. She was born in Bengal and grew up in Aymanam village in Kottayam, Kerala. She was born to Mary Roy a well known social activist who won a landmark Supreme Court verdict that granted Christian women in Kerala the right to their parent's property and fatter a Bengali Hindu tea planter. Arundhiti's parents separated when she was small and she did her formal education in Corpus Christi school run by her mother in Kottayam District, Kerala. When she was just sixteen she left her home and settled in Delhi. There she did her degree in architecture at the Delhi school of Architecture. During this period she met Gerard de Cunha, a fellow architecture student and married him. Their marriage lasted for only four years. After a brief stint in the field of architecture, she found that it was not for her. She left for Goa making a life out at the beach, got tired of it after a few months and came back to Delhi. She took a job at the National Institute of Urban Affairs, met Pradeep Krishen, a film director now her husband who offered her a small role in "Massey Saab". She went to Italy on a scholarship for eight months to study the restoration of monuments. She realized that she was a writer during her stay in Italy.

After she returned from Italy she worked with Pradeep Krishen and they planned an episode for Doordarshan called the *Banyan Tree*, which didn't materalize and was shelved by the producers after shooting 2-3 episodes. She wrote and starred in *In which Anne Gives it Those Ores,* a film on college life in India based on her experiences in the University of Delhi and wrote the screenplay for Pradeep Krishen's film *Electric Moon* (1992). She quickly became known for her work as screenwriter. Then she wrote a series of essays called *The Great Indian Rape Trick,* which attracted media attention in defence of former dacoit *Phoolan Devi,* who she felt had been exploited by Shaker Kapoor's film *Bandit Queen.* Then came her debut novel *The God of Small Things,* which shot her into prominence in 1997, by winning the prestigious Booker Prize in London and becoming an international best seller. The book, which took almost five years to complete, gives an insite into the social and political life in a village in South India through the eyes of seven year old twins and how it effects/disrupts their small lives. The book won $ 20,000 as prize and sold nearly 400'000 copies globally by October that year.

In the years following her success, she has turned to activism, writing *The Cost of Living,* a book comparing two essays, *The Greater Common Good (1999)* and *The End of Imagination (1998),* the former against Indian Government's massive dam projects, which displaced millions of poor people and the latter, its testing of the Nuclear weapons. She has been an active participant in public demonstrations against the construction of the Sardar Sarover Dam on the Narmada river in Western India and has devoted substantial amount, around one million rupees, equivaent to the Booker Prize money for the cause. She was even arrested along with other protesters for campaigning for the cause. *Power Politics* her latest book published takes on Enron, the power corporation based in Houston trying to take over Maharashtra's power sector. She has also spoken on and published several articles such as *Promotion of Equal Rights,* supporting equal rights for lower castes in India and *War on Terrirorism (2001)* against the Iraq war. Roy was awarded the *Sydney Peace Prize* in May 2004 for her work in social campaigns and her advocacy of non-violence. In January 2006 she was awarded the *Sahitya Academy* award for her collection of essays on contemporary issues, *The Algebra of Infinite Justice* but she declined to accept it.

Yamini Krishnamurthi (1940-)

Yamni Purna Tilaka Krishnamurthi alias Yamni Krishnamurthi is an accomplished Bharathanatyam and Kutchipudi dancer who has dedicated her life to Indian classical dance for many decades. Born in Madanapalli, Andhra Pradesh, she hails from an eminent family, which was more literati than artistically inclined. Yamni's father, M. Krishnamurthi, was a Sanskrit scholar and grandfather was an expert in Urdu poetry.

Yamni enrolled as a student of Bharat Natyam at the age of five in Kalashreshtra School of Dance, Chennai (previously known as Madras) and her initial training was under Rukmini Devi Arundale. After acquiring a structural base at Kalashreasta, she went on to higher studies under renouned masters as Kanchipuram Ellappa Pillai, Thanwar Kittappa Pillai, Dhandayudhappani Pillai and Mylappore Gouri Amma. She trained in Kutchipuri under Vedantanam Laxumi Narayana Shastri, Chinta Krishnamurthi and Pasumarthi Venugopal Krishna Sharma. In addition to Bharat Natyam and Kutchipuri she learnt Odissi from Pankaj Charan Das and Kelucharan Mohapatra. She was trained in Carnatic vocal music by M.D. Ramanathan and learnt the Veena from Kalpakam Swaminathan.

Yamni gave her debut in 1957 in Chenni where her charishma and stage presence were recognized when she was only seventeen. By 1960 she became one of the most admired dancers in the country. Her performances brought about national and international recogninition to the classical styles of Bharat Natyam and Kutchipuri. Yamni played a significant role in popularizing Kutchipuri, which was then emerging as a solo dance form of Andhra Pradesh.

A multi-faceted artist, Yamni received *Padmashree* in 1968 and *Sangeet Natak Academy Award* in 1997. Tirumala Tirupati Devasthanam, one of the most sacroscent temples of India, bestowed the epithet, *Asthans Nartaki* on her.Along with stage performances Yamni made a thirteen part serial for Doordarshan on dance. She started *Yamni School of Dance* in 1960 in Delhi. She also wrote a book *A Passion for Dance,* which was well received by the critics. She is working on a ballet, titled *The Gandhian Order of Life* and another on Tagore and Subramanya Bharati and her depction of the Goddess Kali.

Kiran Majumdar Shaw:

Dr. Kiran Majumdar Shaw, born on 23 March 1953 in Bangalore, is an Indian entrepreneur. She is the Chairman and Managing Director of Biocon Ltd. In 2004, she became India's richest woman. She was educated at the Bishop Cotton Girl's School and Mount Camel College at Bangalore. After obtaining a B. Sc. Honors Degree in Zoology from Bangalore University in 1973, she joined the Ballarat University in Melborne, Australia and qualified as a master brewer in 1975 to become India's first woman Brew master. Her father encouraged her in this profession as he himself was a Brew master. Her professional career started with the position of trainee brewer. In 1978 she joined as Trainee Manager with Biocon Biochemicals Limited in Ireland. Collaborating with the same Irish firm, she founded Biochem India with a capital of Rs. 10,000/- in her garage in 1978. The initial operation was to extract an enxyme from papaya. Her application for loans was turned down by banks on three counts: biotechnology was a new word yet, the company lacked assets and most importantly, women entrepreneurs were still a rarity. On account of the last reason she faced problems in recruiting as well. Over the years the company grew under her stewardship and today is the biggest biopharmaceutical firm in India. In 2004 Biochem went for an IPO and the issue was ove-subscribed by over 30 times. Post IPO , Shaw held close to 40 % of the stock of the company and was regarded as India's richest woman with an estimated worth of Rs. 2,100 crore. She is a civic activist, especially with respect to municipal administration in Bangalore. She is also an art collector. She has authored *Ale and Arty,* a Coffee table book about brewing beer illustrated by paintings of some of India's renouned artists. Famous brewing families and beer firms are the subject of the book. In 1998 she married John Shaw an expatriate manager and Indofile from Scotland at Madura Coats the same year and joined Biocom as Director for International Business and the Vice Chairman of the Board.

Smt. Pratibha Devisingh Patil:

Smt. Patil was born on December 19, 1934 in Nadgaon village of Jalgaon District, Maharashtra. She assumed the office of the President of India on July 25, 2007. She is the first woman to have been elected to this august office. Immediately prior to being elected as the President of India, Smt. Patil was the Governor of Rajasthan from November 8, 2004 till June 21, 2007.

Smt. Patil received her education from RR Vidyalaya, Jalgaon and later obtained her Master's Degree in Political Science and Economics from the Mooljee Jetha College, Jalgaon. Later, she obtained a degree of Bachelor of Laws (L.L.B.) from Government Law College, Bombay (Mumbai). While in college she took active part in sports, excelled in table tennis and won several awards at various Inter-Collegiate tournaments. Even as an MLA, she pursued her studies as a law student.

Smt. Patil started her professional career as a practicing lawyer at the Jalgaon District Court and simultaneously devoted herself to various social activities, especially, for the upliftment of poor women.

At the young age of 27 she successfully contested her first election to the Maharashtra State Legislature. Subsequently she was continuously elected four times as MLA from the Eldabad constituency till 1985. Thereafter she served as Member of Parliament in the Rajya Sabha (the upper house) from 1985 to 1990 and later elected as Member of Parliament to the 10th Lok

Sabha in the 1991 General Elections from the Amravti constituency. She enjoys the unique distinction of not having lost a single election that she contested till date.

Smt. Patil has held various positions:

- Deputy Minister, Public Health, Prohibition, Tourism, Housing and Parliamentary Affairs, Government of Maharashtra from 1967 to 1972.

- Cabinet Minister, Social Welfare, Government of Maharashtra from 1972 to 1974.

- Cabinet Minister, Public Health and Social Welfare, Government of Maharashtra from 1974 to 1975.

- Cabinet Minister, Prohibition, Rehabilitation and Cultural Affairs, Government of Maharashtra, 1975 to 1976.

- Cabinet Minister, Education, Government of Maharashtra, 1977 to 1978;

- Cabinet Minister, Urban Development and Housing, Government of Maharashtra from 1982 to 1983;

- Cabinet Minister, Civil Supplies and Social Welfare, Government of Maharashtra from 1983 to 1985.

Smt. Patil is married to Dr. Devisingh Ramsingh Shekhawat, a Ph.D. from the Haffkine Institute of Mumbai in Chemistry.

CHAPTER 8
CONCLUDING REMARKS

The status of women of India has been traced over the long and interesting history; discussed from all perspectives and it is appropriate to comment on the subject and predict the future of women in this great and ancient country. In the beginning during the Vedic times the population of India was small, the land available was plentiful and very fertile and productive, which it still is. The Aryans, therefore, enjoyed much better prosperity than the present condition in which the population has grown exponentionally and the resources are falling significantly short of the demands. The prosperity in the ancient times had been a big factor in the way of life of the Aryans during those times and the freedom, which the women engoyed is partly due to the abundance of resources. The society did not consider a girl child as an unwanted burden. The Aryans who were trying to establish themselves in their newly acquired areas, were fighting wars with the natives and trying to establish themselves; acquisition of land for agriculture and domestic animals, such as cows and cattle were their basic necessities. They desired to have brave sons to fight battles and to protect and expand their land their land acquisitions. They, therefore, prayed for having brave sons and grandsons rather than daughters. However, daughters were given equal opportunities for getting education and acquisition of skills as they chose. They enjoyed freedom in choosing their lovers and husbands and had prominent part to play in decision making in their family affairs as well as in society. Women occupied responsible positions in the society and enjoyed as much respect as men. This status of women continued in the post-Vedic period and during the Puranic and epic periods as well. But there was a gradual decline in the overall status of women and women's freedom also gradually got curtailed.

After the last great epic, the *Mahabharatha,* the society felt the need to restrict the women in many ways as can be seen from the Manu Smiriti in which it states that a woman ought to be under the control of a male throughout her life, be it be the father, then husband and then her son. The Brahmians who held the power to make rules and regulations, started giving new interpretations to the ideals of the Vedas based on the changed social environment. This imposed further restrictions on the freedom of women. Opportunities for women to get educated became restricted. Marriages of girls before maturity started happening. To educate a girl who was to only going to do the household work was considered unnecessary. So only very elementary education was then provided to young girls who were then married off. They were given some training to make them capable of looking after household chores such as cooking, cleaning, gardening and taking care of animals etc.

The marriages of young girls at an early age and curtailment of her education probably was motivated by economy, the incursions by foreigners and a greater concentration of power and resulting corruption of the Brahmins, the priest class. All these factors in various degrees resulted in the poor woman being subjected to a very restricted life. The condition of women gradually became so bad that it was described as being worse than a Shudra or a slave. Abot the same time two religions, Jainism and Buddhism were born, both of which promised equal respect for women. They admitted women to their Order and allowed them to perform religious rituals just as their male counterparts. This attracted a lot of Hindu women as well as Sudras to join these religions. Jainism and Buddhism dominated north India during the Mauryan and Gupta empires. Even though these religions were preferred by the rulers of that time, they never forced or interfered with Hinduism and allowed the Hindus complete freedom of conducting their religious affairs. The Hindu priest class continued to dominate and they exercised their religious authority to continue to suppress women during this period in the history of India.

It was the coming on the scene of Shri Adi Shankaracharya, the greatest philosopher of Hindu religios philosophy of all time that the influence of Buddhism subsided in the Indian sub-continent. The sharpness and strength of the *Adwaita philosophy* was so great that the principles of Buddhism seemed to fade away. Buddhism, therefore gained popularity in adjoining countries where it still thrives. Jainism underwent certain modifications from its original philosophy and got much closer to Hinduism and therefore continued in certain parts of India.

The era that followed proved much more dangerous and oppressive for all women of India. It was the arrival of the Mughals through the cracks in the Himalayas. They repeatedly attacked the northwest frontier, gradually attacking deeper into Indian teritory. This was an enemy the likes of which the population had never confronted before since they came with a completely different religious philosophy which allowed them to abduct and rape women with impunity. Conversion of Hindus to Islam was ordered by their religion. Any body who was not Muslim was called a *Kafir* or an infidel and in accordance with their belief ought to be either converted to Islam or killed. This filled the entire country with an air of terror. Women's freedom got further restricted. They could not move freely and adopted *purdah* behind it they could hide themselves. Muslims did not educate their women and considered them nothing more than property and that had a degrading effect on women of India. The Moghul ruled India for many centuries. The local kings and chieftains were not strong enough to resist and fight the mighty Mughal armies. The religions of Buddhism and Jainism, which emphasized non-violence to such an extent that the hearts of the worriers had become soft and the desire to fight had become much weak. In addition, internal divisions and jelousy further weakened the Hindu forces. In any case, the Mughal Empire got disintegrated and the British East India Company, which came to India as traders, started becoming powerful. It eventually captured all of India in 1857 and India became a colony of the British Empire. The condition of Indian women during that time and how the British treated them till 1857 has been described in detail. Women of India were filling the harams of British soldiers to satisfy their lust. This was a shameful situation for India that a small country like Britain conquered such a large and populous country like India and used the women as their mistresses!

The British conquest of India had one positive side: it integrated all the Indian sub-continent. In the years' which followed, great sons of India strived for independence and mixed with the struggle for independence was also a want for granting greater freedom to the Indian woman: greater opportunities for education, for providing her basic human rights, for getting rid of all the evil social traditions which had restricted and persecuted Indian women for the past many centuries. Great social reformers, listed in the appendix, did heroic work in the emancipation of women. Good legislation, some during the British rule and quite a bit later after India became independent, was passed to protect women from abuse and discrimination. Provisions were made to promote education and employment. The evil traditions of Sati were declared illegal. There is enough good legislation now in force to protect the Indian woman and to improve her in all respects. The problem is that the rural areas of India where the population is still uneducated and old beliefs and superstitions still dominate the thinking, things have not really changed from what they used to be. In addition, there is wide spread corruption at all levels of government, which promotes male domination and prevents the progress of women. There are fprces at work in certain areas, which would prefer women to remain uneducated and remain at home just doing house work and obey the orders of the matriarch. On the other hand, there are the urban dwellers who have made considerable progress in educating women and allowing them to seek work and be a productive part of the society. In this area of the population the primary motivation for educating women has been economical, that is, to use her as an additional source of income. The male domination and lack of freedom in matters of marriage, dowery and other evil things such as "bride burning" and female fctocide are prevailan in this the so-called urban educated society.

The real change in the status of woman of India is not going to take place unless the leaders of India in all spheres of life change their view of women; the male psyche has to change drastically in that they must regard women as respectable and their equal and behave accordingly. This change is not going to take place in the near future. A country, which has been myred into centuries of religious conditioning affecting; a long and hard period of subjucation under foreign rule-first the Mughals and then the British-a period of approximately one millineum, hardly having any comparison any where in the world- has drastically affected their way of life and thinking and is going to require a long time to recover. Poverty, corruption and extreme greed is holding India back in its desire to become progressive and women's emencipation and progress is held up on account of the fact that people in general have not yet come out of the old mindset. India also suffers from corruption, which is a great impedent in its progress, especially those of women who are subject to male domination and are still bound by the outdated shackles of religious traditions, social collective practices and beliefs, which play an important role in preventing women's progress. The psyche of the people of India has been moulded by its past history, as mentioned earlier and is deep rooted and such deep- rooted mentalities are difficult to eradicate. Education for both men and women is absolutely essential in effecting improvement. Unfortunately a considerably large population of India is still uneducated and illiterate. When men, who are the head of the family, are illiterate, they prevent the girls from getting educated and generations after generations are passing without getting education and the problem persists. India must make serious efforts in spreading literacy and education. It should also inform women about their rights as enshrined in the constitution and the protection, which they can get from the government if their rights are violated. But there is a lot of corruption in the government. The local police and others would not help. This is another reason why progress is held up.

A recent article by Stephanie Nolan in the Globe and Mail, a leading national newspaper of Canada, describes the latest conditions in India and what sort of impression it creates on a foreigner, in this particular case a represpectable foreign worker, who has moved from South Africa to India. One would have expected that she might find society in India more cultured and advanced as compared to the country from where she moved. But based on what she writes, it is not the case. I quote:

"Sub-Saharan Africa, of course, is no bastion of gender equality—I covered horrific incidents of mass rape, child marriage and female genetial mutulation. Yet somehow I am reminded more incessantly of sexism here. It started when I signed our lease, and had to provide either my father's name or my husband's. I had to adjust to the fact that every repair person, shopkeeper and many potential staff members utterly ignore anything I say to them, waiting for the voice of authority, to tell them that they really ought to do.

I have in a few short weeks here, seen men casually whack their wives for some apparent infraction; watched police officials thrash female street children, apparently for sport; and heard educated, upper-class Indian women in a children's park talk freely about which chic clinic doctor will break the law and revealthe sex of a fetus, so they could abort in the unfortunate event they should be carrying a girl."

"A few weeks ago, I visited a rural area with some fantastic doctors and rural health experts, all women, who were traveling with a very junior colleague and when I asked gently, what he was doing with them, since he never spoke or took a note, they shrugged in resigned way and said it wouldn't be safe or seemly for women to be traveling without a man."

"In African villages, even the poorest woman moved freely, looked me in the eye and shook my hand; here women pull their saree ends over their faces and shrink from my *namaste* :; they will not sit, stand or open their doors until father or husband decrees. In thehandful of places that I have been in north India, most women won't speak to me at all, refusing to answer gentle questions about where they get water or the age of their children, ducking their heads and nodding toward the husband who must speak for them. In rural areas I meet family after family where only the sons go to school, the men consume most of every meal and gaunt girls and women hang back waiting for what is left. *It is all hard on the soul.*"

"Yet if African problems sometimes wore me down with their intractability, the sense that nothing had or would change for a thousand years, India feels different. Last week I was in Kerala in the south—that state best known for repeatedly electing a Marxist government. Here they have universal literacy, and right away, I noticed a difference with the women: they move freely, even in rural areas, and they approached eager to talk and ask me questions."

Further:"Men stare at me incessantly, with an assessing curiosity that is not friendly. Young men follow me in the street even when I am carrying my young son. When I am alone, they call out to me, or make sucking noises, in India it is known by the dismissive term "Eve teasing". It is pervasive, unrelenting sexual harassment by strangers. It is allenating and unpleasant. New friends here tell me it can, if you are unlucky and caught alone, easily escalate from harassment to assault. One foreign journalist colleague, walking with her male colleague, also a foreigner, was recently set upon—at noon in a crowded market—by men who groped her so aggressively, she had to run away and a week later, kad livid purple bruises from the fondling."

An account such as this makes a person of Indian origin, living in Canada for the past about forty years and wants to feel and talk with pride about the great culture of his country of origin, fees ashamed and quite concerned. After completing the reading of this article in the public library, I raised my head and looked around to see if people were looking at me any differently. I had to pretend that they had probably not read it and pretending to be confident, replaced the newspaper in its slot.

India is now regarded as a great emerging economy, being the fifth in the world and is hoping to become the leading economy in the world. The rate at which the GDP is increasing per year is about 8 percent or so within the past fiftee years or so, which is quite remarkable. The growth is due to India's great performance in the IT sector and certain other manufacturing sectors. This has resulted in a large middle class, about three million, who are enjoying the prosperity, the good life and their children, including girls, are receiving good education but the rest of the population, about eight hundred million, who live in the sixthousand villages, are a completely different story. They suffer from powerty and are still caught up in the centuries old thinking. If India wishes to be a "first world" country, it would, no doubt, have to liberate and educate its women. This is a vast human resource, which India has not been able to tap on account of factors already mentioned. It is a daunting task but it has to be done and done soon. There is no time to waste. India has already wasted a lot of time since gaining independence.

India has been and is a patriarchal and patrilineal society right from the beginning, except for a small area in the South. This, of course, implies that a woman, however important her role is within the family, is always going to be at a subordinate position within the family unit. This position of the woman also determines her position in the society in general. A man, howsoever his level of education or ability might be, will not easily accept the authority of a woman and would be reluctant to work under her. Superimpose the division of the society into the caste system, the situation then becomes even more unacceptable to men. In spite of the efforts of innumerable reformers to correct the situation, the caste system still remains strong and the masculine superiority is also quite strong. These things seem fairly deeply entrenched into the Indian society. Most western societies are also based on patriarchal and patrilineal systems. Even with the freedom, which exists in the West, men still dominate. To expect the women to enjoy *equal status* with men is a fairly ambitious expectation. With the women becoming educated and getting technologically advanced, their status will change but only to a certain extent.

It is my sincere hope that leaders in India will seriously undertake the task of educating the women, especially in the rural areas and takle this problem with ehthusiasm and bring about a change in India, which is so badly needed.

APPENDIX I
SOME SELECTED HYMNS FROM RIG VEDA PERTAINING TO WOMEN'S ISSUES: (Taken from reference 3, and translated into English).

NOTE: Numerical nomenclature for stanzas: 1.48.1 means Mandala 1, Sukta 48 and Stanza 1.

1.48.1:"Usha", that is the time of the morning, just prior to the Sunrise, i.e. dawn, wakes up everybody, fills them with energy and happiness and presents them with big things of enjoyment and in the evening lets them stop all the work and puts them to rest. Similarly, the parents should encourage their daughters to obtain education of high standard.

1/48.2: One who marries a woman, whose level of education is equal to his, enjoys a happy life.

1/48.9: Just as Usha brings to light all things, large and small, a learned daughter similarly brings glory to both her mother and father's dynasties.

1.48.14: Partial translation: Learned people, do great favor by explaining various subjects; "Usha" brings to light all the objects. Similarly, an educated woman decorates the whole world.

1.49.2: Just as the Sunlight makes every thing beautiful, similarly, a learned woman makes the whole household beautiful and happy giving birth to sons, taking care of all the household work. Recognizing this, one ought to be obliged to her

1.49.4: Learned people should know that a woman possesses the same virtues as "Usha" and they should preach this to everybody

1.50.1: Religious parents should wed their educated daughter(s) to a gentleman (men) of equivalent education and learning: just like a pair of trained horses in a chariot, and just like the beams of light emanating from the Sun

1.56.1:A teacher should marry a well- educated woman and just as he teaches his male pupils, his wife should teach female pupils. By doing this the fear and sadness due to learning of wrong things can be avoided

1.56.2: It is proper for all boys and girls to practice celibacy and completely learn all the subjects during their youth. They should then marry according to their choice with those of similar qualities, nature, and work, by careful mutual examination and with love. And in turn, those with complete education should teach girls and boys in accordance with their professions, for example, the "Khatriays" (worrier class) should be taught public administration, the "Vaishyas" (business/farming/commerce class) be taught their skills; and the "Shudras", (Service/labor class) their required skills

1.71. 3 : Just as the "Vaishyas" accumulate wealth by doing business in conformity with the principles of the Dharma, the daughters, prior to marriage should practice celibacy (*bramhacharya*) and obtain complete knowledge and skills from female teachers and after marriage contribute in the collective well being of the society. It should be understood that the time after marriage is not suitable for studies. Never think that any man or woman has no right to get educated; conversely, everybody got the right to get education.

1.71. 4: Without education a woman can never be happy. An uneducated man makes the life of an educated wife miserable and the reverse is also true. Therefore, there is happiness in getting educated and marry with love, of your own choice to enjoy life.

1.71.5: All parents should educate their children. Just as the brilliant Sun brightens everything and delights everybody, the educated sons and daughters make everybody happy.

1.71. 9: Partial interpretation: Just as a king can not successfully run his kingdom without truth, wealth, science and knowledge; women and men can not be happy without constantly increasing their knowledge and physical strength.

1.112.19: Those men and women desirous of happiness should practice celibacy, complete their education and then get married in accordance with mutual compatibility. This is only appropriate. Otherwise, they ought to continue their celibacy and further education because a marriage without compatibility, agreeable character and equal education will result in unhappiness

1.113.7: When a young man, having practiced celibacy, has followed the right path, is knowledgeable and well educated, marries a woman of equivalent knowledge and education, having also practiced celibacy, is beautiful and of good nature, and who is going to provide happiness, is strong and brave, then only they can enjoy a happy life

1.113. 8: Women, who wish to enjoy a happy life, should follow the teachings of the Vedic Dharma, should be pure and virgin and should make their husbands happy. And they should produce beautiful children whom they should bring up with the teaching of truth, good quality education. This way they may always enjoy happy life

1.113.9: Just as Usha (Dawn), a close relative of the Sun makes the life of all living beings pleasant and happy, a gentle and educated woman makes her husband happy and is able to produce fine children. Other cruel wives are not able to accomplish this

1.113.2: The morning time, Usha (Dawn), spreads light everywhere and removes darkness; it makes religious people happy and makes the life of thieves etc difficult. And makes all living beings happy; similarly. Similarly, a woman who is well educated, well versed in religion, is bright, and is equipped with fine virtues, will provide her husband with off springs, and give them good education, free them from the darkness of ignorance and bring glory to the dynasty

1.113.13: Oh woman! Just as the morning time of dawn, never fails to brighten all things in the morning, noon and in the evening, (the three "sandhyas", considered important in the Hindu religion), you also should always, with

conviction, with education and truth in behavior, become wealthy and have sons and grand sons etc, and always be happy
.

1.113.16: Just as the dawn wakes up all in the morning and removes darkness and just as the "Usha" of the evening makes everybody quit all the activities and puts them to sleep, i.e., like a mother who looks after all the creatures well and engages them in activities, an educated, gentle woman is quite similar in character.

1.113.17: When women and men, with good mutual conviction, having received good education and learning, and having gathered good quality materials such as food and other necessary things, spend their lives in happiness, then only the "Grastha Ashram" (married family life) is supposed to be completely happy.

1.113.20: Only those well educated parents are able to properly protect their offspring and provide them with good education; the families of those men who treat Their wives with respect and those women, in turn also treat their husbands with respect are blessed with all kinds of happiness and sadness and sorrow disappears from their lives.

1.114. 1: When persons who are truthful and are followers of the Dharma, are well educated, teach young men and similarly when women who are well educated, follow the teachings of the Dharma, and are truthful teach celibate receptive young girls, then these men and women get internal and physical strength and make this world a happier place.

1.116.10: Administrators and preachers should protect the young boys and girls who are engaged in studies and actively receiving education and encourage them to learn and obtain good education; They should prevent boys to marry before age 25 and the girls before the age of 16. Beyond these ages, they should be allowed to marry in accordance with their mutual choice and consent; men up to the age of 48 and the women after achieving the age of 24. This is helpful in increasing their internal strength and also physical strength.

1.116.13: Oh! The learned ones! Just as the educated persons marry the learned women and successfully go through the "Grahastha Ashram", that is, the married life, similarly, gather all the intelligent students and educate them and campaign for education. Also, just as the students get happiness after receiving lessons from their teachers; Educated women and men should teach and educate their children and other children and always feel good about it.

1.117.14: Men and women should follow the work done by the sages and practicing celibacy, obtain all the knowledge and learning, and go in all the distant places in the world and be happy.

1.117. 24: The male teachers teaching male students and the female teachers teaching the female students should initiate and engage the students in celibacy and complete their education (it is called the second birth of these students, implying their beginning of student life), and learning about the real life skills, and then returning them over to their families; the students, after returning to their families, ought not to forget what they learned from their teachers.

1.118.1: If men and women get knowledgeable, they can make their life happy
.

1.140. 7: Those learned men who marry learned women always progress and are acquire virtues and do good work in this life as well as in the life thereafter.

1.140. 8: Those girls who practice celibacy and acquire all kinds of knowledge and skills, they become admirable in this world and enjoy happiness not only in this life but also the life in the life, which will follow after their death. Also those learned men who by the strength of their will power and strong physique enjoy healthy old age.

1.165.12: Let those persons who make the men and women well educated, of good natured and of good character, and followers of the path of dharma, be respectable in the society
.

1.167. 5: Just as fire lights every thing, a woman, having acquired all kinds of good knowledge and skills, glorifies her entire dynasty

1.167. 6: All the administrators and those in power should educate their sons and daughters with practicing celibacy and provide them with the best knowledge.They should then let them choose their life partners so that every body will enjoy good and happy life
.

1.167.7: Greatness of men lies in imparting the best education to the boys and girls, for the sake of acquiring strong will power and physique, long life. And produce fortunate off springs, who in turn will spread their admiration

1.173.8: Just as the Sun creates clouds and rain and makes every body happy, similarly, a gentle person with his ever- increasing prosperity also makes all happy. Men should be educated and women should also be equally educated

1.179. 2: Those celibate students who wish to acquire knowledge ought to get education from only those teachers who have good education, are truthful and have control over their senses; and should marry only those celibate women who are equally well educated and are compatible in terms of their nature and character.

1.179. 4: Those men who marry women who lack education and perseverance do not enjoy happiness in life; it is preferable to marry women who are of compatible virtues and nature

1.180.2: The one, whose sister is learned, is always praiseworthy.

2.5. 6: When the girls acquire education and learning and become teachers and become mothers, then they become rich in many ways

2.17. 7 Those women, having acquired learning and then entering the "Grastha Ashram", that is the family life, should respect the able persons and disrespect those who are worthy of disrespect; this will enhance their wealth.

2.17. 9: Oh! The learned people! Let the educated and learned women who follow the path of the "Dharma", teach good education to other female pupils. This will prevent the destruction of the culture and traditions

2.27.12: Those men and women who are very well educated should become judges and should affect progress of men and women; such men and women deserve praise.

2.27. 14: In those cities or countries where learned women are judges for women and learned men are judges for men, experience fearless days and nights and there will be no fear from thieves etc.

:2.30. 8: Just as the king kills the enemies and respects gentlemen and dispenses good judgment, the queen should, in a similar manner, get rid of the cruel women and pass good judgments regarding women

2.31. 5: Just as the men practice celibacy, study and acquire knowledge and become educated, the women should also practice celibacy and become educated in a similar manner.

2.32.5: If a woman of good character and very well educated should marry a distinguished educated gentleman, then all sorts of happiness will befall on them.

2.41.16: All the unmarried girls should learn from well educated and learned women and the learned women should teach the young celibate girls and make every body and us happy and proud

.

2.41.17: All educated persons should encourage their educated wives to teach all the daughters in a nice manner.

2.41.18: Just as the learned persons teach the young celibate boys, the learned women should, similarly, impart good education to young celibate girls

.

2.41.19: All men should keep the teachers of boys and female teachers of girls constantly employed so that there will be dissipation and spread of knowledge and skills in women and men.

2.41. 20: Just as the Sun and the earth always give prosperity to all, the teachers and those giving sermons should spread learning and education in men as well as women in a proper manner

.

2.41 21: Learned and educated women should remain close to teachers and persons giving sermons so that good quality education is given to both men and women in an equitable manner

.

3.1. 3: Men should educate their daughters just as they educate their sons. Just as the brothers study so should the daughters. This will create happiness.

3.1. 6: Those educated women, who marry men of their own choice, and are equally well educated, and with mutual love, produce off springs, to whom they bring up with protection and give them good quality education enjoy happiness. Well-educated men and women together can successfully attain the goals of "Dharma, Artha, Kama and Moksha".

3.30.1: Wise, teachung, following the thought of Order, the sunless gained a grandson from his daughter.

Fain as a sire, to see his child prolife, he sped to meet her with an eager spirit.

3.33.2: The son left not his portion to the brother, he made a home to hold him who should gain it.

3.31.16: A woman who is engrossed in skills and industry just like electricity, and is clever in speech, humble in nature, is going to make everybody happy just as rains make all happy.

3.33.1: Partial meaning: Women, who desire spread of good quality education, pleasant nature, and acquisition of skills, should always teach girls and women.

3.33.2: Just as young women marry young men and desire to get pregnant and just as the rivers all flow in to the oceans and become their part; those women who are teachers and also give sermons should impart complete and best knowledge and education to women.

3.57.6: Men and women should practice celibacy and acquire best education and knowledge and skills and then while they are young, should get married in accordance with their choice with partners who are compatible with respect to their nature, values, and character. They should, thereafter, enjoy the "Grahastha Ashram" (family life).

3.61.1: Oh Women! Just as the morning dawn time wakes up all the living beings and urges them to start working; you should, similarly, devote yourself to your husbands and with compatible attitude, become praiseworthy.

3.61. 2: Just like the early morning time of dawn, which rides the chariot of moon beams, and with its gleaming beauty wakes up everybody, you women, with your high quality education, should be, similarly, serving your husbands with humility.

3.61. 3: Oh good women! Just like the early morning time of dawn illuminates all the areas in all directions, you should, similarly, spread illumination by your excellent behavior.

3.61. 4: Oh women! Just as the dawn is the link for the day, similarly, you should be with your husbands like a shadow, with compatibility and cooperative behavior. And just as the brightness happens with the help of earth, off springs come about by the relationships between husbands and wives.

3.61. 5: Just as by savoring the early morning time, men gain good health and strength, similarly, by marrying a lovely, devoted wife, men become bodily and mentally strong and healthy. In this way by being compatible with each other, mutual love may flourish.

4.5. 7: A daughter who marries a bridegroom of qualifications, comparable to those of hers, and having practiced celibacy, and similarly a celibate who should marry a girl suitable for him; they shall shine just like the stars in the sky.

4.14. 3: If a man marries a woman who is beautiful, lovely, with good virtues, devoted to the husband, then she will illuminate the dynasty just like the morning dawn illuminates everything and will give good quality education the children, while making everybody happy.

4.18. 5: A mother who teaches her children and gets rid of their bad behavior, and gives them good education, makes those children good citizens.

4.33. 2: Anybody who learns from his/her mother up to age five and then from his father until age eight and then from his teacher till as long as age forty-eight, they only become wise, learned, religious and will do good for the community at large.

4.51. 2: Oh "Brahmacharins" ! (Celibates)! The female celibate who possesses great depth (like the clouds full of water), and is a person of few meaningful words, is pious and learned is the only one fit for marriage; after having thoroughly tested.

4.51. 3: Oh males! The girl who is equally well learned as you and is of pleasant nature and of auspicious virtues is the only one fit for becoming a wife.

4.51. 4: The person who accepts a woman who is very strong, rich, beautiful and his equivalent in knowledge and is virgin, will be happy in his life; and by the same token, a women who yearns for a good husband enhances the wealth and knowledge, is capable of making men very happy.

4.51. 5: Those persons who get married to a virtuous woman, beautiful and of similar in nature as their own, and revel in glory and become role models for others.

4.51. 8: Oh men! Only wed those women who are educated, are beautiful and are virtuous, celibate and learned.

SOME IMPORTANT STANZAS FROM ATHARV A VEDA:

The *Atharva Veda* was reviewed, Mandal 8, consisting of 7 *Kandams* for stanzas pertaining to women's issues. There were some stanzas, which provided guidance for the conditions under which marriages ought to be performed, the care which ought tto be taken during pregnancy. Keys to successful and happy married life and education of women have been emphasized. The stanzas are:

FROM KANDAM 1 TO 7:
Explanation of Numerical References: Kandam/Suktam/Padam

1.11.11: At the time of child birth, the husband and other knowledgeable people should pray to God and make offerings, *(Havana),* etc. for the pleasure of the pregnant woman; the woman should practice inhaling and exhaling breath to keep her body flexible so that the delivery may be accomplished easily.

1.11. 3: During the entire time of pregnancy care must be taken to make sure that the mental as well as physical condition of the pregnant woman is kept healthy. By keeping the mother happy and satisfied the child is also born happy.(A relationship between the state of mother's mental and physical condition and that of the child is stated here.). The quarters where the birth is going to take place should be selected in advance and should provide comfortable environment, that is, climatic conditions should be taken into consideration so that both the mother and the new born remain in good healthy conditions.

1.14. 1: Learned men should search for an equally learned wife for marriage; this way he will enjoy wealth and happiness in the world. The daughter-in-law should arrange for the care of her elders such as her in-laws, and her husband and sons and live a happy life.

1.14. 2: The bride's parents say to the bridegroom: "This well-educated, virtuous daughter is being given to you. She will live with your mother, father, brother etc andby her good nature keep everybody happy and may she enjoy a happy life." (Manu Smiriti has stanzas 2/240 and 5/147, which have similar meanings).

1.14. 3: In continuation of stanza 2, The parents of the bride request the parents of the groom by chanting this stanza and tell the bride about the duties of the wife (*Stree Dharma*) , and perform the ceremony of "giving away of the daughter", (*Kanya Daan*).
1.14. 4: In accordance with this mantra, the men and women of the bride's side request the groom and give the daughter wealth, ornaments, clothes etc and bid her farewell with respect.

5.25. 2: Just as the enormous Earth produces jewels from its woumb by the action of the thunder, so should a woman of benovelent nature give birth to learned off-spring from the union with her husband.

5.25. 3: Knowledgeable woman having become pragnent, shoud arrange for herself a good and healthy diet and living environment so that the featus will grow healthy and well fed on a day-today basis.

5.25. 4: Effort must be made to ensure that by the regulation of breathing, (inhaling/exhaling), sun, bodily electricity, fire etc, may benefit the pragnent woman in the proper nurishment of the fetus.

5.25. 6: Educated husband and learned wife, in consultation with a skilful physician, arrange for proper diet and live in proper healthy environment for the pragnent woman and be dedicated to the protection of the fetus.

5.25. 8: Educated man should work hard to earn money and wealth prior to entering the married life (*Grahastha Ashram*) so that he can properly provide for the protection and care of his offspring.

5.25. 9: A woman should be strong and virtuous to be able to give birth to excellent offspring.

5.25.10: An educated woman should be always thinking of the benovelent nature of the almighty God and complete the full term of her pregnancy and then deliver the child.

ADDITIONAL RIG VEDA HYMNS: (Taken from reference 36.)

5.61.8: The idea of equality expresses in the *Rig Veda*: "The home has verily, the foundation in the wife", "The wife and husband being the equal halves of one substance, are equal in every respect; therefore both should join and take equal parts in all work, religious and secular".

10.18.7: Let these unwidowed dames with noble husbands adorn themselves with fragrant balm and ungent.
Decked with fair jewels, tearless, free from sorrow, first let the dames go to where he lieth.

10.18:

> *7.Let these unwidowed dames with noble husbands*
> *Adorn themselves with fragrent balm and unguent.*
> *Decked with fair jewels, tearless, free from sorrow,*
> *First let the dames go up to where he lieth.*
>
> *8 Rise, comeunto the world of life, O woman:*
> *Come, he is lifeless by whose side thou liest.*
> *Wifehood with this thy husband was thy portion,*
> *Who took thy hand and wood thee as a lover.*
>
> *9 From his dead hand I take the bow he carried,*
> *That it may be our power and might and glory.*

(These stanzas are proof that though wives grieved for their dead husbands, the sati tradition, in which the widow sat on the funeral pyre of her dead husband and underwent self-immolation, did not exist during the Vedic period.)

10.27.11: When a man's daughter hath been ever eyeless, who, knowing, will be worth with her for blindness? Which of the two will loose on him his anger-the man who leads her home or he who woos her ?

10.27.12: How many a maid is pleasing to the suiter who fain would marry for her splinded riches? If the girl be both good and fair of feature, she finds, herself, a friend among the people.

10.70.6:

> *Here in this shrine may Dawn and Night,*
> *The daughters of heaven, the skilful*
> *Goddesses, be seated.*
> *In your wide lap, auspicious, willing Ladies*
> *May the Gods seat them with a willing*
> *Spirit.*

10.70.8:

> *On our wide grass, Three Goddesses be*
> *Seated: for you have we prepared and*
> *Made it pleasant.*

> *May Ila, she whose foot drops oil, the*
> *Goddess, taste, man-like, sacrifice and*
> *Well-set presents.*

10.85.26: Let Pusan take thy hand and hence conduct thee; may the two Aswins on their car transport thee. Go to the house to be the householder's mistress and speak as lady to thy gathered people.

10.85.27: Happy be thou and prosper with thy children here; be vigilant to rule thy household in this home. Closely unite thy body with this man, thy lord. So shall ye, of years, address your company.

10.85.44: Come O desired of the gods, beautiful one with tender heart, with the charming look, good towards your husband, kind towards animals, destined to bring forth heroes. May you bring happiness for both our quadrupeds and bipeds.

10.85. 46: Over thy husband's father and thy husband's mother bear full sway. Over the sister of thy lord, over his brothers rule supreme.

The Marriage Hymn, X.85, *Surya's Bridal* :

> *1. Truth is the base that bears the earth;*
> *By Surya are the heavens sustained.*
> *By law the Adityas stand secure, and*
> *Soma holds its place in heaven.*

2.By Soma are the Adityas strong, by Soma
mighty is the earth.
Thus Soma in the midsy of all these
constellations hath his place.

One thinks, when they have brayed the
Plant, that he hath drunk the Soma's
Juice;
Of him whom Brahmins truly know as
Soma no one ever tastes.

Soma secured by sheltering rules, guarded
By hymns in Brhati,
Thou standest listening to the stones:
None tastes of thee who dwells on earth.

When they begin to drink thee then, O
God, thou swellest out again.
Vayu is Soma's guardian God. The Moon
Is that which shapes the years.

Raibhi was her dear bridal friend, and
Narasamsi led her home.
Lovely was Surya's robe: she came to
That which Gatha had adorned.

Thought was the pillow of her couch,
Sight was the unguent for her eyes:
Her treasury was earth and heaven when
Surya went unto her Lord.

8. Hymns were the cross- bars of the pole,
Kurira-metre decked her car:
The bridesmen were the Aswin pair:
Agni was the leader of the train.

9. Soma was he who wooed the maid: the
groomsmen were both Aswins, when
The Sun-God Savitar bestowed his willing
Surya on her Lord.

*10. Her spirit was the bridal car; the cover-
ing thereof was heaven:
Bright were both Steers that drew it,
When Surya approached her husband's
Home.*

*11. Thy Steers were steady, kept in place by
Holy verse and Soma hymn:
All ear were thy two chariot wheels: thy
Path was tremulous in the sky.*

*12. Clean, as thou wentest, were thy wheels:
Wind was the axle fastened there.
Surya, proceeding to her Lord, mounted
A spirit fashioned car.*

*13. The bridal pomp of Surya, which Savitar
Started, moved along.
In Magha days are oxen slain, in Arjunis
They wed the bride.*

*14. When on your three-wheeled chariot, O
Aswins, ye came as wooevers unto Surya's
Bridal.
Then all the Gods agreed to your proposal:
Pusan as Son elected you as fathers.*

*15. O ye Two Lords of lusture, then when ye
To Surya's wooing came,
Where was one chariot wheel of yours?
Where stood ye for the Sire's command?*

*16. The Brahmins, by their seasons, know, O
Surya, those two wheels of thine:
One kept concealed, those only who are
Skilled in highest truths have learned.*

*17. To Surya and the Deities, to Mitra and
To Varuna.
Who know aright the thing that is, this
Adoration have I paid.*

18. By their own power these Twain in close succession
move; They go as playing children round theSacrifice.
One of the Pair beholdeih all existing Things;
the other ordereth seasons andIs born again.

19. He, born fresh, is new ans new for ever:
Ensign of days he goes before the Mornings.
Coming he orders for the Gods theirPortion.
The moon prolongs the daysOf our existence.

20. Mount this, all-shaped gold-hued, with strong wheels,
fashioned of KirnsukaAnd Salmali, light rolling,
Bound for the world of life immortal,
Surya: make for thy lord a happyBridal journey.

21. Rise up from hence: this maiden hath a
Husband. I laud Visvavasu with hymns and homage.
Seek in her father's home another fair one,
And find the portion from of old assigned thee.

22. Rise up from hence, Visvavasu: with
Reverence we worship thee.
Seek thou another willing maid, and with
Her husband leave the bride.

23. Straight in direction be the paths, and thornless,
whereon our fellows travel to the wooing.
Let Aryaman and Bhaga iead us: perfect,
O Gods, the union of the wife and husband.

24. Now from the noose of Varuna I free thee,
Wherewith Most Blessed Savitar hath bound thee.
In Law's seat, to the world of virtuous action,
I give thee up uninjured with thy consort

25. Hence not thence, I send thee free.
I make thee softly fettered there.
That Bountious Indra, she may live
Best in her fortune and her sons.

26. *Let Pusan take thy hand and hence conduct thee;*
May the two Aswins on their car transport thee.
.Go to the house to be the household mistress and
seek as lady to thy gathered people.

27. *Happy be thou and prosper with thy children here:*
Be vigilant to rule thy household in this home.
Closely unite thy body with this man, thy lord.
So shall ye, full of years, address your company.

28. *Her hue is blue and red: the fiend who*
Clingeth close is driven off.
Well thrive the kinsmen of this bride:
The husband id bound fast in bonds.

29. *Give thou the wollen robe away: deal*
Treasure to the Brahman priests.
This female fiend hat got her feet, and
As a wife attends her lord.

30. *Unlovely is his body when it glistens with*
This wicked fiend,
What time the husband wraps about his
Limbs the garments of his wife.

31. *Consumptions, from her people, which*
Follow the bride's resplendent train—
These let the holy Gods again bear to
The place from which they came.

32. *Let not the highway thieves who lie in*
Ambush find the wedded pair.
By pleasant ways let them escape the
Danger, and let foes depart.

33. *Signs of good fortune mark the bride:*
Come all of you and look at her.
Wish her prosperity, and then return
Unto your homes again.

34.Pungent is this, ans bitter this, filled, asIt were,
 with arrow-barbs. Empositioned and not fit for use.
The Brahman who knows Surya well
Deserves the garment of the bride.

35. The fringe, the cloth that decks her head
And then the triply parted robe,--
Behold the hues which Surya wears;
These doet the Brahman purify.

36.I take thy hand in mine for happy
Fortune that thou mayst reach old age
With me thy husband.
Gods, Aryaman, Bhaga, Savitar, Purandhi,
Have given thee to be my household's mistress.

37.O Pusan, send her on as most auspious,
Her who shall be the shaver of my pleasures;
Her who shall twine her loving arms about me,
And welcome all my love and mine embraces.

APPENDIX II
Epithets for women in the Vedas:

It is noteworthy that in the Vedic literature although a woman's prime role is portrayed as a wife only, yet several other aspects of feminine form are also suggested by various names and epithets used to denote a woman. It is quite interesting to derive the exact meaning of these words because it may help in giving a better idea of different roles of woman in home and in society. For instance, a woman as wife is denoted by three words; *jaya, jani, and patni.* Of these, jaya is the woman who gives birth to one's progeny, jani is the mother of children and patni is the co-partner in the religious duties.

Similarly women are designated as:

Aditi: because she is not dependent; (4) *Aghnya* for she is not to be hurt, (5) *Brhati:* for she is large hearted; (6), *Chandra:* because she is happy (7), *Devkama:* since she is pious (8), *Devi:* since she is divine (9 and 10), *Dhruva:* for she is firm,(11),*Havya:* because she is worthy of invocation (12), *Ida:* for she is worshippable (13), *Jota:* because she is illuminating, bright (14), *Kamya:* because she is lovable (15), *Kshama:* for she is tolerant, indulgent, patient (16), *Mahi:* since she is great (17), *Mena:* because she deserves respect (18), *Nari:* because she is not inimical to anyone (19), *Purandhih:* for she is munificent (20), *Ranta:* because she is lovely (21), *Rtavari:* because she is the preserver, forester, of truth (22), *Sanjaya:* because she is victorious (23), *Sarasvati:* since she is scholarly (24), *Simbhi:* since she is courageous (25), *Shiva:* for she is benevolent (26), *Shivatama:* since she is noble (27), *Stri:* since she is modest (29), *Subhaga:* because she is fortunate (30), *Subhdha:* for she is knowledgeable (31), *Sumangali:* since she is auspicious (32), *Suheva:* for she is pleasant (33), *Suvarcha:* since she is splinted (34), *Suyama:* since she is self disciplined (35), *Syona:* for she is noble (36), Virni: since she is mother of brave sons (37), *Vishruta:* since she is learned (38), *Yashasvati:* for she is glorious (39), *Yosha:* because she intermingles with men, she is not isolated. (40).

Women Rishis (rishikas) in the *Rig Veda Samhita*:

Verse: 4.18 revealed to	Aditi
Verse: 10.72 revealed to	Aditrirdakshyani
Verse: 8.91 revealed to	Apala atria
Verse: 10.86 revealed to	Indrani
Verse: 10.85	Urvashi
Verse: 10.134	Godha
Verse: 10.39,10.40	Gosha Kakshivini
Verse: 10.109	Juhurbramhajaya
Verse: 10.184	Tvashta Garbhakarta
Verse: 10.107	Dakshina Prajapatya
Verse: 10.154	Yami
Verse: 10.10	Yami Vaivasvati
Verse: 10.127	Ratrirbharadvaji
Verse: 1.171	Lopamudra
Verse: 10.28	Vasukrapatni
Verse: 10.125	Vagambhrni
Verse: 5.28	Vishvavara Atreyi
Verse: 8.1	Sashvatyangirasi
Verse: 10.151	Shradhda Kamayani
Verse: 10.159	Shachi Paulomi
Verse: 10.189	Sarparajni
Verse: 9.86	Sikata Nivavari
Verse: 10.85	Surya Savitri
Verse: 1.126	Romasha
Verse: 10.108	Sarama Devashumi
Verse: 9.104	Shikhandinyava Psarasau Kashyapan
Verse: 10.142	Jarita Sharngah
Verse: 8.71	Sudhitirangirash
Verse: 10.153	Indra Mataro.

(This list is not complete)

References from the Vedas:

1. Rig Veda, 10.125; 2. Rig Veda, 10.27.12, 3. Rig Veda, 10.85; 4. Nirukta, 4.22; 5. Yajur Veda, 8.43; 6. Yajur Veda, 11.64; 7. Yajur Veda, 8.43, 8. Atharva Veda, 14.1.47, 9. Atharva Veda, 14.1.45, 10. Yahur Veda, 4.23, 11.

Yajur Veda, 11.64, 12. Yajur Veda, 8.43, 13. Yajur Veda, 8.43, 14. Yajur Veda, 8.43, 15. Yajur Veda, 8.43, 16. Atharva Veda, 12.1,29, 17. Yajur Veda, 8.43, 18. Nirukta, 3.21.2, 19. Atharva Veda, 14.1.59, 20. Yajur Veda, 22.22, 21. Yajur Veda, 8.43, 22. Rig Veda, 2.41.18, 23. Rig Veda, 10.159.3, 24. Yajur Veda, 20.84, 25. Yajur Veda, 5.12, 26. Atharva Veda, 14.1.64, 27. Rig Veda, 10.85.37, 28. Rig Veda, 8.33.9, 29. Nirukta, 2.21.2, 30. Yajur Veda, 8.43, 31. Atharva Veda, 14.2.75, 32. Atharva Veda, 14.2.26, 33. Atharva Veda, 14.2.26, 34. Atharva Veda, 14.4.47, 35. Atharva Veda, 14.2.18, 36, Atharva Veda, 14.2.27.

NOTE: This article is taken from: "Rishikas in the Vedas—Hindupedia, the Hindu Encyclopedia.

APPENDIX III
Statements Made By Some Important Indian Thinkers And Philosophers Regarding Women's Education:(Ref. 22)

Mahershi Dayanand Saraswati: (1825-1883)

"In ancient India, Gargi and other ladies—jewels among women-were highly educated and perfect scholars of the Veda. This is clearly written in Satpatha Brahmana.

Now if the husband be well-educated and the wife ignorant or vice versa, there will be constant state of warfare in the house. Besides, if women were not to study, where will the teachers for girl's schools come from? Nor would ever the affairs of State, the administration of justice and the duties of married life, that are required of both husband and wife (such as keeping each other happy, the wife having supreme control over all household matters) be carried on properly without thorough education of men and women."

Swami Vivekananda (1863-1902):

"Writing down smrities, etc. and binding them by hard rules, in a serious vein, the men have turned the women into mere manufacturing machines. If you do not raise the women who are living embodiment of the Devine Mother, don't think that you have any other way to rise.

"All nations have attained greatness by paying proper respects to women. That country and that nation which does not respect the women have never become great, nor will ever be in future."

"Women have all the time been trained in helplessness, serving dependence on others and so they are good only to weep their eyes at the slightest approach of a mishap or danger. Along with other things they should require spirit of valour and heroism. In the present day it has become necessary for them also to learn self-defence. See how grand was the Queen of Jhanshi."

(The complete works of Swami Vivakananda)

Dr. S. Radha Krishnan (1888-1975):

"Women are human-beings and have as much right to full development as men have. In regard to opportunities for intelluctual and spiritual development, we should not emphasize the sex of women even as we do not emphasize the sex of men. The fact that we are human- beings is infinitely more important than the physiological pecularities, which distinguish us from one another. In all human-beings, irrespective of their sex, the same drama of the flesh and the spirit, of finititude and transcendence takes place."

"The position pf women in any society, is a true index of its cultural and spiritual level. Men, who are responsible for many of the views about women, have woven fantastic stories about the latter's glamour and instability and their inferiority to men as well as their mystry and sanctity. Because oriental women do not greatly resort to self-assertive bluster, we need not argue, that they are slaves. There is nothing more attractive than modesty, nothing more shining than shyness in a woman. The feminity of woman is not a matter of race or nationality. It belongs to their inmost nature. It is my hope that our women, while participating in public work, will retain their essential qualities, which have helped to civilize their race."

"You are living in an age when there are great opportunities for women in social work, public life and administration. Society requires women of disciplined minds and restrained manners. Wharever line of work you undertake, you should bring to it an honest, disciplined mind. You will then succeed and have the joy of your work."

"Our civilization became arrested and one of the main sign of that decay is the subjection of our women."

"After the independence several legislative measures have been enacted with a view to the equal treatment of women and men. But the legislative measures are not enough. The climate of opinion has to change and women themselves have to exert their utmost to improve their mantal stature."

(From occasional speeches and Writings).

Mahatma Gandhi (1869-1948):

"As for women's education I am not sure whether it should be different from men's and when it should begin. But I am strongly of opinion that women should have the same facilities as men and even special facilities where necessary."
(Gandhi, M.K., True Education)

From *Sri Guru Granth Sahib:*

"We are born of women, we are conceived in the womb of women, we are engaged and married to women. We make friendship with women and the lineage continued because of women. When one woman dies, we take another one, we are bound with the world through woman. Why should we talk ill of her, who gives birth to kings? The woman is born from woman; there is none without her. Only the One True Lord is without woman." (Guru Nanak Dev. Var Asa, pg. 473)

REFERENCES AND BIBLIOGRAPHY

WOMEN OF INDIA THEIR STATUS
(From Vedic Times to Present)

1.Rigvedic India by Abinas Chandra Das, Second Ed., Revised, R. Cambray & Co., 15, College Square, Calcutta. 1927.

2. A Survey Of Hinduism by Klaus K. Klostermier. Second Ed., State University Of New York Press, Albany, 1994. ISBN 0-7914-2109-0
.

(An excellent Reference. Contains: Part I: Hinduism Development and Essence, Part II: Trimarga: The Three Hindu Paths To Liberation, Part III: The Structural Supports Of Hinduism, Part IV: The Meeting Of East and West In Modern India.)

3. Rig Ved Hindi Bhshsya, Pratham Mandal, by Maharshi Dayananda Saraswati, Prince Ofsett Printers, New Delhi, Third Ed.

4. "From Eve to Dawn, A History of Women", by Marilyn French Volume I, McArthur & Company, Toronto, Ontario 2002.

5. "From Eve to Dawn, A History of Women", by Marilyn French Volume III, Chapter 15, "Anti- Imperial Revolution in India. McArthur & Company, Toronto, 2003.

6."Bhartya Nari", by Sane Guruji, Sadhana Prakashna, Pune, second edition, September, 1962.

7. "Shodash Sanskar Darshan", by K. M. Bapat, Shastri. Published by Ramesh Vitthal Raghuvanshi, Shri GajBookDepot, Kabutarkhana, Dadar, Mumbai, 28.

8. "The Wonder That Was India", Volume II, 1200 to 1700, by S. A. A. Rizvi, 2005 Edition, published by Picador, an imprint of Pan Macmillan Ltd., 2o New Wharf Road, London NI 9RR.

9. "The Real Beginning of Bilingualism in India", McCrum, et. Al., 1988:325. (Lord William Bentnick, governer general of India, passes a decree based on the recommendation of Lord Macaulay, which recommended: creation of a class of persons, Indian in blood and colour, but English in taste, in opinion,in morals and in intellect".)

10. "The Greenwood Encyclopedia of Women's Issues Worldwide", Asia and Oceania. Editor-in-Chief: Lynn Walter, Volume Editor: Manisha Desai. Greenwood Press, Westport, Connecticut. Chapter 7, India. By Deepa S. Reddy

11. "The Origions Of The Sati System" by Dr. Jotsna Kamat. Obtained through Google internet search.

12. " Gandhi and Status Of Women." By Jotsna Bapat. Excerpts from a lecture given by her at the Gandhi Peace Foundation in December, 1998.

13 Women in Medieval Karnataka" by Dr. Jotsna Kamat.Information obtained via Google Internet Search
.
14. "Indian Women and Patriarchy", by Maria Mies, Concept Publishing, New Delhi..

15 "Purdah, The Status of Indian Woman" by S. Das. Ess Ess Publications, New Delhi 110002, India, 1979 Ed.

16." The Resurgence of Indian Women" by Aruna Asaf Ali in association with G.N.S.Raghvan, under the auspices of Nehru Memorial Museum and Library. Radiant Publishers, 1991. Nadiant Publishers, 1991. New Delhi.

17. "Indian Women Forge Ahead" Case studies of women activists, Editors: Jessie B. Tellis-Nayak, Marlyn Lobo Brito. Published by Indian Social Institute, 10 Industrial Area, Lodhi Road, New Delhi-110 003.

18. "From The Seams Of History", Essays on Indian Women. Edited by Bhaati Ray. Delhi, Oxford University Press, Printed in India at Paul's Press, New Delhi 110020, and published by Neil O'Brian, Oxford University Press YMCA Library Building, Jai Singh Road, New Delhi 110001.

19. "Status Of Indian Women, A Historical Perspective." By B.R.Sharma. Uppal Publishing House, 3, Ansari Road, Daryaganj, New Delhi, 110 002, 1992.

20. "Annals And Antiquities Of Rajasthan" By Colonel James Todd, 1820.

21."The Indian Woman in Perspective." By Shoma A. Chatterji. Published by Ajanta Publications, P.Box 2192 Malka Ganj, Delhi 110007.

22. "Indian Women: Education And Status." By J.C.Aggarwal, Arya Book Depot, Karol Bagh, New Delhi, 110005.

23. "Dharma's Daughters" By Sara S. Mitter. Rutgers University Press, New Brunswick, New Jersey.

24. An article by Ranjit Devraj dated Aug. 2002, in India Together, entitled, "Fighting the Veil". http://www.indiatogether.org/women/articles/veil10802. htm

25. "Unequal Citizens: Muslim Women in India" , by Zoya Hasan and Ritu Menon. Oxford University Press, New Delhi, 2004. referred from internet : http://www.hinduonnet.com/fline/fl2119/stories/200440924002810300. htm

26. "Indian Women In The Smrities" by Ramnika Jalali, Vinod Publishers & Distributers, P.B. No. 130, Pacca Danga, Jammu-180001, J & K (India)

27. "Beyond the Veil, Indian Women in the Raj", by Pran Nevile. Nevine Books, New Delhi, distributed by Variety Book Depot, A.V.G. Bhavan, M-3 Cannaught Circus, New Delhi, 110 001, India.

28. "Women in Sikhism" ; Quotes from Sri Guru Granth Sahib and statements by various Gurus. http://www.sikhs.org/women.

29. "Indian Women Through the Ages." By P. Thomas, Asia Publishing House, Printed in India, by C Srinivasan at The Statesman Press, 4, Chauranghee Square, Calcutta, 1.

30. "Atharva Veda", From *Pratham Khand to Saptam Khand,* Hindi translation by Khemkaran Trivedi. Published by Sarvadeshik Arya Pratinidhi Sabha, Maharshi Dayanand Bhavan, Ramlila Maidan, New Delhi, 1.

31. "Ghate's Lectures on Rigveda", Revised and enlarged by Dr. V.S.Sukthankar, Oriental Book Agency, 15, Shukarwar, Poona-2.

32. "Rigveda A Historical Analysis", Shrikant G. Talageri, Aditya Prakashan, New Delhi
,
33. "Early Life In Ancient India". From 200 BC to 700 AD. By Jeannine Auboyer, translated from French by Simon Watson Taylor. Phoenix Press, 5, Upper Saint Martin's Lane, London. WC2H 9EA, 1965.

34. Surendra Kumar, Vishuddha Manusmiriti, Arsh Sahitya Prachar Trust, Delhi, Fourth Edition.

35. "The Hymns of the Rig Veda", Translated with a popular commentary, by Ralph T.H. Griffith. Edited by Prof. J.L. Shastri. Motilal Banarsidas, Delhi, 1973.

36. "History And Culture Of The Indian People, The Vedic Age", General editor, R.C.Majumdar, George Allen & Unwin Ltd., London, 1952.

37. "The Indo-Aryans of Ancient South Asia", Language, Material Culture and Ethenicity. Edited by George Erdosy. Walter de Gruyter, Berlin-New York, 1995.

38. "The Vedic Age", Bhartya Ithasa Samiti's History And Culture of The Indian People. General editor, R.C. Majumdar, Assistant editor, D. Pusalker. George Allen and Unwin Ltd. London Second Ed. 1952. Vol. I.

39. "Vedic Hymns" Translated by F. Max Muller. Part I: Hymns to the Maruts, Rudra, Vayu and Vata. Motilal Banarasidass, Delhi, 1964.

40. "Vedic Hymns" Translated by Hermann Oldenberg. Part II, Hymns to Agni (Mandalas I-V). Motilal Banarasidass, Delhi, 1964.

41. "Ghate's Lectures on Rig Veda", Revised and Enlarged by Dr. V.S.Sukthankar, Oriental Book Agency, Shukarawar, Poona, 2. Revised Ed. 1959. Chapter X, The Social Life in the Rig Veda.

42. The Rig Veda: the oldest literature of the Indians. Author/Editor: Kaegl, Adolf, 1849-1923, Published by New Delhi Amerato Book Agency, 1975.

43. Hymns of the Rig Veda: Selected and inetrically translated by A.A.MacDonell. Author/Editor: MacDonnell, Arthur Anthony, 1854-1930. Published: Calcutta Association Press (YMCA) London, Oxford University Press, 1922.

Internet References:
http://www.Stephen-krapp.com/woman-in-vedic-culture.htm
http://www.vedah.com/org/literature/essence/women&Rushikas.osp
http://www.geocities.com/nemhasekha/stahusofindianwomen.htm

http://sfy.com/news/othernews/fullstory.php?dz13170729
http://www.surichat.nl/forum/index.php?topic=14696.65wap2
http://groups.msn.com/hindu-history/nawarchives.msnw?
action=get-message&mview=Q&TD-Message=181

http://ssubbanna.sulekha.com/blog/post/2007/10/rig-veda-position-of-women-2-2.htm

ACKNOWLEDGEMENTS:

I am grateful to the staff of the Burlington Central Library for assisting me in procuring the necessary references. The McMaster University, Hamilton, is full of references pertaining to Indology and *Vedas*. I am also grateful to them for lending me books at no cost.

I am also grateful to my dear wife, Tara, for her patience and support during the writing of this book.